M

Lost Splendor

The Amazing Memoirs of the Man Who Killed Rasputin

Lost Splendor

Prince Felix Youssoupoff

Translated from the French by
Ann Green and Nicholas Katkoff

HELEN MARX BOOKS ◆ NEW YORK

First published in 1953 by
G. P. Putnam's Sons, New York

LCCN 2001132727
ISBN: 9781885983664

Design and composition by Melissa Ehn at
Wilsted & Taylor Publishing Services

FRONTISPIECE: The author, in the costume
of a sixteenth-century boyard (1910)

contents

introduction

This is the history of my family, set against a background of oriental savagery and magnificence, starting with the Golden Horde of the Tartars, through the Grand Duchy of Moscow to the Imperial Court of St. Petersburg, and ending in exile in a foreign land.

The family records disappeared during the Revolution, and as no other documents were available I was obliged to refer almost exclusively to a work written by my grandfather in 1886 for all data concerning the origin and history of my ancestors.

I have written very frankly about my own life, telling alike of joys and sorrows, of days of glory and days of tribulation, without keeping back any of my experiences.

I would have preferred to avoid politics, but as I have lived in a troubled period I cannot write my recollections without alluding to the dramatic events in which I took part.

This first volume deals with our carefree life before the first World War and the Revolution of 1917; a second will tell the story of our exile in foreign lands.

An abyss separates these two periods, and it is only because of a deep trust in the Almighty that we have never questioned His justice. Absolute faith in Him has alone made it possible for us to live through these years of trial without ever losing hope.

Lost Splendor

Prince Youssoupoff, the author's father,
and his two sons in Tcherkess uniform (1892)

chapter I

According to our records, my family was founded by a certain Aboubekir ben Raïoc who lived in the sixth century and who was said to be a descendant of the Prophet Ali, a nephew of Mahomet. Aboubekir was the supreme head of all Moslems and bore the titles of Emir el Omra, Prince of Princes, Sultan of Sultans, and Khan, thus uniting religious and political authority in his person. His descendants also exercised the same supreme authority in Egypt, Antioch, and Constantinople. Some of them are buried in Mecca, in the neighborhood of the celebrated Caaba stone.

Termess, one of Aboubekir's descendants, emigrated from Arabia to the shores of the Azov and Caspian seas. He held vast tracts of land between the River Don and the Ural Mountains where the Nogaïskaia-Orda* was eventually constituted.

In the fourteenth century, one of the descendants of Termess, Edigue Manguite, who was considered one of the greatest strategists of his time, took part in all the campaigns of Tamerlane, the founder of the second Mongolian Empire. He fought the Khan of Kaptchak who had rebelled against Tamerlane after having been his ally. Later, Edigue Manguite went south to the shores of the Black Sea where he founded the Krimskaïa-Orda, or Crimean Khanate. He lived to a great age, but after his death there was such strife among his heirs that most of them perished in a general massacre.

***Orda* or *Horde*: the name given to the nomadic tribes of Tartary. The city of Kazan, mentioned later, was long the capital of the Golden Horde, which was the most westerly kingdom founded by the Mongols and was several times dismembered during the fourteenth and fifteenth centuries.

Toward the end of the fifteenth century, Moussa-Mourza, great-grandson of Edigue, became the supreme chief of the powerful Nogaïskaia-Orda. Allied to the Grand Duke Ivan III, he fought and destroyed the Kaptchak Khanate, which was a rival clan stemming from the old Golden Horde.

He was succeeded by his eldest son Shik-Shamaï, but the latter was soon replaced by his brother Youssouf.

Khan Youssouf was one of the most powerful and intelligent princes of his day. Czar Ivan the Terrible, who was his faithful ally for twenty years, regarded the Nogaïskaia-Orda as a kingdom, and treated its chief as a sovereign. The two allies exchanged sumptuous gifts: saddles and armor studded with precious stones, magnificent ermine and sable furs, tents lined with rare silks brought from distant lands. The Czar called his ally "my friend, my brother." Youssouf remarked in a letter to the Czar: "He who has a thousand friends should count them for one, but he who has one enemy must count him for a thousand."

Youssouf had eight sons and one daughter, Soumbeca, who was Queen of Kazan, a princess as famous for her beauty as for her quick wits and bold, passionate nature. Queen Soumbeca was married three times: her second and third husbands had each murdered his predecessor to seize the throne of Kazan. Her first husband was King Enalei whom she married when she was fourteen. He was killed by Safa-Guirei, the son of the Khan of Crimea, who promptly married the widow. Proclaimed King of Kazan, Safa-Guirei was in turn murdered by his brother, who became the next King of Kazan and Soumbeca's third husband. He was soon driven from power and forced to take refuge in Moscow. Soumbeca was at last able to reign in peace for several years, but, when dispute broke out between Ivan the Terrible and Youssouf, the City of Kazan was besieged, and surrendered to superior Russian forces, and Queen Soumbeca was taken prisoner. The celebrated cathedral of Saint Basil the Blessed was erected in Moscow to commemorate the capture of Kazan, and its eight cupolas are symbolical of the eight days the siege lasted.

Ivan the Terrible, who admired Queen Soumbeca's bravery,

treated her with the greatest consideration. He sent a richly bedizened flotilla down the Volga to bring her and her son to Moscow, and gave them apartments in the Kremlin.

The Czar was not the only one to fall under his captive's charm. She very soon conquered all hearts at court, and the Russian people adored her, for in their eyes she was a fabulous princess out of a fairy tale.

Meanwhile, Khan Youssouf grieved over his daughter's and grandson's imprisonment by the Czar and constantly demanded their release. Ivan the Terrible took not the slightest notice of the old man's entreaties and threats. He did not even answer his messages, but merely remarked to his intimates: "His Highness Khan Youssouf is fuming with rage." Deeply offended, Youssouf was preparing to resume the war when his brother Ishmael murdered him.

Captivity in no way impaired Soumbeca's taste for power. She begged the Czar to allow her to divorce her last husband, who was still in exile in Moscow, in order to marry the new King of Kazan. Ivan the Terrible refused her request, and Soumbeca died a captive at the age of thirty-seven. But such a woman could never be forgotten. During the eighteenth and nineteenth centuries, her memory inspired several great Russian writers and composers. *Soumbeca and the Conquest of Kazan*, a ballet by Glinka, in which the part of the Queen was taken by the famous ballerina Istomina, had an enormous success in St. Petersburg in 1832.

After Youssouf's death, his descendants quarreled unceasingly until the end of the seventeenth century. His great-grandson Abdoul Mirza, on his conversion to the Orthodox faith, took the name of Dimitri and received the title of Prince Youssoupoff from Czar Feodor. The new prince, who was renowned for his courage, took part in all the Czar's campaigns against Poland and the Khan of Crimea. These wars ended victoriously for Russia, to whom all her former territories were restored.

Nevertheless, Prince Youssoupoff was disgraced and stripped of half his possessions for serving the Metropolitan of Moscow a goose disguised as fish when the prelate dined with him on a fast day.

Prince Nicolas Borissovitch, great-grandson of Prince Dimitri, relates that one evening, when he was the guest of Catherine the Great at the Winter Palace, she asked him if he knew how to carve a goose. He replied: "How could I be ignorant of anything concerning a fowl that cost us half our fortune?"

The Empress wished to hear the story and was much amused by it. "Your ancestor only got what he deserved," she said, "and what's left of your fortune should amply suffice you, for you could well afford to keep me and all my family."

Prince Gregory, son of Prince Dimitri, was one of Peter the Great's most intimate advisers. He rebuilt the fleet and took an active part in the Czar's wars, as well as in government reforms. Exceptional capacities and a keen intelligence earned him the friendship and regard of his sovereign.

His son Boris followed in his father's footsteps. He was sent to France when he was only twenty to study the French Navy, and on his return became the Czar's intimate adviser. Like his father before him, he took a great interest in social reforms.

During the reign of the Empress Anne, Prince Boris Gregorievitch was made Governor General of Moscow and, during that of the Empress Elisabeth head of the Imperial Schools. He was so popular with his pupils that they considered him more as a friend than as a master. He picked out the most gifted among the boys and formed a company of amateur actors. They gave performances of classical plays and also of works written by the boys themselves. One youth was conspicuous for his talent: Soumarokoff, later to become an author and one of my ancestors in the paternal line.

The Empress Elisabeth, when she heard of this theatrical company which was a real novelty (as none composed of all-Russian actors then existed), wished to see a performance at the Winter Palace. The Sovereign was so charmed by the boys' acting that she herself saw to their costumes, and lent her own dresses and jewels to those who acted the women's parts. At the instigation of Prince Boris, the Empress signed a decree in 1756 which gave St. Petersburg its first public theater.

These artistic activities did not cause the Prince to neglect affairs of State. He was particularly interested in economic questions, and created a river navigation system which established communications between Lake Lagoda and the Don and Oka rivers.

The eldest son of Prince Boris was my great-great-grandfather, Prince Nicolas Borissovitch. He deserves a chapter all to himself.

Prince Nicolas Youssoupoff
(1751–1831)

chapter II

Prince Nicolas is one of the most striking of my ancestors. Gifted with a remarkable personality, keenly intelligent and very erudite, he was a great traveler, spoke five languages, and corresponded with most of the famous men of his day. In addition to this he was a great patron of the arts, as well as the friend and counselor of Catherine the Great and her successors the Czars Paul I, Alexander I, and Nicolas I.

When he was seven, his name was put down for one of the Imperial Guards regiments, and he received a commission at sixteen. Later, he reached the highest dignities of state and was given all the most coveted decorations of his time, even the diamond and pearl shoulder ornament usually reserved for members of reigning families. In 1798 he was Grand Commander of the Orders of Malta and of St. John of Jerusalem. It has even been asserted that he received other more intimate if less dazzling favors from Catherine the Great.

Prince Nicolas spent a considerable part of his life abroad. There he met the greatest artists of his day, and remained in correspondence with them when he returned to Russia.

When he went to stay in Paris, Prince Nicolas was often invited to receptions given at the Palace of Versailles and at the Trianon. Louis XVI and Marie Antoinette were very fond of him and presented him with a Sèvres dinner service with a floral design on a dark brown ground, one of the finest specimens produced by the Royal Manufactory, and originally intended for the Dauphin. No one had any idea what had become of this service, till in 1912 I was visited by two French professors who were making a study of Sèvres porcelain. This led me to make investigations, and in a far corner of one of our furniture warehouses, where it had been stored for more than a century, I found the Sèvres service presented to my great-great-grandfather by Louis XVI.

Prince Nicolas prided himself on his friendship with Frederick the Great of Prussia and with the Emperor Joseph II of Austria. He was also a friend of Voltaire, Diderot, d'Alembert, and Beaumarchais; the last-mentioned composed an ode in his honor.

In 1795, Prince Nicolas married Tatiana Engelhardt, one of Prince Potemkin's five nieces.

Tatiana was a charmer from early childhood. When she was twelve, the Empress Catherine took the child under her wing and kept her beside her constantly. Princess Tatiana soon conquered all hearts at court and, as she grew to womanhood, had numerous suitors.

At that time an Englishwoman, as famous for her beauty as for her eccentricity, came to St. Petersburg. She was the Duchess of Kingston, sometimes known as the Countess of Bristol. On the bridge of her luxuriously decorated and appointed yacht, she had arranged an exotic garden stocked with rare birds.

The Duchess of Kingston took a great fancy to Tatiana. The day before she left Russia, the Duchess asked leave of the Empress to take her protégée back to England with her, promising to make her sole heiress to her immense fortune. Catherine told Tatiana about this proposal, but, although she was much attached to the Duchess, Tatiana refused to leave her country and her empress.

She was twenty-four when she married Prince Nicolas Youssoupoff, who was over forty. At first their marriage was a very happy one, and a son named Boris was born to them. In St. Petersburg, in Moscow, and at Arkhangelskoïe, their summer residence, the couple were always surrounded by artists, poets, and musicians. Alexander Pushkin was one of their intimate friends. The poet spent part of his youth in a suite of rooms which the Prince and Princess had given his parents in their Moscow house.

Princess Tatiana was not only a perfect hostess, as gracious as she was witty, but also proved to be an excellent business woman. Under her wise administration her husband's fortune increased, while the

Princess Tatiana Youssoupoff (1769–1841).
She wears the Peregrina pearl in her ear.

Princess Tatiana Youssoupoff,
by Winterhalter

standard of living of the peasants on the Youssoupoff estates was much improved. She was gentle and kindly. "When God tries us," she used to say, "it is for the sole purpose of enabling us to exercise our faith and patience." Notwithstanding her many virtues she loved beautiful clothes. She was particularly fond of jewelry, and her collection became the nucleus of a larger one which was to become famous. She bought a diamond called the "Polar Star," several sets of jewels which came from the French Crown, the jewels of the Queen of Naples and, lastly, the unique and splendid "Peregrina," a celebrated pearl which had belonged to Philip II of Spain and, in ancient times, or so tradition has it, to Cleopatra.

The Prince, who loved his wife after his own fashion, gave her an unlimited amount of money to spend. His peculiar nature showed even in his gifts. On one of her birthdays he gave his wife all the statues and stone urns which adorned the park at Arkhangelskoïe; on another occasion, he made her a present of animals and birds to stock the zoological gardens which she had planned and created on the estate. But their happy relations did not last. In his old age Prince Nicolas turned into a profligate. The Princess, wishing to leave a place where her husband lived like a pasha in the midst of his seraglio, retired to a small pavilion, called "Caprice," which she had built in the park of Arkhangelskoïe. Renouncing the world and its pomp, she gave herself up to her son's education and to good works. She survived her husband by ten years and died in 1841 at the age of seventy-two, having kept to the last the rare qualities which had made her famous.

After years spent in traveling through Europe and the Near East, Prince Nicolas returned to Russia and applied himself diligently to furthering the fine arts. He began the installation of the Hermitage Museum and of his own picture gallery at Arkhangelskoïe, which he had recently acquired. He built a theater in the park of the estate where his private company of actors, his musicians, and his own ballet dancers, gave performances that were long remembered in Moscow. Arkhangelskoïe became an art center that attracted foreigners as well as Russians. It was then that Catherine the Great,

TOP: *Arkhangelskoïe—the court of honor*
ABOVE: *Arkhangelskoïe—façade on the park*

who appreciated Prince Nicolas' taste and ability, gave him the management of all the imperial theaters.

Two factories, one for porcelain, the other for glass, were built by the Prince on his estate of Arkhangelskoïe. He sent to the Sèvres manufactory for decorators, workmen, and raw materials, and kept the entire output for his private use, chiefly to give as presents to friends and distinguished visitors. Porcelain with the trade-mark "Arkhangelskoïe 1828–1830" is much sought after nowadays by collectors. Unfortunately fire destroyed the factory and warehouses and a great quantity of Arkhangelskoïe porcelain was lost as well as a magnificent "rose du Barry" service of Sèvres, bought by the Prince on one of his journeys to Paris.

In 1799, Prince Nicolas returned to Italy where he spent several years as ambassador to the courts of Sardinia, Rome, Naples, and Sicily.

During his last stay in Paris, in 1804, he often met Napoleon I. He had the entrée to the Imperial box in every Parisian theater. When he was about to leave France, the Prince was presented by the Emperor of the French with two large Sèvres vases and three tapestries representing Meleager's Hunt.

On his return to Russia, the Prince continued to embellish his Arkhangelskoïe estate. In memory of Catherine the Great, he had a temple erected in the park on the pediment of which were inscribed the words: *Dea Caterinea*. Inside the temple, a bronze statue representing the Empress as Minerva stood on a marble pedestal. A tripod placed before the statue supported an urn in which perfumes and aromatic plants burned. On the wall, these words were engraved in Italian:

> *Tu cui concede il cielo e dietti il fato, voler il giusto e poter cio che vuoi.*
>
> (Thou who didst receive from heaven the desire for justice, and from destiny the power to enforce it.)

An Eastern prince who was making a short stay in Moscow having expressed the desire to visit Arkhangelskoïe, Prince Nicolas had a wall built in front of the chapel in order to conceal it from his visitor, for he could not bear the idea that an infidel might enter it. The wall is curiously topped with small pinnacles of Oriental design and was, so they say, erected in two days by the Prince's serfs.

His head steward was a Frenchman called Deroussy. He humored all his master's imperious whims, but his cruelty to the peasants made them hate him. One fine evening they hurled him from the top of a tower and threw his body into the river. The culprits were arrested, each received fifteen lashes with the knout, their nostrils were torn off, the word "murderer" was branded on their faces with a red-hot iron; after which they were sent to Siberia in chains.

A great number of gardeners were needed for the upkeep of the park. Prince Nicolas, who wished Arkhangelskoïe to be a residence dedicated solely to luxury and beauty, forbade the cultivation of cereals on his land. He bought wheat from a neighboring estate for his peasants' needs, and the latter were employed only in maintaining and improving his gardens.

The park was laid out in the purest French style. Three long terraces adorned with statues and marble urns led down to the river. In the center, long hornbeam hedges bordered a sweeping lawn, and fountains played on every side. Four pavilions stood on the river bank, connected by hothouses over two hundred yards long. In the winter garden among the orange and palm trees were seats and marble fountains. Exotic birds and flowers gave the illusion of eternal summer, even while, from the tall casement windows, one saw the park lying shrouded in snow. The Prince's zoological gardens were stocked with specimens of rare animals which he had brought from foreign countries. Catherine the Great presented him with a whole family of Tibetan camels, and while these animals were on their way from Tsarskoïe-Selo a special courier rode each day to Arkhangelskoïe to keep the Prince informed of their state of health.

Tradition has it that every day, on the last stroke of noon, an eagle flew from the park to the château, and that the fish in the ponds had gold rings in their gills.

In 1812 Prince Nicolas was obliged to leave Arkhangelskoïe and take refuge at Tourachkin where the Russian armies had fallen back before the advancing French troops. For long months he was without

TOP: *Arkhangelskoïe—view of the terraces*
ABOVE: *Arkhangelskoïe—one of the terraces*

news of his estates. When the war ended, he returned to Moscow to find his house intact, but Arkhangelskoïe seriously damaged. All the statues in the park were mutilated and the trees uprooted. On discovering that the noses of his mythological deities had all been broken, the prince exclaimed: "Those pigs of Frenchmen have given my entire Olympus syphilis!" In the château itself, all the doors and windows had been taken away, and most of the furniture and objets d'art lay in heaps on the floor. The destruction of his beloved collection proved too much for the Prince, and he took to his bed.

Prince Nicolas led a life of splendor at Arkhangelskoïe where hunting parties, balls, and theatrical performances were given continually. His enormous fortune allowed him to gratify his slightest whims and fancies and, where these were concerned, he spent without stint. He was, however, petty-minded to the point of avarice in minor daily expenses. This stinginess was to cost him dear. He most unwisely heated his stoves with sawdust to save wood, and one day the interior of the château was completely destroyed by fire.

One of his friends in Moscow describes the accident thus:

"Here is the latest news from Moscow: the magnificent château of Arkhangelskoïe has been burned down, and this misfortune is due to the old prince's avarice, for he insisted on using sawdust instead of wood to heat his stoves. There is, alas, but a step from sawdust to ashes. The greater part of the library and many pictures have been destroyed. To save them from the flames, paintings and objets d'art were thrown out of the windows. As a result, the arms and feet of Canova's celebrated group, Love and Psyche, were broken. Poor Youssoupoff! How could he be so stupid? I think that Arkhangelskoïe will never forgive him its gaping wounds, to say nothing of its desecration by a whole harem of dancers and prostitutes."

All Moscow gossiped about the scandalous life led by old Youssoupoff. Separated from his wife for many years, he kept an incredible number of mistresses, dancers and peasant girls. An habitué of the Arkhangelskoïe theater used to relate that when the whole ballet was on the stage the Prince waved his cane and suddenly all the dancers appeared completely naked. The *première danseuse* was his favorite, and he showered on her magnificent gifts, but his great passion was for a very beautiful Frenchwoman who unfortunately drank. She led him a terrible dance, and when she was intoxicated their quarrels often degenerated into a battle royal. China and ornaments were smashed to pieces, and the wretched Prince lived in a state of continual terror; nothing could soothe his irascible mistress but the promise of some splendid gift. His last intrigue was with a girl of eighteen. He was then eighty.

The Prince's journeys were complicated affairs. He never traveled without his intimate friends, his mistresses of the moment, a numerous staff of servants, his musicians and their instruments, not to mention his favorite dogs, monkeys, parrots, and part of his library. Preparations lasted for weeks, and at least ten coaches, each drawn by six horses, were required to convey the Prince and his retinue. He never omitted to have a salute fired from his own guns whenever he left Moscow for his summer residence and upon his arrival at his destination.

Prince Nicolas died in 1831, aged eighty. He was buried on his estate of Spaskoïe-Selo, near Moscow.

I cannot end this short biography of my great-great-grandfather without devoting a few lines to the estate which was his masterpiece. "Arkhangelskoïe," he used to say, "is not run for profit, but is a source of expense and joy."

I have known more magnificent and imposing places, visited many a royal or princely residence, but nowhere have I seen a house as finely proportioned as Arkhangelskoïe. And nowhere have I found man's handiwork so happily united with that of nature. The names of the architects who actually built this masterpiece are unknown. Arkhangelskoïe first belonged to a Prince Galitzin who began the construction of the château but, having lost a great deal of money, was obliged to part with it and sold it to Prince Youssoupoff. The latter continued the building of the house but made important changes in the original plans. These had been drawn up by the French architect Guerne, but as he never came to Russia himself his ideas were doubtless carried out by Russian architects.

In all probability, when Prince Nicolas became the owner of Arkhangelskoïe he himself superintended the work of construction with the aid of an Italian, Pietro Gonzago, a well-known architect and stage decorator of the period. Prince Nicolas often asked him to his house at St. Petersburg, and also commissioned him to paint scenery for his private theater. It is more than probable that the Italian artist helped in the decoration of Arkhangelskoïe.

A detailed description is necessary in order to give an idea of the house. I will describe it, just as I knew it.

A long, straight avenue led through a forest of pine trees to a circular courtyard round which ran a colonnade. On the ground floor of the château, great columned halls with frescoed ceilings were adorned with statues and fine pictures. Two rooms were specially reserved for the works of Tiepolo and Hubert Robert. In spite of their imposing proportions, all these rooms were friendly and intimate, thanks to the beautiful old furniture and a profusion of plants and flowers. A rotunda intended for receptions had doors opening onto the park. All the visitors who came to Arkhangelskoïe admired the view from this room; terraces and a long green lawn lined with statues stretched to the horizon and seemed to fade into the shadowy blue of the forest.

The left wing contained the dining room and my parents' private rooms. On the floor above were my rooms, my brother's and the guest rooms. In the right wing were the reception rooms and a library of thirty-five thousand volumes, among which were five hundred Elzevir editions and a Bible dating from 1462. All these volumes were in their original bindings, with this bookplate: "*Ex biblioteca Arkhangelina.*"

In my childhood I was afraid to wander around the library, for it contained a life-sized automaton representing Jean Jacques Rousseau, dressed in an eighteenth-century French costume; the figure was seated at a table, and a spring would put it in motion.

Near by was a collection of ancient carriages. I particularly remember a wooden coach, carved, gilded, and decorated with panels painted by Boucher. On raising a cushion of the back seat, a closet stool was disclosed. Prince Nicolas, who had been obliged to attend the Czar Paul I's coronation in spite of illness, had had this facility built into his state coach.

In 1912 when I modernized the private apartments of the château, I had to be on the spot to superintend the work. I took advantage of this to look through the storerooms, the basement, and the attics and discovered some wonderful treasures. I found a great roll of dusty canvases which turned out to be the stage scenery painted by Pietro Gonzago. I had these placed in the theater where they were most effective.

I also found whole crates full of crystal and porcelain from the Arkhangelskoïe factory. I took this treasure trove to St. Petersburg where it adorned the cabinets in my dining room.

After the death of Prince Nicolas, Arkhangelskoïe went to his son, Prince Boris. He was far from possessing his father's personality and had quite a different nature. His independence, integrity, and great frankness brought him more enemies than friends. Neither rank nor fortune played any part in his choice of friends; all that mattered to him was their worth and honesty.

On one occasion, when he was about to entertain the Czar and Czarina, the court minister struck out several names on the list of guests. The Prince refused to accept this. "When I have the great honor of receiving my Emperor," he said, "all my friends should be considered fit to share it."

During the famine of 1854 Prince Boris made himself responsible for the maintenance of his peasants. Naturally he was adored by them.

He took great pains with the administration of the fabulous fortune he had inherited. Prince Nicolas had long hesitated whether he should leave Arkhangelskoïe to his son or to the state. He realized that if ever it belonged to Prince Boris the whole character of the place would be altered. And sure enough, no sooner was the old Prince dead than his son at once turned Arkhangelskoïe into a profit-making concern. Most of the works of art were removed to St. Petersburg, the animals from the zoological gardens were sold, actors, dancers, and musicians dismissed. The Emperor Nicolas tried to intervene, but it was too late; irreparable harm had been done.

When Prince Boris died, his widow inherited his whole fortune. He had married Zenaïde Ivanovna Narishkin, who later became Comtesse de Chauveau. Their only son, Prince Nicolas, was my mother's father.

◆ ◆ ◆ ◆ ◆ ◆ ◆ ◆ ◆ ◆ chapter III

I *was born on March 24, 1887, in our house* on the Moïka Canal, at St. Petersburg. The evening before, my mother went to a ball at the Winter Palace and danced the whole night through. Our friends thought this was a sign that I would be gay, and a good dancer. They were right as to the gaiety, but wrong about the dancing.

I was christened Felix. My godfather was my mother's father, Prince Nicolas Youssoupoff, and my godmother was my great-grandmother, the Comtesse de Chauveau. During the christening, which took place in our chapel, the priest almost drowned me in the baptismal font, into which, according to the Orthodox rite, I had to be plunged three times. It seems that I was revived with the greatest difficulty.

I was so puny on coming into the world that the doctors did not think I would live more than twenty-four hours, and so ugly that my brother Nicolas, then aged five, cried out on seeing me: "Disgusting! Throw him out of the window."

My mother, who had already three sons, two of whom had died in infancy, was so certain I would be a girl that she had ordered a pink layette for me. To make up for her disappointment, she dressed me as a girl until I was five years old. Far from making me feel ashamed, this, on the contrary, made me very vain. I used to call out to passers-by in the street: "Look, isn't Baby pretty?"

One of my earliest memories is connected with a visit to the Berlin zoo, during a stay in that city with my parents.

On that fateful day I wore, for the first time, a sailor suit which my mother had just bought me, and a sailor hat trimmed with ribbons. I carried a little cane, and thus attired off I went with my nurse, as proud as a peacock.

We had no sooner entered the park than I noticed some small carts drawn by ostriches, and I badgered my nurse into allowing me to get into one. All went well at first, then suddenly the ostrich bolted and careered madly down the drive with me clinging to the seat as the cart swung from side to side. The bird came to a stop on reaching its cage. The guards and my poor nurse rushed up and lifted out a terrified little boy who had lost his hat and his smile in the adventure.

While I was a student at Oxford, I passed through Berlin and, remembering the zoo, felt an urge to visit it again. I gave some peanuts to an enormous female ape called Missie, and she took such a fancy to me that the keeper offered to let me enter her cage along with him. I accepted without much enthusiasm, and Missie showed her joy by embracing me in her long arms and hugging me to her hairy bosom. These transports of affection were not very enjoyable, and my one idea was to escape but, when I turned to go, Missie started to scream at the top of her voice; to pacify her, the keeper decided we should all three go for a walk. So I offered my arm to my new-found friend and promenaded through the park with her, to the joy of the passers-by who stopped to photograph us.

I never failed, whenever I was in Berlin, to pay my girl friend a visit. One day, I found the cage empty: "Missie is dead," said the keeper, and his eyes filled with tears. I was as moved as he was. This ended my visits to the Berlin zoo.

When a child, I had the rare good fortune of knowing one of my great-grandmothers, Zenaïde Ivanovna, Princess Youssoupoff, later Comtesse de Chauveau by a second marriage. I was only ten when she died, but she still remains deeply impressed upon my memory.

She was one of the most beautiful women of her generation. She had led a very gay life and had had numerous love affairs, among them a romantic attachment for a young revolutionary whom she followed to Finland where he was interned in the Sveaborg Fortress.

Princess Zenaïde Youssoupoff,
later Comtesse de Chauveau (1797–1897)

She bought a house on a hill facing the prison in order to be able to gaze at her beloved's window from her room.

When her son married, she gave the young couple her house on the Moïka Canal in St. Petersburg and went to live in Liteinaïa Street in a smaller replica of the Moïka residence.

When I was sorting her papers long after her death, I discovered, among a mass of correspondence with the greatest names of her day, a series of letters from the Emperor Nicolas I, which left no doubt as to the nature of their relations. In one of these letters the Czar offered her the Hermitage, a pavilion in the park of Tsarskoïe-Selo and invited her to spend the summer there, in order to be nearer him. A draft of her reply was pinned to his letter. Princess Youssoupoff thanked the Czar for his charming attention, but refused his gift, saying that she was used to living in her own houses, and the number of her estates was amply sufficient for her needs. However, she bought a piece of land adjoining the Imperial Palace and built a pavilion on it which was an exact copy of the one offered by the Czar. Both the Emperor and his wife frequently visited her there.

Two or three years later, having quarreled with the Czar, she went abroad. She settled down in Paris and bought a house in the Parc des Princes. All Paris of the Second Empire flocked there. Napoleon III took a great fancy to her, but his advances met with no response. At one of the balls given at the Tuileries, a handsome young Frenchman of modest extraction was introduced to her. His name was Chauveau. She was greatly taken by the good-looking young man, married him, bought him the Château de Kériolet, in Brittany, and obtained for him the title of Comte, and for herself that of Marquise de Serre. The Comte de Chauveau died soon after their marriage, bequeathing the Château de Kériolet to his mistress. The Comtesse, furiously angry, bought the château from her rival at an exorbitant price and gave it to the state on condition that it should be turned into a museum.

We used to visit my great-grandmother in Paris every year. She lived alone with a companion in her house in the Parc des Princes. We used to stay in a pavilion connected to her house by a subterranean passage, and never called on her except in the evening. I can see her now, enthroned majestically in a huge armchair, the back of which was decorated with three coronets, the emblems of her triple rank of princess, marchioness, and countess. In spite of her extreme old age, she was still beautiful and had retained an imposing appearance and aristocratic bearing. Always very carefully made up and perfumed, she wore a red wig and an impressive number of pearl necklaces.

She was strangely mean about some little things. For instance, she invariably offered us moldy chocolates, which she kept in a box made of rock crystal studded with precious stones. I was the only one who would eat them, and I really believe this was the reason why I was her favorite. On seeing me accept what everyone else refused, Granny would caress me affectionately, saying: "I like this child."

She was a hundred years old when she died in Paris, in 1897. She left my mother all her jewels, my brother the house in Parc des Princes, and to me her houses in St. Petersburg and Moscow.

In 1925, when I was a refugee in Paris, I read in a Russian newspaper that the Bolsheviks, while searching our house at St. Petersburg, had discovered a secret door in my great-grandmother's bedroom; this door led to a room in which was a coffin containing the skeleton of a man. I pondered over this mysterious discovery for a long time. Could the skeleton have been that of the young revolutionary she had loved? Had she hidden him in her home, after helping him to escape? I recollected that years before, while going through my great-grandmother's papers in this very room, I had felt strangely ill at ease and even asked my manservant to stay with me so that I should not be alone.

The house in the Parc des Princes remained vacant for a long time; it was rented and finally sold to the Grand Duke Paul Alexandrovitch. After the Grand Duke's death, it became a girls' school, the Cours Dupanloup, which my daughter attended long afterward.

My mother's father, Prince Nicolas Youssoupoff, son of Comtesse de Chauveau by her first husband, was a man of great ability, considerable attainments, and a most peculiar character.

On graduating from the University of St. Petersburg, where he had been an exceptionally brilliant student, he entered the service of the state and devoted the rest of his life to working for the welfare of Russia.

In 1854, during the Crimean War, he armed and equipped two infantry battalions.

During the Russo-Turkish War, my grandfather presented the army with a hospital train. He was deeply interested in public welfare. He founded and organized a number of charitable institutions, and took a particular interest in the Institute for Deaf-mutes. His character was full of contradictions. He would spend most generously for charities, yet showed an incredible stinginess in all the minor details of daily life. When traveling, for instance, he always stayed at third-rate hotels and asked for the cheapest rooms. On leaving, he went down the back stairs in order to avoid tipping the staff who waited for him in vain. Being both hard to please and very touchy, he was dreaded by one and all. It was misery for my mother to travel with him. In St. Petersburg, to reduce the expense of his receptions, he closed some of the drawing rooms to save the cost of lighting them, thus obliging his guests to huddle together in overcrowded rooms. The Dowager Empress, who remembered my grandfather's eccentricities, told us that when he gave a supper party the tables were set with gold and silver dishes, but that artificial fruits were placed among the real ones in the bowls. In spite of these petty economies, the general effect of his receptions was one of matchless splendor. It was at one of these, in 1875, that the historic interview between the Emperor Alexander II and the French general Le Flo took place.

After the France-Prussian War, Bismarck again became very aggressive, and did not conceal his determination to "finish with France, once and for all." Much alarmed, the French government sent General Le Flo to St. Petersburg to ask for the Czar's intervention to avoid a conflict. My grandfather was asked to give a party at which the French envoy could meet the Czar.

That evening a French play was given in our private theater. It was arranged that after the performance the Czar would stand in the recess of a window in the foyer, and that General Le Flo would join him. When my grandfather saw them together, he said to my mother: "You are present on a historic occasion. The fate of France hangs upon this interview."

Alexander II promised to intervene, and warned Bismarck that Russia was ready to mobilize if Germany persisted in her militant attitude.

My grandfather loved the arts passionately, and helped artists all his life. He was a great lover of music, and an accomplished violinist whose fine collection of violins included an Amati and a Stradivarius. My mother took it for granted that I had inherited my grandfather's talent, and she insisted on my taking violin lessons with a professor of the Academy of Music. To encourage me, even the Stradivarius was brought out. But all was in vain, and my career as a violinist soon came to an end.

The collections begun in the eighteenth century by Prince Nicolas were added to and enriched by his grandson, who also had a love for objets d'art. The glass cases in his study contained a large collection of snuff boxes, rock crystal cups filled with precious stones, and other bric-à-brac. He had inherited a passion for jewels from his grandmother, Princess Tatiana. He always carried a doeskin purse full of unset gems which he loved to handle and display to his friends. I well remember that in my childhood I used to play with one of his pearls and roll it about on a table; it was a specimen of such perfect shape and luster that my family thought it too beautiful to be pierced!

My grandfather was the author of several books including an important work on our family history. He had married the Countess Tatiana Alexandrovna de Ribeaupierre; I never knew her, as she died before my mother was married. She was so delicate that my grandparents spent a good deal of time abroad, at watering places and in Switzerland where they owned an estate on the Lake of Geneva. As a result of these frequent absences, their Russian estates were sadly neglected, and my parents had to spend a lot of time and money on putting them in order.

My grandfather died at Baden-Baden after a long illness. I remember seeing him there when I was a child. My brother and I often paid him a morning visit at his modest hotel. We used to find him sitting in a high-backed armchair, his legs wrapped in a plaid. Beside him, on a table littered with bottles and medicines, he always kept a flask of Malaga and a box of biscuits. It was with him that I had my first glass of wine.

My Grandmother Ribeaupierre was as good as she was intelligent and witty. She must have been very beautiful, judging by the portrait Winterhalter painted of her. She liked to surround herself with attendants whom we Russians call *prijivalki*, vague persons whose duties were ill defined and who were to be found in most old family homes where they formed part of the household. Thus, for instance, the sole duty of a certain Anna Artamonovna was to watch over a very beautiful sable muff which my grandmother never wore but used to keep in a cardboard box. When Anna died, my grandmother opened the box: the muff had disappeared and in its place was a note written by the deceased:

"Forgive me, Lord Jesus Christ! Have mercy on Your servant Anna for her voluntary and involuntary sins!"

My grandmother took great pains over her daughter's education. By the age of seven, my mother was well versed in social usage. She knew how to welcome guests and carry on a conversation. Once when my grandmother was expecting a visit from an ambassador, she asked her daughter, who was still a small child, to entertain him till she came downstairs. My mother laid herself out to please the old gentleman, offered him tea, biscuits, cigarettes . . . she labored in vain! The ambassador, as he waited in majestic silence for the mistress of the house to appear, paid no attention to the child. Having shot all her arrows, my mother could think of nothing else she could do for her guest until she had a sudden inspiration and asked: "Perhaps you'd like to go to the bathroom?"

Of my grandparents on my father's side, I knew only my grandmother. My grandfather, Felix Elston, died long before my parents' marriage. He was said to be the son of Frederick William IV, King of Prussia, and Countess Tiesenhausen, maid of honor to the Empress

Alexandra, the King's sister. The Empress went to Prussia to visit her brother, taking her maid of honor with her. The King fell violently in love with the maid of honor and wanted to marry her. Some say that the affair ended in a morganatic marriage, others that the young woman refused to marry him as she did not wish to leave the Empress. However, she must have yielded to the King's pressing suit, and their secret love affair resulted in the birth of a son, Felix Elston. Spiteful contemporaries construed this name as the contraction of three French words: *elle s' étonne* (she is astonished), which supposedly expressed the feelings of the young mother.

My grandfather lived in Germany until he was sixteen; he then came to Russia where he entered the Army. He was later given the command of the Don Cossacks.

He married Helen Sergeïevna, Countess Soumarokoff, who was the last of her line. On account of this, the Czar granted Grandfather Elston the right to take his wife's name and title. The same favor was granted to my father when he married the last of the Youssoupoffs.

My grandmother Elston was a tiny, dainty old lady, round as a dumpling, with a sweet face and the kindest of hearts. Her whimsical nature often showed itself in the most unexpected ways. For instance, she filled the many pockets of her innumerable petticoats with a jumble of oddments which she labeled "useful presents for my friends." The result was an extraordinary collection of slippers, toothbrushes, medicines, and various toilet accessories, some of them very intimate ones indeed. She used to display them before our guests, and would scrutinize their faces to try to discover which object would suit them best. My parents had to resort to various stratagems to keep her in her room while we were entertaining strangers.

She had two manias: collecting stamps and breeding silkworms. The worms overran the house; they crawled all over the armchairs, and our guests would squash them when they sat down, and of course ruined their clothes.

When we stayed in the Crimea my grandmother's chief interest lay in the garden, where there was plenty of scope for her originality. She decided that snails were good fertilizer for rose trees. She would scour the estate for them, and on returning home would trample her

The author's father as commandant of horse guards (1906)

harvest underfoot until it was reduced to a gluey pulp which she then presented to the gardeners, who immediately threw it away. However, as they wished to please my grandmother, they never failed a few weeks later to bring her the choicest fruit and flowers, obtained, so they said, thanks to the snail-fertilizer.

Her charity was boundless. When she had given away all she had, she continued to help the poor by begging from her friends. She was very fond of my brother and myself, although she was often the victim of our hoaxes. One of our favorite games consisted in taking her up in the lift and stopping it between two floors. When the poor woman, beside herself with fear, shrieked for help, we would stage a rescue which she never failed to reward. We played the same trick on visitors we disliked, but we never rescued them until the servants, hearing their cries, came running to their help.

A few moments before her death, Grandmother, true to her strange passion, asked for her silkworms and after gazing at them for the last time passed peacefully away.

The motto of the Soumarokoffs is: "Straight ahead." All his life my father was faithful to it, and in consequence was morally far superior to most of his associates. Physically he was tall, good-looking, and slim with dark eyes and black hair. Although he grew heavier with age, he never lost his fine bearing. He had more common sense than real intelligence, and his inferiors and subordinates loved him for his kindness. But he showed little tact in dealing with his superiors, and his frankness sometimes got him into trouble.

He had a love for soldiering which dated from his earliest youth. He entered the regiment of Chevaliers-Gardes which he later commanded until he was appointed aide-de-camp general to the Emperor. Toward the end of 1914, the Czar entrusted him with a mission abroad and on his return made him Governor General of Moscow.

My father was ill equipped to administer the immense fortune which my mother brought him on their marriage, and he made many bad investments. As he grew older, he showed signs of eccentricity which recalled those of his mother. His nature was so different from my mother's that he never really understood her. He was above all a soldier, and had no taste for the intellectual circles which would have suited his wife so well. Out of love for him, she sacrificed her personal inclinations and gave up much which might have helped to make life pleasant for her.

Our relations with our father were always very distant. They merely consisted in kissing his hand morning and evening. He knew nothing of our life, and neither my brother nor I ever really talked frankly with him.

My mother was lovely. She was slim and had wonderful poise; she had very black hair, a soft olive complexion and deep blue eyes as bright as stars; she was clever, cultured, and artistic, and above all she had an exquisitely kind heart. No one could resist her charm, and far from being vain and proud of her exceptional gifts she was modesty and simplicity itself. "The more you have," she used to tell us, "the more you owe to others. Be modest, and if you do happen to have any advantages don't let those who are less favored know it."

She had had numerous suitors from every country in Europe. But she refused all offers, even those of royalty, as she was determined to choose her own husband. My grandfather, who in his mind's eye saw his daughter on a throne, lamented her lack of ambition. He was bitterly disappointed when he found that she had decided to marry Count Felix Soumarokoff Elston, a mere officer in the Guards.

My mother had a natural gift for dancing and acting which would have enabled her to vie with the best professionals. At a great fancy-dress court ball where all the guests had to appear as sixteenth-century boyars, the Czar asked her to perform the Russian national dance. Although she had not rehearsed with the orchestra, she improvised so skillfully that the musicians followed her movements with ease. She took five curtain calls.

Stanislavsky, the famous manager of the Moscow theater, after seeing her act in a charity performance of *Les Romanesques*, a play by Edmond Rostand, begged her to enter his company, insisting that her right place was on the stage.

Wherever my mother appeared she brought a delightful feeling of light and well-being. Her eyes shone with kindliness and

Princess Zenaïde Youssoupoff,
the author's mother

sweetness. She dressed with quiet elegance, was not fond of jewelry, and although she owned the most beautiful gems wore them only on great occasions.

The Infanta Eulalia, aunt of King Alfonso XIII of Spain, once came to Russia on a visit and my parents gave a reception for her in our house at Moscow. In her memoirs, the Infanta gives a description of my mother:

> *Of all the parties given in my honor, none impressed me more than that of Princess Youssoupoff. The princess was a most lovely woman, whose marvelous beauty stands out as typical of a period. She lived in extraordinary luxury, in a setting of unsurpassed splendor, surrounded by works of art of the purest Byzantine style, in a great palace the windows of which gave onto the city of a thousand cupolas. The magnificence and luxury of Russia, blended with the refinement and distinction of France, reached its culminating point in the Youssoupoff palace. At the reception in question, the Princess wore a court gown studded with the finest diamonds and pearls. Tall, exquisitely beautiful, she wore a* kokoshnik *set with enormous pearls and equally large diamonds, worth a fortune. A dazzling array of fantastic jewels from the East and the West completed her costume: ropes of pearls, massive gold bracelets of ancient design, pendants of turquoises and pearls, multicolored, glittering rings. . . . All these gave to Princess Youssoupoff the majestic splendor of a Byzantine Empress. [The* kokoshnik *is our court tiara.]*

On another official occasion, things turned out quite differently. My parents accompanied the Grand Duke Serge and the Grand Duchess Elisabeth to England to attend Queen Victoria's Jubilee celebrations. The wearing of jewels was obligatory at the Court of St. James, and the Grand Duke had asked my mother to bring her finest sets. A large red leather bag containing the jewels was entrusted to a manservant. On the evening of her arrival at Windsor Castle, when my mother was dressing for dinner, she asked her maid for the jewels, but the bag could not be found. So Princess Youssoupoff appeared in a sumptuous gown without a single jewel. The bag was found next day in the rooms of a German princess whose luggage had also gone astray.

When I was a small child, my greatest pleasure was to see my mother in evening dress. I remember particularly a dress of apricot velvet trimmed with sable which she wore at a dinner given in our house on the Moïka in honor of Li-Hung-Chang, a Chinese statesman who was making a short stay in St. Petersburg. To complete her toilette, she wore a set of diamonds and black pearls. At this dinner, my mother became acquainted with one of the stranger forms of Chinese politeness. At the end of the meal, two of Li-Hung-Chang's Chinese attendants brought in a silver basin, two peacock feathers and a napkin. The Mandarin took one of the feathers, tickled his throat with it . . . and vomited his entire dinner into the basin. My mother was horrified, and turned an inquiring glance upon the diplomat seated on her left, who had lived in the East for many years.

"Princess," said he, "you should consider yourself highly flattered, for such behavior on the part of Li-Hung-Chang is a tribute to your delicious food; it is meant to convey his Excellency's readiness to start his dinner all over again."

My mother was a great favorite with the Imperial family, particularly with the Grand Duchess Elisabeth, the Czarina's sister. She was deeply devoted to the Czar, but her friendship with the Czarina did not last. My mother was too independent to conceal her opinions, even at the risk of causing displeasure. Under the influence of certain members of her immediate circle the Czarina ceased to see her.

In 1917 the court dentist, Dr. Kastritzky, on his return from Tobolsk where the Imperial family was imprisoned, brought us a last message from the Czar:

"When you see Princess Youssoupoff, tell her that I now see how right she was. If I had listened to her, many tragic events might have been averted."

Ministers of state and politicians appreciated my mother's clear-sightedness and the sureness of her judgment. She might have played the part of a descendant of her great-grandfather, Prince Nicolas, and become the center of a political *salon,* but her retiring nature prevented her from doing this. Her dignified reserve increased the regard that everyone had for her.

My mother cared nothing for money, and allowed my father to

The author with his parents and brother (1889)

use hers as he pleased, confining her personal activities to works of charity and to the well-being of our peasants. If she had married a different type of man, she would probably have played an important role not only in Russia but in Europe.

There was a gap of five years between my brother Nicolas and myself; this at first hampered our intimacy, but by the time I was sixteen we had become fast friends. Nicolas went to school and then to the University of St. Petersburg. He liked military life no better than I did, and refused to become a soldier. However, his character differed from mine and resembled my father's. From my mother he inherited a gift of music, literature, and the arts. At twenty-two he directed a company of amateur comedians who gave private performances. This greatly shocked my father, who always refused to allow him to act in our own theater. Nicolas attempted to enroll me in his company, but the first part I was given was that of a gnome, and this so wounded my vanity that I took an immediate dislike to the stage.

My brother was a tall, slender boy with black hair, expressive brown eyes, thick eyebrows, and a wide sensuous mouth. He had a very fine baritone voice and accompanied himself on the guitar.

As he grew up, he became overbearing and arrogant. He had little regard for other people's opinions, and did exactly what he pleased. He loathed the kind of people who came to our house, and in that I agreed with him entirely. To relieve the boredom we felt in the company of these self-sufficient hypocrites, we learned to communicate with each other silently by imperceptible lip movements. We became so expert that we could make fun of the guests under their very noses, but this trick was finally discovered and earned us the enmity of a great many people.

Arkhangelskoïe—interior of the rotunda

chapter IV

In 1896, when the Emperor Nicolas II came to the throne, we went to Arkhangelskoïe early in May to entertain the numerous guests who came to take part in the coronation festivities. Among these were the Crown Prince of Rumania and his wife, Princess Marie. In their honor, my parents sent for a Rumanian orchestra which was then very fashionable in Moscow. One of the musicians was a certain Stefanesco, a remarkable cymbal* player, who later became one of my intimate friends. He often came with me on my travels. I was extremely fond of listening to him play, which he often did for me alone the whole night through.

The Grand Duke Serge and the Grand Duchess Elisabeth had also invited a number of friends and relations to Elinskoïe, their estate, which was only about three miles away from ours. So they were often present at the receptions at Arkhangelskoïe. The Emperor and Empress also came to these receptions, which were almost as magnificent as the court balls.

For these festivities we opened our private theater. My parents sent to St. Petersburg for the Italian Opera, with Mazzini, Madame Arnoldson, and the *corps de ballet*. One evening, a few moments before the curtain went up on *Faust*, my mother was told that Mme. Arnoldson refused to sing because, in the garden scene, the *parterres* were filled with real flowers and their scent made her feel ill. The flowers had to be replaced by shrubs before she would go on. I shall never forget another performance at our theater: all the guests were

*A string instrument used in Rumanian and Hungarian orchestras.

seated in boxes, the stalls were removed, and in their place was a garden of tea roses whose fragrance filled the air.

After the performance everyone met on the terrace, where supper was served at tables lighted by tall candelabra. This was followed by a marvelous display of fireworks, an enchanting sight so dazzling to me as a small boy that I hoped I would never be sent to bed.

My parents and their guests went to Moscow a few days before the coronation to take part in another round of fetes. Our house in Moscow, originally a sort of super hunting lodge belonging to Ivan the Terrible, had retained its sixteenth-century character; great vaulted halls, medieval furniture, richly wrought gold and silver plate. All this oriental splendor was a wonderful setting for the receptions given by my parents. Foreign princes who had been to them declared that they had never seen anything like them.

My brother and I were left behind at Arkhangelskoïe, for we were considered too young to take part in these festivities. But we were allowed to go to Moscow for the coronation. I have only to close my eyes now to see once more the brilliantly illuminated Kremlin, its red and green roofs and golden cupolas.

On the morning of the coronation, we watched the procession leave the Imperial Palace for the Ouspensky Cathedral. After the ceremony, the Czar and the two Czarinas wearing their coronation robes and crowns, followed by the Imperial family and all the foreign princes, left the cathedral to return to the palace. The sun was particularly bright that day, and played on the gold and gems of the glittering costumes. Such a sight could be seen only in Russia. When the Czar and the two Czarinas appeared before their people, they were verily the Lord's anointed.

Who could then have foreseen that twenty-two years later nothing would remain of all this majesty and splendor?

It is said that while dressing the Czarina for the ceremony one of her women pricked her finger on the clasp of the Imperial cloak, and that a drop of blood fell on the ermine. . . .

Three days later, the dreadful Khodinka tragedy plunged the whole of Russia into mourning. Many considered this a bad omen for the dawning reign.* Most of the receptions planned to follow the coronation were canceled. However, on the bad advice of some of his counselors, Nicolas II decided to attend a ball given that evening at the French Embassy. There was deep dissension between the Grand Dukes. The three brothers of the Grand Duke Serge, then Governor General of Moscow, wanted to minimize the importance of a catastrophe for which he was to some extent responsible; they claimed that the program of coronation festivities should go on as arranged. The four "Mikhaïlovitchi" (my future father-in-law, the Grand Duke Alexander, and his brothers) firmly opposed this point of view, and for this were accused of conspiring against their elders.

After the coronation, my parents returned to Arkhangelskoïe with their guests, including Prince Ferdinand of Rumania and Princess Marie. Prince Ferdinand was the nephew of King Carol I. I remember King Carol perfectly, for he often came to see my mother. He was handsome and had a kingly look, with hair turning gray and the features of an eagle. It was said that he cared only for politics and money, and neglected his wife, the Princess of Wied, who was well known as a writer under the pen name of Carmen Sylva. As they had no children, Prince Ferdinand was heir to the throne. He was an attractive man, but devoid of personality, extremely timid and undecided in both public and private life. He would have been rather a handsome man had his ears not stuck out, which spoiled his looks. He had married Princess Marie of Great Britain, the eldest daughter of the Duchess of Saxe-Coburg-Gotha, sister of the Emperor Alexander III.

Princess Marie was already famous for her beauty: she had wonderful eyes of such a rare shade of grayish blue that it was impossible to forget them. Her figure was tall and slender as a young poplar, and she bewitched me so completely that I followed her about like a shadow. I spent sleepless nights conjuring up her lovely face. Once, she kissed me; I was so happy that I refused to let my face be washed

*Through lack of organization, during a distribution of the Czar's gifts to the people, a terrible stampede took place and thousands of persons were trampled to death.

that night. She was much amused to hear about this act of boyish infatuation, and many years later when I met her again at a dinner given in London at the Austrian Embassy, she reminded me of the incident.

It was at the time of the coronation that I witnessed a scene which deeply impressed my childish imagination. One day as we sat at a table, a noise was heard in the adjoining room. The door opened, and a very handsome young man on horseback rode in. He carried a bunch of roses which he threw at my mother's feet. It was Prince Gritzko Wittgenstein, an officer of the Czar's escort, a most attractive man, well known for his extravagances and doted on by all women, old and young. My father was furious at the young officer's audacity, and forbade him to enter his house again.

I could not understand my father's anger. I was indignant that he should have insulted a man who, in my eyes, was a hero, the reincarnation of the knights of yore, a cavalier who fearlessly declared his love by such a noble gesture!

Chapter V

In my early youth, I was a prey to every disease known to childhood and remained small and sickly for a long time. I was ashamed of my skinniness, and longed to find a means of fattening out. Then, one day, I happened to see an advertisement which gave me high hopes. It extolled the merits of *Pilules Orientales*, a French patent medicine warranted to turn the flattest-breasted lady into a harem beauty of opulent charms. I managed to get hold of a box of these pills and took them on the sly, but, alas, without result. The doctor who attended me saw them in my bedroom and asked what they were for. When I told him of my disappointment he was much amused, but advised me to discontinue the treatment.

I was in the hands of several doctors, but I had a marked preference for Dr. Korovin, whom I nicknamed Uncle Moo (*korova* in Russian means cow). When, from my bed, I heard his footsteps coming down the corridor, I used to "moo" and he, not to be outdone, gave an answering bellow. Like most old-fashioned doctors, he never used a stethoscope but put a towel on my chest to which he laid his ear. I loved the smell of his hair lotion; for years I thought that all doctors' heads must necessarily have a nice smell.

I was a difficult child. Today, after so many years, I still think remorsefully of all those who wore themselves out in an effort to bring me up properly. First on the list was a German nurse who had been with my brothers, and who went off her head. This was partly due to her unrequited passion for my father's secretary, and partly no doubt to my bad temper. My parents had to send her to a mental home, and I was handed over to my mother's former governess, Mademoiselle

Versiloff, a charming, good, and devoted woman, who had become one of the family.

I was a very bad pupil. My governess, thinking that a little competition might do me good, organized classes so that I could work with other children; but I remained lazy and uninterested, and my bad example had a most disastrous effect upon my fellow pupils. Late in life Mlle Versiloff married my brother's Swiss tutor, M. Penard, a kindly, scholarly man whom I remember with great affection. He is now ninety-six years old and lives in Geneva. His letters bring me echoes of a faraway past, when I so often used to put his good nature and patience to the test.

After a drunken German who went to bed every night with a bottle of champagne, there followed a succession of Russian, French, English, Swiss, and German tutors, to say nothing of a Roman Catholic priest who afterward taught the Queen of Rumania's children. Many years later, the Queen told me that the memory of me was still a nightmare to the wretched priest, and she wanted to know if what he had told her about me was true. I had to admit that nothing could be truer! I still remember my music teacher whose finger I bit so savagely that the poor woman was unable to play the piano for a year.

We had no real cousins on my mother's side. The Koutouzoff, Cantacuzène, Ribeaupierre, and Stakhovitch families were distant relatives, and though we saw little of them we were on excellent terms with each other. It was the same with our first cousins, Helen and Michael Soumarokoff, who lived almost entirely abroad on account of their father's bad health. Our closest companions were Michael, Wladimir, and Irene Lazareff, the children of my father's sister, and also Uncle Soumarokoff Elston's two daughters, Catherine and Zenaïde.

We all fell in love with Catherine, who was very pretty. Her sister was less good-looking, but so nice that everyone adored her. Michael, the eldest Lazareff boy, was about the same age as my brother, and was very witty and extremely intelligent, but his brother Wladimir had a sort of comical charm of his own that made him irresistible. His merry, expressive face and turned-up nose made him look

The author with his parents
and brother (1901)

rather like a clown, but he was full of fun and exuberance, and was the life and soul of all our parties. He was generous to a fault, but his levity prevented him from taking anything seriously. He laughed at everybody and everything, and thought of nothing but amusement. Together he and I played the maddest pranks; I still think of them with amusement and, I must say, without remorse. His sister Irene had the same happy nature; she had many admirers, attracted by her beautiful Egyptian profile and long green eyes.

The children of the Minister of Justice, Mouraviev, and those of the Secretary of State, Taneïev, also belonged to the group of young people who met on Sundays and holidays at our house on the Moïka. Once a week M. Troïtsky, the fashionable dancing master, initiated us into the mysteries of the waltz and the quadrille. Slender, affected, perfumed, his hair covered with pomatum, his well-brushed gray beard parted in the middle, he used to come mincing in, always attired in a beautifully cut dress suit, with a flower in his buttonhole, patent leather pumps, and white gloves.

My usual partner was Choura Mouraviev who was as charming as she was clever. I was a poor dancer, but she endured my clumsiness with the utmost sweetness, and never resented my treading so repeatedly on her toes. Time has not weakened our friendship.

There was a dance every Saturday at the Taneïevs. These parties were large and very gay. Anna, the eldest Taneïev girl, was tall and stout with a puffy, shiny face, and no charm whatever. Although she was not at all intelligent, she was extremely crafty and rather sly. It was quite a problem to find partners for her. No one could have foreseen that this unattractive girl would one day become the intimate friend and evil genius of the Czarina. It was largely to her that Rasputin owed his amazing rise to favor.

I had reached the age when, to a child, everything is followed by a big question mark. I used to pester my friends with questions on every sort of subject, such as, for example, the origin of the world. When I was told that everything came from God, I wanted to know who God was.

"The invisible Power that lives in Heaven."

The answer was too vague to satisfy me, and for a long time I used to gaze at the sky, hoping to discover some image or revelation that would give me a clearer idea of the Divinity.

But when I tried to solve the mystery of childbirth, it seemed to me that the explanations I got were even more confusing. People talked of marriages, of a sacrament established by Christ. They said I was too young to understand such things, but that later on I would discover their meaning for myself. Such vague replies did not satisfy me. Left to myself, I tried to solve these riddles after my own fashion. I pictured God as the King of Kings, seated on a golden throne amidst the clouds, surrounded by a court of archangels. And, thinking that the birds must be the purveyors of this Heavenly Court, I used to set aside part of my food and put a plateful on the window sill. I was delighted when I found the plate empty, for this convinced me that the King of Kings had accepted my offering.

As for the enigma of procreation, I solved it in the same simple manner. Being sure, for instance, that an egg laid by a hen was nothing but a fragment detached from the rooster's body, and that this fragment was instantly replaced, I deduced that the same phenomenon occurred with human beings. The difference between the sexes, which I had noticed on statues and by a study of my own anatomy, had led me to this strange conclusion, with which I was quite satisfied. Then, one day, the truth was brutally revealed to me by a chance encounter at Contrexéville, where my mother was taking the waters. I was then about twelve. I had gone out alone one evening after dinner, for a walk in the park. I happened to pass a summer house, and glancing through the window I saw a very pretty young woman in the arms of a stalwart youth. A strange emotion swept over me as I watched them embracing with such obvious pleasure. I tiptoed closer to gaze at the handsome couple, who were of course unaware of my presence.

On returning to the hotel, I told my mother of my experience; she seemed upset and quickly changed the subject.

Troubled and fascinated by what I had seen, I spent a sleepless night. The next day, at the same hour, I went back to the summer house only to find it empty. I was just going home when I met the young man coming up the path. I went up to him and asked him point-blank whether he had an appointment with the girl that evening. He stared at me in astonishment, then began to laugh and asked why I wished to know. When I confessed that I had watched them in the summer house, he told me he was expecting the girl at his hotel that same evening, and asked me to join them there. Imagine my feelings on receiving this invitation.

Everything conspired to make things easy for me. My mother was tired and went to bed early, and my father had an engagement to play cards with some friends; furthermore, the young man's hotel was near ours. He was sitting on the veranda waiting for me. He congratulated me on my punctuality and took me to his room, and had just begun to tell me that he was from the Argentine when his girl friend appeared.

I don't know how long I was with them. When I got home, I threw myself fully dressed onto my bed and fell into a deep sleep. That fateful evening, I had received an answer to the question that had mystified me. As for the Argentinean to whom I owed my initiation, he had disappeared the next day and I never saw him again.

My first impulse was to go to my mother and tell her everything, but a feeling of modesty and apprehension held me back. I was so amazed by what I had learned that, in my youthful ignorance, I failed to discriminate between the sexes. In my imagination, I began to picture men and women I knew in the most ridiculous postures. Did they really all behave in such a strange fashion? I was seized with giddiness, as fantastic pictures floated through my mind. A little later, when I told all this to my brother, I was surprised to find him completely uninterested in the questions that so engrossed me. So I retired within myself and never again touched on this matter to anyone.

In 1900 I left for Paris with my family to see the World Exposition. I have only a very vague memory of it, and of being dragged there morning and afternoon, in the hottest weather, to visit stands that did not interest me in the least. I used to reach home tired out and came to detest the Exposition. One day, when my patience was exhausted, I suddenly noticed a fire hose which I at once seized and, turning it on the crowd, copiously watered all those who attempted to approach me. There were screams, a stampede, and a general panic. Policemen rushed up, tore the hose from my hands, and took me, with my entire family, to the police station. A long discussion ensued, and much waving of hands, but it was at last decided that the heat had gone to my head and we were finally released after paying a heavy fine. To punish me, my parents deprived me of the pleasure of returning to the Exposition, never dreaming that this was the one thing I wanted. I was, however, allowed to wander about Paris alone and completely free: I went to bars and struck up friendships with all sorts of people. But the first time that I brought some of my new acquaintances to the hotel, my horrified parents forbade me ever to go out alone again.

A visit to Versailles and the Trianons impressed me enormously. I was not very familiar with the story of Louis XVI and Marie Antoinette, but when I heard all the details of their tragic end I became devoutly attached to their memory. I hung their portraits in my room and always kept fresh flowers before them.

When my parents went abroad, they were generally accompanied by one friend or another. On this occasion it was General Bernoff, whom everyone for some unknown reason called "Aunt Votia," who went with them. He looked exactly like a fat seal, very ugly, with such long mustaches that he could have tied them round his head—and he was so proud of his mustaches! He was really kindness itself, a most benevolent old gentleman who fell in with all my father's whims. In fact, my father could not do without him. General Bernoff had a trick of always using the words "in there" in season and, more frequently, out of season. No one had the least idea what the words corresponded to in his mind. But he said it once too often. At a review, he was in command of a regiment of the Guards which, swords drawn, was to ride at full gallop past the Czar. When the time came to give the order to charge, he cried: "In there!" and charged at full speed, not noticing that his men, confused by the unfamiliar order, remained standing at attention.

Russian officers, even when off duty, always wore uniform. They were unused to civilian clothes, and when they wore them always looked stiff and strange as if they were disguised. My father was no exception to this rule and once found himself in a most embarrassing situation. He and his friend Bernoff had taken some of my mother's jewels to Boucheron, the jeweler in the Rue de la Paix, to have them reset. Seeing these valuable gems in the hands of two such suspicious-looking characters, Boucheron thought it best to send for the police. The jeweler apologized profusely when my father and General Bernoff produced their identity papers, but he could scarcely be blamed.

Once when I was walking in the Rue de la Paix with my mother I saw some dogs for sale. I took such a fancy to a small brown ball of fur with a black nose, who answered to the name of Napoleon, that I begged my mother to buy it for me. To my joy, she consented, but as I felt it disrespectful to call my dog after such a famous man I named it Gugusse.

For eighteen years, Gugusse was my devoted and inseparable companion. He soon became quite famous, for everyone knew and loved him, from members of the Imperial family to the least of our peasants. He was a real Parisian guttersnipe who loved to be dressed up, put on an air of importance when he was photographed, adored candy and champagne. . . . He was most amusing when slightly tipsy. He used to suffer from flatulence and would trot to the fireplace, stick his backside into the hearth, and look up with an apologetic expression.

Gugusse loved some people and hated others, and nothing could stop him from showing his dislike by relieving himself on the trousers or the skirts of his enemies. He had such an aversion for one of my mother's friends that we were obliged to shut him up whenever she called at the house. She came one day in a lovely gown of pink velvet, a Worth creation. Unfortunately, we had forgotten to lock up Gugusse; no sooner had she entered the room than he made a dash for her. The gown was ruined and the poor lady had hysterics.

Gugusse could have performed in a circus. Dressed as a jockey, he would ride a tiny pony or, with a pipe stuck between his teeth, would pretend to smoke. He used to love going out with the guns, and would bring in game like a retriever.

The head of the Holy Synod* called on my mother one day and, to my mind, stayed far too long. I resolved that Gugusse should create a diversion. I made him up as an old cocotte, sparing neither powder nor paint, rigged him out in a dress and wig, and pushed him into the drawing room. Gugusse seemed to understand what was expected of him, for he made a sensational entry on his hind legs, to the dismay of our visitor who very quickly took his leave, which was exactly what I wanted.

I was never parted from my dog: he went everywhere with me and slept on a cushion by my bed. When Seroff, the well-known artist, painted my portrait, he insisted that Gugusse should be in the picture, saying that the dog was his best model.

Gugusse reached the ripe old age of eighteen and when he died I buried him in the garden of our house on the Moïka.

The Grand Duke Michael Nicolaïevitch and his youngest son, the Grand Duke Alexis, used to spend a few days with us each summer at Arkhangelskoïe. The Grand Duke Michael was the last surviving son of Czar Nicolas I. He had fought in the Crimean, Caucasian, and Turkish wars and filled, with great distinction, the post of Viceroy of the Caucasus for twenty-two years. Later on, he was appointed Inspector General of Artillery and was President of the Council of the Empire. He was loved and respected by all.

The Grand Duke Alexis was ten years older than I, and during my childhood always used to bring me toys. I remember particularly a rubber harlequin which could be blown out to twice my size. I loved it, but my pleasure was short-lived for, alas, Tipti, my little squirrel, soon tore it to pieces.

The Grand Duke Michael liked to watch my brother and myself playing tennis. Settled comfortably in a big armchair, he used to watch the game for hours. As I played very badly and sent the ball in all directions but the right one, it one day struck the Grand Duke in

*Supreme Council of the Russian Orthodox Church.

The author at seventeen, by Seroff

the eye with such violence that one of the greatest specialists in Moscow had to be called in to save the eye.

I behaved in the same clumsy fashion at Pavlovsk, the summer residence of the Grand Duke Constantine Constantinovitch. Among the people present were his sister, Queen Olga of Greece, and his mother, the Grand Duchess Alexandra Iosifovna. Everyone had the deepest respect for this venerable old lady who, when she was promenaded through the park in a wheel chair, surrounded by her family, had the air of a high ecclesiastical dignitary heading a procession.

This imposing company sallied forth from the château one day while the Grand Duke's children, Prince Christopher (Queen Olga's youngest son), and I were playing ball on the lawn. With my usual clumsiness, I sent the ball with a masterly kick toward the august group and struck the venerable lady full in the face.

At St. Petersburg, the Grand Duke Constantine lived in the Marble Palace, a very fine marble edifice built by Catherine the Great for her favorite, Prince Orloff. I often played there with the Grand Duke's children. One day they had the idea of reenacting the funeral of President Félix Faure, whose Christian name was the same as mine. I dutifully pretended to be dead during the whole ceremony but, once released from the box which served me as a coffin, I was so ill-tempered that I fell upon the "undertakers" and gave them such a trouncing that every one of them had a black eye for days. I was never again invited to the Marble Palace or to Pavlovsk.

I used to walk in my sleep until I was about fifteen. One night, at Arkhangelskoïe, a bird's call or some such small noise awakened me as I was straddling the balustrade that surrounded the terraced roof. I was terrified to find myself perched in mid-air, but a manservant heard my screams and rescued me from my precarious position. I felt so grateful to him that I asked my parents to attach him to my service. From that day on, Ivan never left me, and I considered him more a friend than a servant. He was with me until 1917. As he was away on holiday when the Revolution broke out, he was unable to rejoin me, and I could never find out what became of him.

* * *

In 1902, my parents decided to send me on a tour of Italy with an old professor of art, Adrian Prakhoff. The professor's appearance was so comic that it was impossible for him to pass unnoticed. Short, squat, his big head framed by a leonine shock of hair, his beard dyed red, he looked like a clown. We had decided to call each other Don Adriano and Don Felice. The journey began at Venice and ended in Sicily. It was most instructive but not, perhaps, in the way intended by my parents.

I suffered greatly from the heat, and was not in the mood to admire the artistic beauties of Italy. Don Adriano, on the contrary, briskly inspected churches and museums without showing the least trace of fatigue. He stopped for hours before every picture, and gave a lecture in French, with the most atrocious accent, for the benefit of anyone present. We were always followed by groups of tourists, obviously dazzled by his eloquence. As for me, I never enjoyed improving my mind in public, and I cursed the perspiring crowd, armed with cameras, that dogged our heels.

Don Adriano had adopted a costume which he considered suitable for the climate: a white alpaca suit, straw hat, and a sunshade lined with apple green. We never went out without an escort of street urchins and, although I was so young, I felt quite certain that this ridiculous-looking personage was not the ideal companion for an expedition through Venice in a gondola!

At Naples, we stopped at the Hôtel de Vésuve. The heat was appalling and I refused to go out before nightfall. The professor had a number of friends in town and spent his days with them while I stayed alone in the hotel. In the evening, when the heat abated somewhat, I used to sit on a balcony and amuse myself by watching the passers-by. I even occasionally exchanged a few words with them, but my scanty knowledge of Italian did not take me very far. One evening, a cab stopped in front of the hotel and two ladies alighted. I spoke to the coachman, a pleasant-looking young man who understood a little French. I confided to him that I was dreadfully bored and would like to visit Naples by night. He offered to be my guide and show me round the city and said he would call for me that night at eleven. By then the professor was in bed and asleep. I tiptoed from my room, and without worrying about the fact that I hadn't a penny in my pocket jumped into the cab and off we went. After driving along some deserted streets the coachman stopped before a door at the end of a dark alley. On entering the house, I was surprised to see a quantity of stuffed animals—among them a large crocodile—hanging from the ceiling by strings. I thought for a moment that my guide had brought me to a natural history museum. I realized my mistake when a stout, outrageously made-up woman covered with imitation jewelry advanced to meet us. I felt a little embarrassed, but the coachman, very much at his ease, ordered champagne and sat down on one side of me while the woman settled down on the other. In an atmosphere heavy with the odor of perspiration and cheap scent, women filed past us ... women of all colors, including Negresses. Some were completely naked, others were dressed as Turkish beauties, sailors, or little girls. They swung their hips and cast alluring glances at me; I became more and more embarrassed, even rather frightened. Madame and the coachman drank copiously and I began to do the same. From time to time she kissed me, exclaiming: *"Che bello bambino!"*

All of a sudden, the door opened and I was petrified to see my professor appear. Madame rushed to meet him and greeted him as an old friend of the house, clasping him to her broad bosom. As for me, I tried to hide behind the coachman's back, but Don Adriano had already seen me. His face lit up with a big smile and, coming up to me, he embraced me effusively, crying: "Don Felice! Don Felice!" The onlookers looked at us in astonishment; the coachman was the first to recover. He filled a glass of champagne and, raising it, cried *"Evviva! Evviva,"* and my cicerone and I received a frenzied ovation.

I don't know how late it was when the party ended, but I awoke next morning with a splitting headache. From then on, I no longer remained alone in my hotel. In the afternoons as soon as the heat abated I visited museums with my professor, and in the evenings we "did" Naples in the company of the obliging coachman.

From Naples we went to Sicily to visit Palermo, Taormina, and Catania. In the still air the heat was unbearable: the smoke rose in a straight line from Etna's snow-covered summit. As I longed for the cool mountain air, I suggested a climb to the crater. Don Adriano showed little enthusiasm, but I finally persuaded him, and off we went on donkeys, accompanied by guides. The ascent seemed endless, and when we reached the crater the professor was half dead with fatigue. We dismounted to admire the magnificent view when suddenly we felt the ground under our feet becoming hotter and hotter, while steam leaked through it in places. Panic-stricken, we jumped on our donkeys and started down the slope, when our guides, much amused by our terror, called us back, explaining that this was quite normal and that there was no cause for alarm. We spent the night in a shelter which was so cold that we could not sleep. Next day we agreed that the heat on the plain was far easier to bear than the cold in the mountains and decided to return to Catania without further delay. An accident which might have had a tragic ending marked our departure. When skirting the crater, the professor's donkey slipped, and he fell and rolled into the abyss. Luckily Don Adriano was able to grasp at a protruding rock, which gave the guides time to come to his rescue. They hauled him up, more dead than alive.

Before returning to Russia we spent a few days in Rome. It is most regrettable that I should not have profited more by our journey. Venice and Florence impressed me greatly, but I was too young to appreciate, or even take in, so much beauty, and my memories of this first trip to Italy were not, as we have seen, particularly artistic.

chapter VI

The war with Japan, one of the most terrible blunders made during the reign of Nicolas II, had disastrous consequences and marked the beginning of our misfortunes. Russia was not prepared for war, and those who encouraged the Czar in his purpose betrayed their sovereign as well as their country.

Russia's enemies took advantage of the general dissatisfaction to set the Government and the masses against each other. Strikes broke out almost everywhere; there were several attempts on the lives of members of the Imperial family and of high government officials. The Czar was forced to compromise and give the country a constitutional government by establishing the Duma. The Czarina violently opposed this; she did not realize the seriousness of the situation, and would not admit that there was no other solution.*

The Duma was opened on April 27, 1906. This was a moment of great anxiety for all, as everyone knew that the Duma was a two-edged sword which could prove either helpful or disastrous to Russia, according to the course of events.

At one o'clock the Imperial family went in great state to St. George's Hall in the Winter Palace. It was the first time that any room in this place had ever seen such a mixed crowd of queerly dressed people. After the Te Deum had been sung, the Czar delivered the inaugural speech. This first session made a painful impression on most of those present and filled them with dark forebodings.

If all the members of the Duma had been loyal Russians actuated

*The old Duma, composed solely of boyars (nobles), was suppressed by Peter the Great when he proclaimed himself absolute monarch.

only by patriotic motives, the assembly might have done great service to the Government; but certain questionable and destructive elements made it a hotbed of revolutionary ideas.

The political atmosphere grew heavier and heavier; the Duma was periodically dissolved, and attempts on the lives of prominent people grew more and more frequent.

Fresh complications arose when Goutchkoff, a member of the Junior Party, delivered a violent speech against the Government and the Grand Dukes. He thought it intolerable that the most important offices of state, and those which entailed the greatest responsibilities, should be entrusted to members of the Imperial family, for, he said, political immunity allowed their mistresses or their protégées to carry out dubious transactions with impunity.

The King of Montenegro's two daughters, the Grand Duchess Militza and her sister the Grand Duchess Anastasia Nicolaïevna, played leading parts at the Court of Russia during this period. The first married the Grand Duke Peter Nicolaïevitch, the second married Prince Leuchtenberg and afterward the Grand Duke Nicolas Nicolaïevitch. In St. Petersburg, these two princesses were called "the black peril." They were much interested in occultism and lived surrounded by soothsayers and questionable prophets. It was through them that a French charlatan named Philippe, and later Rasputin, had access to the Imperial Court. Their palace was the central point of the powers of evil which so tragically bewitched our unhappy Czar and Czarina and plunged our country into the abyss.

One day as my father was walking by the seaside in the Crimea, he met the Grand Duchess Militza driving with a stranger. My father bowed, but she did not respond. Meeting her by chance a few days later, he asked her why she had cut him. "You couldn't have seen me," said the Grand Duchess, "for I was with Dr. Philippe, and when he wears a hat he is invisible and so are those who are with him."

One of the Grand Duchess's sisters told me that as a child she had once hidden behind a curtain and seen Philippe enter the room; to her astonishment, all those present knelt and kissed his hand.

The Bible, in Leviticus 20:6, says: "And the soul that turneth after such as have familiar spirits, and after wizards, to go a whoring after them, I will even set my face against that soul, and will cut him off from among his people."

The two Grand Duchesses discovered their imprudence too late, and then tried in vain to open the eyes of the Czar and Czarina.

During the summer of 1906, it was learned in St. Petersburg that an attempt had been made upon the life of Prime Minister Stolypin at his country house; it was said that a great many people had been killed.

As we knew that my mother had meant to call on the Prime Minister that afternoon, we were frantic with anxiety until she came home. She told us that the attempt had taken place a few minutes after she left, and that she heard the explosion just after getting into her carriage. Stolypin himself had not been hurt, but one of his daughters was seriously injured by the bomb.

A little later it was rumored that another attempt had been made, this time upon the Imperial family, which was cruising in the Finnish Archipelago aboard the yacht *Standart,* as it did each autumn.

Exactly what happened was never known. Some said that the yacht struck a mine laid by revolutionaries, others that it had run onto some rocks, and that only the fact that the ship was sailing at low speed averted a catastrophe. However that may be, the Imperial party returned safe and sound aboard the *Polar Star,* which the Dowager Empress sent to bring them home.

That same summer, King Edward VII and Queen Alexandra of England were expected on a visit. Their meeting with the Czar and the Czarina was to take place at Reval. When the royal couple reached Reval on the *Victoria and Albert,* King Edward, who had neglected to try on the Russian uniform in which he was to meet the Czar, discovered it was so tight that he could not button it; a tailor was summoned hastily but found it impossible to make the necessary alterations at such short notice. So the King went to lunch aboard the *Polar Star* in a state of semi-suffocation and in a very bad temper.

This interview between the Czar and the King of England greatly alarmed public opinion in Germany. Germany considered it dangerous for Russia to trust England, whom she regarded as Russia's bitterest enemy. Many Russians shared this opinion; they were the ones who disapproved of the alliance concluded with France by Alexander III, urging that an empire could not be allied to a republic against another empire, and that only an alliance between Russia, France, and Germany could guarantee peace in Europe.

The Imperial family returned to Reval to receive M. Fallières, President of the French Republic, but the reception given him lacked the splendor which had marked that of the King and Queen of England. This did not escape the French, who were, it seems, extremely displeased.

◆ ◆ ◆ ◆ ◆ ◆ ◆ ◆ ◆ ◆ chapter VII

Our movements during the course of the year always followed the same invariable order: we spent the winter between St. Petersburg, Tsarskoïe-Selo, and Moscow; in summer we were at Arkhangelskoïe; the autumn found us at our Rakitnoïe estate for the shooting, and toward the end of October we left for the Crimea.

We seldom went abroad, but my parents sometimes took my brother and myself on a tour of their various estates which were scattered all over Russia; some were so far away that we never went there at all. One of our estates in the Caucasus stretched for one hundred and twenty-five miles along the Caspian Sea; crude petroleum was so abundant that the soil seemed soaked with it, and the peasants used it to grease their cart wheels.

For these long trips, our private car was attached to the train; it was so comfortable that we were far better off in it while visiting our estates than we would have been in houses which had often not been lived in for years. The coach was entered by a vestibule which in summer was turned into a sort of veranda containing an aviary; the songs of the birds drowned the train's monotonous rumble. The dining-drawing room—which would now be called a living room—was paneled in mahogany, the chairs were upholstered in green leather and the windows curtained in yellow silk. Next came my parents' bedroom, then my brother's and mine, both very cheerful with chintzes and light wood paneling, and then the bathroom. Several compartments reserved for friends followed our private apartments. Our staff of servants, always very numerous, occupied compartments next the kitchen at the far end of the coach. Another car fitted up in much the same way was stationed at the Russo-German frontier for our journeys abroad, but we never used it.

On all our journeys we were accompanied by a host of people without whom my father could not exist. My mother would have preferred rather less commotion, but she was always very nice to my father's friends. As for my brother and myself, we loathed them, for they deprived us of our mother's company. I must admit that they disliked us just as much as we disliked them.

St. Petersburg, called the "Venice of the North" because of its situation in the Neva estuary, was one of the finest capitals in Europe. It is difficult to imagine the beauty of the Neva River with its quays of pink granite and the splendid palaces that bordered it. The genius of Peter the Great and Catherine II was apparent everywhere, in the beautiful monuments, wide avenues, and lovely buildings.

The railings of the garden in front of the Winter Palace were designed for the Empress Alexandra by a German architect. The palace, built at the beginning of the eighteenth century by the Empress Elisabeth, is the masterpiece of the famous architect Rastrelli. The railings are hideous, but no matter what was done to disfigure the Winter Palace, it always retained its majestic dignity.

St. Petersburg was not entirely Russian; a European influence was introduced by the empresses and grand duchesses who, for nearly two hundred years, were foreign princesses—most often German—and also by the presence of the diplomatic corps. With the exception of a few families that kept up the traditions of old Russia, most of the aristocracy who lived there were very cosmopolitan. They had a snobbish infatuation for foreign countries, and loved to visit them. It was considered good form to have one's laundry done in London or Paris. Most of my mother's contemporaries affected to speak French only, and spoke Russian with a foreign accent. My brother and I found this most irritating, and always answered old ladies in Russian when they addressed us in French. We were considered ill-mannered and boorish, but we did not mind that as we preferred more bohemian circles where we had a far better time than in their strait-laced company.

Here, as everywhere, civil servants were for the most part corrupt and unscrupulous, obsequious to their superiors, indifferent to everything but personal advantage, and totally lacking in patriotism. As to the "intelligentsia," they were a focus of disorder and anarchy, and a serious danger to the country. This group tried to spread dissension between the people on the one hand and the Government and the aristocracy on the other, by sowing seeds of envy and hatred. When the representatives of this group assumed power during the Kerensky period, they proved how incapable they were of governing.

The Imperial theaters of St. Petersburg and Moscow deserved their reputation for excellence. Until the middle of the eighteenth century the Russian theater, properly speaking, did not exist, for most of the actors were foreigners. The first national theater was created in 1756 during the reign of the Empress Elisabeth, at the instigation of her chief adviser, Prince Boris Youssoupoff. The Russian theater received fresh impetus when Catherine the Great entrusted the management of all the Imperial theaters to my great-great-grandfather. It can be said that the influence of Prince Nicolas is at the root of the development of the Russian stage, and the high level of its artistic quality has been maintained to this day in spite of tragic upheavals. Everything crumbled in Russia except the theater.

Thanks to Diaghilev, who was the first to call the attention of Europe to the riches of Russian art, both Russian opera and the Russian ballet have acquired a world-wide reputation. Who does not recall the enthusiasm with which their first appearance was greeted at the Châtelet in Paris? Diaghilev had been at pains to bring with him the most outstanding artists: Chaliapin, the unforgettable "Boris Godounov"; decorative artists such as Bakst and Alexander Benois; peerless dancers such as Nijinsky, Pavlova, Karsavina, and many others. These artists were soon as celebrated abroad as in Russia, and several of them trained pupils who still keep up the tradition of the Imperial ballet. But our comedies, and Russian dramatic art in general, are less well known in foreign countries. Only in Russia could our great actors be heard in the national classic repertoire or in that inspired by folklore. Plays by Ostrovsky, Chekov, and Gorki were always great favorites; Nicolas and I never missed a good play, and we knew most of the performers personally.

Our house in St. Petersburg stood on the Moïka Canal. Its exterior was chiefly remarkable for its fine proportions. A very handsome semicircular inner court with a colonnade led to the garden.

The house was a present from Catherine the Great to my great-great-grandmother, Princess Tatiana. It was a real museum, filled with works of art, a place one could visit again and again without ever tiring of its beauties. Only some of the drawing rooms, ballrooms, and galleries had retained their eighteenth-century appearance. The picture galleries led to a small Louis XV theater. In the foyer next to it, supper was served after the performance. Sometimes great receptions were held at which the guests numbered up to two thousand people. On these occasions supper was served in the galleries, and the foyer was reserved for the Imperial family. These receptions were always a source of amazement to foreign guests. They were astonished that hot suppers in Sèvres services, or in gold and silver dishes, could be served to so great a number of guests in a private house.

Paul, our old butler, reserved for himself alone the privilege of waiting on the Czar. As he was very old and a trifle blind, he often spilled wine on the tablecloth. He had retired from service when the last of the Moïka receptions to be honored by the presence of our sovereign took place, and the event had been carefully concealed from him. The Czar noticed Paul's absence, and smilingly remarked to my mother that on this occasion the tablecloth stood a chance of remaining clean. He had not finished speaking when the old man appeared like a ghost, his breast covered with decorations, to take a shaky stand behind the Czar's armchair. He remained there, in his old place, throughout the meal. In order to avoid mishaps, Nicolas II carefully held the old man's arm when being helped to wine.

Paul was in our service for over sixty years. He knew all my parents' friends and acquaintances, and treated them according to his own personal likes and dislikes without regard to their rank or quality. A guest who was not in his good graces was sure to go short of wine or dessert. When General Kouropatkin, who commanded the ill-fated expedition to the Far East in 1905, was our guest, our old butler marked his contempt by turning his back on him, spitting on the floor, and refusing to wait on him at table.

I can still see Gregory, our head porter, in his feathered cocked hat and carrying a halberd. He was less harsh with the unfortunate General. One day during the first World War, when we were entertaining the Dowager Empress, Gregory came up to her and said: "Does Your Majesty know why General Kouropatkin's name has been forgotten in the choice of the Army's commanding officers? If he had been given a command he might have atoned for his mistake in Japan." The Empress repeated this to her son, and two weeks later we heard that General Kouropatkin had been given a division!

Our servants were devoted to us and took their duties very much to heart. At a time when houses were still lighted by candles and lamps, a considerable staff was needed to attend to the lighting. The manservant who was in charge of the staff was so grieved when electric lighting was introduced that he drowned his sorrows in drink and died from its effects shortly after.

Our personnel was recruited from all parts of the world: Arabs, Tartars, and Kalmucks brightened the house with their multicolored costumes. They were all under the direction of Gregory Boujinsky. This faithful servant showed the extent of his devotion when the Bolsheviks came to plunder our property. He died under the most atrocious torture without revealing to his tormentors the hiding places in which our jewels and most precious possessions were concealed. Although the fact that these hiding places were discovered a few years later made his sacrifice vain, its value is in no way impaired, and I wish to pay a tribute in these pages to the heroic fidelity of Gregory Boujinsky who remained staunch, and preferred a horrible death to betraying his master's secrets.

The basement of the Moïka Palace was a labyrinth of rooms lined with sheets of steel, with a special device for flooding them in case of fire. These cellars contained not only innumerable bottles of the finest wines, but the plate and china used for big receptions, as well as a great many objets d'art for which no room had been found in the galleries and drawing rooms. There were enough of them to stock a museum, and I was shocked to see them lying in the dust, abandoned and forgotten.

My father's apartments, which looked out on the Moïka Canal, were on the ground floor of the house. They were extremely ugly but crowded with objets d'art and valuable curios: paintings by great masters, miniatures, bronzes, porcelains, snuff boxes, etc. . . . I was not much of a connoisseur at that time, but had a passion for precious stones, which was probably hereditary. One of the showcases contained three little statues which I particularly liked: a Buddha cut from a lump of ruby matrix, a Venus carved out of a huge sapphire, and a bronze Negro holding a basket filled with precious stones.

Next to my father's study was a Moorish room looking onto the garden, entirely covered with mosaics, and copied exactly from an apartment in the Alhambra. In the center was a fountain surrounded by marble columns; along the walls were divans draped in Persian fabrics. I was very much taken with this room because of its voluptuous oriental atmosphere, and liked to sit and dream there. In my father's absence I would get up *tableaux vivants*, assemble all the oriental servants, and disguise myself as a sultan. Seated on a divan wearing my mother's jewels, I fancied myself a satrap surrounded by his slaves. One day I staged a scene to represent the punishment of a disobedient slave; Ali, one of our Arab servants, was the slave. He lay prone at my feet, pretending to beg for mercy, and, just as I raised a dagger to stab the culprit, the door opened and my father appeared. Quite indifferent to my histrionic talent, he flew into a violent rage: "Clear out, all of you!" There was a general scurry as Pasha and slaves jostled each other to escape from the room, and from that day on I was forbidden to set foot in that delectable place.

On the other side of my father's rooms, at the end of a suite of drawing rooms, was the music room where a collection of violins slept in deep peace, for no one ever practiced or played there.

My mother's rooms were on the first floor and looked out on the garden. This floor also included state chambers, drawing rooms, ballrooms, and galleries at the end of which was the theater. My paternal grandmother and my brother and I lived on the second floor, which also contained a chapel.

The real center of the house was my mother's suite of rooms. It seemed as though they were filled with her radiant personality and pervaded by her grace and beauty. Her bedroom was hung with blue damask, the furniture was of inlaid rosewood; long cabinets contained her jewels. On reception days, the doors were left open, and everyone could admire her magnificent jewelry. There was something mysterious about that room: a woman's voice would be heard calling each person in the house by name. The maids used to run in, thinking that their mistress needed them, and were scared to find the rooms empty. My brother and I heard the voice several times.

The furniture of the *petit salon* had belonged to Marie Antoinette; paintings by Boucher, Fragonard, Watteau, Hubert Robert, and Greuze hung on the walls, the rock crystal chandelier had graced Mme. de Pompadour's boudoir, the most lovely knickknacks were scattered on the tables or displayed in cabinets: gold and enameled snuff boxes, ashtrays of amethyst, topaz and jade with gem-incrusted gold settings. My mother usually sat in this room, which was always filled with flowers. When she spent an evening at home and was alone, my brother and I dined with her. We had our meal on a round table lit by crystal candelabra. A fire burned brightly in the hearth, the rings on my mother's slender fingers sparkled in the fitful candlelight, and I still recall with a heartache these evenings of happy intimacy. That charming little *salon,* the exquisite background of an exquisite woman will remain forever in my memory; those were moments of perfect happiness. It would have been impossible then for us to foresee, or even to imagine, the misfortunes that were to overtake us.

As Christmas drew near, there was great activity at the Moïka. Preparations lasted several days. Perched on ladders, all of us, including the servants, decorated the big tree, which reached to the ceiling. The glittering glass balls and "angels' hair" had a special fascination for our oriental servants. Excitement rose to a high pitch as tradesmen delivered the presents chosen for our guests. On Christmas Day these friends, who were mostly children of our own age, arrived with empty suitcases which they took home filled with gifts. When the presents had been distributed, we all had chocolate and delicious cakes, after which the children went to the playroom where the great attraction was a miniature switchback railway.

We had a very good time, but the party usually ended in a fight; I was in the front line of battle, delighted to have the opportunity of soundly thrashing the playmates I disliked and who were smaller than I!

On the following day, another Christmas tree was prepared for our servants and their families. A month before this, the servants had made out a list of the presents each one wanted, and this list was given to my mother. Ali, the young Arab who had played the part of the culprit slave in the memorable performance I gave in the Moorish room, once asked for a "shiny toy," which turned out to be the tiara of diamonds and pearls that my mother had worn one evening when she attended a ball at the Winter Palace. Ali had been literally dazzled on seeing my mother—who usually wore very simple clothes—dressed for court, and blazing with jewelry. He probably mistook her for a goddess, for he fell on his knees before her and was with great difficulty induced to rise.

Easter was celebrated in great state. Our very intimate friends and most of our servants came with us to the Holy Week services, as well as to the Easter midnight Mass in our private chapel. Many guests joined us at the supper which followed this Mass. Like all good Orthodox Churchmen we were supposed to have fasted for seven weeks, so Easter night's supper was always a gargantuan feast with suckling pigs, geese, pheasants, and torrents of champagne—then Easter cakes adorned with paper roses and surrounded by a ring of colored eggs. Most of us were ill the next day as a result.

After supper we always went down to the servants' quarters with our parents. My mother was careful that the servants should always be well fed, and their fare differed very little from ours. We wished them a happy Easter and kissed each one three times, according to the old Russian custom.

One of my father's whims consisted in continually changing dining rooms. Almost every day we dined in a different room, and this complicated the table service to an uncommon degree. Nicolas and

I, who were often late, were sometimes obliged to run all over the house before discovering where dinner was being served.

My parents kept open house, and no one ever had the least idea how many guests would be present at meals. A number of those who invaded our house at mealtimes, sometimes bringing their children, were poverty-stricken people who were more or less supported by wealthier families, turn and turn about. Such persons were excusable, others less so. As, for instance, a very rich old lady who, although she owned a fine house, made it a practice to be a perpetual guest at other people's tables. She always arrived toward the end of the meal and exclaimed with incredible impudence on entering: "Now the wild beasts have finished, I shall be able to lunch in peace."

General Bernoff, whom I have already mentioned, and Princess Galitzin, one of my mother's friends, hated each other cordially and never lost an opportunity of baiting each other at table or anywhere else. One evening when the General was in a particularly bad mood he refused to take Princess Vera home, as had been arranged. "Get along with you," he said to her; "you'll be just as stupid when you reach home as when you left here." She had rheumatism in her right thumb and was forever sucking it, hoping to lull the pain; I always refused to kiss her hand. Her celibacy was a source of continual regret to her: "I'm sorry I have remained an old maid," she would say to my mother; "now I shall never know how 'it' is done."

Each winter, my Aunt Lazareff stayed with us for several months in St. Petersburg. She was always accompanied by her children, Michael, Wladimir, and Irene. Wladimir was about my age and I have already written about this companion and accomplice of my youthful escapades. The last of our practical jokes ended in our being separated for years.

We must have been twelve or thirteen when one evening during our parents' absence we suddenly thought of going out disguised as women. My mother's wardrobe supplied us with all we needed for this fine scheme. Once dressed, made up, adorned with jewelry and muffled in fur-lined velvet pelisses that were much too long for us, we slipped out by a secret staircase and sallied forth to wake up my mother's hairdresser. As we said we were going to a fancy-dress ball, he agreed to lend us wigs.

Thus attired, we prowled around the city. We soon attracted the attention of passers-by on the Nevsky Prospect, which was the hunting ground of all the St. Petersburg prostitutes. To get rid of the men who accosted us, we replied in French: "We are already engaged," and pursued our dignified way. We hoped to escape them for good and all by entering The Bear, a fashionable restaurant. Forgetting to leave our pelisses in the cloakroom, we took a table and ordered supper. It was atrociously hot in the restaurant, and we were stifled in our furs. Everyone stared at us with great curiosity; some officers sent us a note, inviting us to have supper with them in a private room. The champagne began to go to my head: removing a long string of pearls, I made it into a lasso and amused myself by aiming it at the heads of people seated at a neighboring table. Naturally, the string broke, and the pearls scattered all over the floor, to the joy of those present. Finding ourselves the cynosure of all eyes, we became uneasy and thought it would be prudent to slip away. We had found most of the pearls, and were on our way to the door when the headwaiter came with the bill. As we had not a penny, we were obliged to see the manager and confess. The good man proved most indulgent, was very much amused by our adventure, and even lent us the money to take a carriage home. On arriving at the Moïka, we found every door closed; I called outside my faithful Ivan's window, and he was convulsed with laughter to see us in our ridiculous getup. But the next day things took a bad turn. The manager of The Bear sent my father the missing pearls and the supper bill.

Wladimir and I were confined to our rooms for ten days and strictly forbidden to leave them. A short time afterward, my aunt left, taking her children with her, and several years passed before I saw my cousin again.

chapter VIII

I preferred Moscow to St. Petersburg.

The Muscovites had escaped the influence of Western civilization and had remained essentially Russian; Moscow was the real capital of the Russia of the Czars.

Families of the old aristocracy led the same simple, patriarchal existence in their fine town houses as they did in their summer residences in the country. Imbued with century-old traditions, they had little contact with St. Petersburg, which they considered too cosmopolitan.

The rich merchants, who were all of peasant origin, formed a class of their own. Their beautiful, spacious houses often contained extremely valuable collections. Many of these merchants still wore the Russian blouse, wide trousers, and great top-boots, though their wives ordered their clothes from the best French dressmakers, wore the finest jewelry, and rivaled in elegance the great ladies of St. Petersburg.

The Muscovites kept open house. Visitors were taken straight to the dining room, where they found a table permanently laid with *zakouskis* and various kinds of vodka. No matter what the hour, one was obliged to eat and drink.

Most rich families had estates just outside the city, where they lived according to the time-honored customs of old Muscovy and practiced its traditional hospitality. Friends who had come there for a few days could just as well stay for the rest of their lives, and their children after them for several generations.

Like Janus, Moscow was double-faced: on one side was the holy city with its innumerable golden-domed, brightly painted churches;

chapels where thousands of candles burned before icons; convents concealed behind high walls, and crowds of the faithful thronging all places of worship. On the other side was a gay, lively, noisy town bent on luxury and pleasure, and even profligacy. A motley crowd moved along the brightly-lit streets and, swift as arrows, the smart *lihachis* sped by with a jingle of bells. The *lihachis* were luxurious one-horse hackney carriages, extremely light and speedy, driven by well-dressed young coachmen who were not always unaware of the adventures on which their clients were setting out.

A mixture of piety and dissipation, of religion and self-indulgence, was characteristic of Moscow. The Muscovites reveled in the grosser forms of pleasure, but they prayed as much as they sinned.

Moscow was a great industrial center, and also very rich in intellectual and artistic resources.

The opera company and the ballet at the Grand Theater could compete with those of St. Petersburg. The Little Theater's repertory of drama and comedy was much the same as that of the Alexander Theater, and the acting was of the first order. One generation of artists after another maintained its high traditions. Toward the end of the last century, Stanislavsky created the Art Theater; he was a manager and producer of genius, and was greatly assisted by such men as Nemirovitch Danchenko and Gordon Craig. A surpassing gift for training actors enabled him to achieve a unique ensemble in which even the most insignificant parts were taken by first-class performers. There was nothing conventional in the stage scenery; it was the reflected image of life itself.

I was an enthusiastic and assiduous habitué of Moscow theaters. Often too, I went to hear the gypsies at the Yar and Strelna restaurants; they were far superior to those of St. Petersburg. The name of Varia Panina is remembered by all who had the good fortune to hear her sing. Even when she was well on in years, this very ugly woman, always dressed in black, cast a spell over her audience with her deep, pathetic voice. At the end of her life she married an army cadet of eighteen. On her deathbed, she asked her brother to accompany her on the guitar while she sang one of her greatest successes, "The Swan Song," and breathed her last on the final note.

* * *

Our Moscow house was built in 1551 by Czar Ivan the Terrible. The Czar used it as a hunting lodge, for it was then surrounded by forests. An underground passage connected it with the Kremlin. It was designed by Barna and Postnik, the architects to whom Moscow owes the celebrated church of St. Basil the Blessed. To make sure that they would never duplicate this wonderful building, Ivan the Terrible rewarded the architects by cutting off their tongues and arms and putting out their eyes. This pitiless monarch's fits of cruelty were always followed by remorse and penance; apart from his crimes he was an extremely intelligent man and a great statesman.

The Czar never stayed long in this house; he used it for his fabulous entertainments, and then returned to the Kremlin through the underground passage. This labyrinth of galleries had several exits which allowed him to put in sudden appearances at places where he was least expected.

He owned a library which was unique of its kind and in order to preserve it from fire—then a very frequent danger—he had it walled into the underground passage. It is known, from historical evidence, that it is still there, but, as portions of the passage have caved in, all attempts to trace it have been in vain.

After the death of Ivan the Terrible the house remained empty for almost a century and a half; in 1729 Peter II gave it to Prince Gregory Youssoupoff.

During the restorations carried out by my parents at the close of the last century, one of the entrances to this passage was discovered. On going into it, they found a long gallery with rows of skeletons chained to the walls!

The house was painted in bright colors after the old Muscovite style. It stood between a formal courtyard and a garden. All the rooms were vaulted and decorated with frescoes. The largest room contained a collection of very fine gold and silver plate; the walls were hung with portraits of the czars in carved frames. The rest of the house was a network of innumerable small rooms, dark passages, and diminutive staircases leading to secret dungeons. Thick carpets

TOP: *Youssoupoff house in Moscow*
ABOVE: *Inside the house in Moscow*

stifled every sound, and the silence added to the atmosphere of mystery which pervaded the house.

Everything in it conjured up the memory of the terrible Czar. On the third floor, on the very spot where there is now a chapel, there used to be grilled niches containing skeletons. I thought that the souls of these poor creatures must haunt the place, and my childhood was obsessed by the terror of seeing the ghost of some murdered wretch.

We were not fond of this house, for its tragic past was too vivid, and we never stayed long in Moscow. When my father was made Governor General of the city we lived in a wing connected to the house by a winter garden. The house itself was used only for parties and receptions.

Certain Muscovites were most eccentric, and my father liked to surround himself with these oddities and found them entertaining. Most of them belonged to various societies of which he was the honorary president: dog clubs, bird fanciers, associations, and, in particular, a bee-keeping organization, all the members of which belonged to a widespread sect of castrates, the *Skoptzis*. One of these, old Mochalkin, who directed the organization, often came to see my father. He had a soprano voice and the face of an old woman, and altogether his appearance rather frightened me. But it was quite another matter when my father took us to visit the bee-keeping center. About a hundred *Skoptzis* gathered to greet us. We were given a delicious lunch followed by a very fine concert. All the performers were men with feminine voices; imagine a hundred old ladies dressed as men, singing popular songs with children's voices. It was at once touching, sad, and rather funny.

Another strange person was a round, bald-headed little man called Alferoff. He had had a shady past as a pianist in a brothel and as a dealer in birds. In the exercise of this last calling, he got into trouble with the police for dyeing humble barnyard fowls in lively colors and palming them off as exotic birds.

He always showed us the deepest respect when he came to our house, even to the point of kneeling and remaining in that position until we entered the room. Once, when the servants had forgotten to tell us he had called, he waited for one hour on his knees. During meals, he always rose when one of us addressed him and would not sit down until he had answered. Engaging him in conversation became a pastime of which I never tired, and I never gave the poor man time to eat. When visiting us, he wore an old dress suit that had once been black but which time had changed to a dirty green; it was probably the suit in which he used to play dance music for ladies of easy virtue. His stiff collar was so high that it concealed part of his ears; round his neck hung a huge silver medal which had been struck to commemorate the coronation of Nicolas II; his breast was covered with small medals, which were prizes he had won at bird shows for his so-called exotic specimens.

My father sometimes took us to see a parish priest in whose house a number of cages filled with nightingales hung from the ceiling. Our host set these birds singing by means of homemade instruments which he struck one against the other. He directed the singers like the leader of an orchestra, making them stop or start off again at will; he could even make each bird perform a solo. I have never heard anything like it since.

At Moscow, as at St. Petersburg, my parents kept open house. We knew a woman, a well-known miser, who contrived to be invited to meals in different houses every day of the week, except Saturdays. She would congratulate her hostess extravagantly on the excellence of the cooking and end by asking for anything that remained. Without even waiting for an answer, she called a servant and had the food put in her carriage. On Saturdays she invited her friends to her house to partake of a meal composed of a week's leftovers from their own tables.

Summer saw us back at Arkhangelskoïe; we had many guests, and some of them stayed for the whole season.

My liking for them depended entirely on the degree of interest they took in our beloved estate. I had a violent hatred for those who were indifferent to its beauties and merely came to eat, drink, and play cards. To me their presence was a desecration. To escape from them I used to take refuge in the park, wandering among the groves

Arkhangelskoïe—
"the silver drawing room"

and fountains, never tiring of a landscape where art and nature harmonized so perfectly. Its serenity brought me peace and quiet, and in its romantic setting my imagination had free play. I used to pretend I was my great-great-grandfather, Prince Nicolas—absolute monarch of Arkhangelskoïe. I would go to our private theater and, seated in a box, would watch an imaginary performance in which the finest artists played, sang, and danced for me. Sometimes I myself would go on the stage and sing, and be so carried away by my imagination that the ghosts of past audiences seemed to come to life and applaud me. When I awoke from my dreams, it was as though my personality had been split in two: one part of me jeering at such nonsense, the other grieving that the spell was broken.

Arkhangelskoïe had a friend and admirer after my own heart in the person of Seroff, the artist who came to paint our portraits in 1904.

He was a delightful man. Of all the artists I have ever met in Russia or elsewhere, my memory of him is the most precious and vivid. His admiration for Arkhangelskoïe, which revealed his acute sensibility, was the basis of our friendship. In an interval between sittings, we sometimes went into the park, sat down on a bench under the trees, and had long talks. His advanced ideas influenced the development of my mind considerably. I must add that in his opinion there would have been no cause for a Revolution if all rich people had been like my parents.

Seroff had a great respect for his art and never consented to paint a portrait unless the model interested him. He refused to paint a very fashionable lady of St. Petersburg whose face did not inspire him. However, he finally yielded to the lady's entreaties but, after the last sitting, he added to the portrait an enormous hat, which concealed three-quarters of her face. When the model protested, he replied that the hat was the most interesting part of the portrait.

He was too independent and too disinterested to conceal his feelings. He once told me that when he was painting the Czar's portrait the Czarina exasperated him by continual criticisms; so much so that one day, losing all patience, he handed her his palette and brushes and suggested that she should finish the work herself.

This portrait, the best ever painted of Nicolas II, was ripped to pieces during the 1917 Revolution, when a frenzied mob invaded the Winter Palace. An officer, who was a friend of mine, brought me a few shreds of it which I have reverently kept.

Seroff was very much pleased with the portrait he painted of me. Diaghilev asked us to allow him to include it in the exhibition of Russian art which he organized in Venice in 1907, but it brought me so much notoriety that my parents were annoyed and requested Diaghilev to withdraw it from the exhibition.

Every Sunday after church my parents received the peasants and their families in the courtyard in front of the château. The children were given refreshments, and their parents presented their requests and grievances. These were always treated with great kindness and their requests were rarely refused.

Great popular festivals, in which singing and dancing by the peasants played an important part, took place in July. Everyone enjoyed these festivals; my brother and I were particularly enthusiastic and looked forward to them impatiently each year.

Our foreign guests were always surprised by the spirit of fraternity that existed between us and our peasants. This was the result of our straightforward dealings with them, and never made them less respectful to us. The painter François Flameng, who stayed with us at Arkhangelskoïe, was particularly impressed by this. He was so delighted with his visit to us that he said to my mother, on taking leave: "Promise me, Princess, that when my artistic career is over you will allow me to become the honorary pig of Arkhangelskoïe!"

One year, toward the end of the holidays, my brother and I had a strange experience, the mystery of which was never solved. We were leaving by the midnight train from Moscow to St. Petersburg. After dinner we said good-by to our parents and entered the sleigh which was to take us to Moscow. Our road led through a forest called the Silver Forest which stretched for miles without a single dwelling or sign of human life. It was a clear, lovely moonlit night. Suddenly in the heart of the forest, the horses reared, and to our stupefaction we saw a train pass silently between the trees. The coaches were brilliantly lit and we could distinguish the people seated in them. Our servants crossed themselves, and one of them exclaimed under his breath: "The powers of evil!" Nicolas and I were dumbfounded; no railroad crossed the forest and yet we had all seen the mysterious train glide by.

We had frequent contacts with Ilinskoïe, the estate belonging to the Grand Duke Serge Alexandrovitch and the Grand Duchess Elisabeth Feodorovna. Their house was tastefully arranged in the style of an English country house: chintz-covered armchairs and a profusion of flowers. The Grand Duke's entourage lived in pavilions in the park.

It was at Ilinskoïe, when I was still a child, that I met the Grand Duke Dimitri Pavlovitch and his sister the Grand Duchess Marie Pavlovna, both of whom lived with their uncle and aunt. Their mother, Princess Alexandra of Greece, had died in their infancy and their father, the Grand Duke Paul Alexandrovitch, had been obliged to leave Russia after his morganatic marriage to Mme Pistohlcors, later Princess Paley.

The Grand Duke's court was composed of the most heterogenous elements; it was very gay and the most unexpected things happened there. One of its most diverting personalities was Princess Wassiltchikoff who was as tall as a drum major, weighed over four hundred pounds, and in her stentorian voice used the language of the guardroom. Nothing amused her more than to show off her muscular strength. Anyone passing within her reach risked being snatched up as easily as a newborn babe, to the joy of all present. The princess often chose my father for a victim, and he did not appreciate the joke in the least.

Prince and Princess Scherbatoff were other neighbors of ours, who always welcomed their guests most graciously. Their daughter Marie, beautiful, intelligent, and charming, later married Count Tchernicheff-Besobrasoff. She was always one of our most intimate friends, and neither age nor the misfortunes she has suffered have in any way affected her fine qualities.

Spaskoïe-Selo, one of the oldest estates belonging to my family, was also near Moscow. Prince Nicolas Borissovitch lived there before buying Arkhangelskoïe.

I never knew why this estate had been abandoned and reduced to the sad neglect in which I found it when I visited the place in 1912.

On the border of a forest of fir trees, a large palace embellished by a colonnade stood on a height; the building seemed to be in perfect harmony with the magnificent site. But, as I drew nearer, I was horrified to see that nothing was left of it but ruins! The doors and windows had disappeared; I picked my way through rubble, for the ceiling had caved in; here and there I discovered the remains of past glories: fine stucco ornamentation, paintings, or rather traces of paintings, in delicate colors. I passed through suites of rooms, each one more beautiful than the other, where stumps of marble columns lay on the ground like severed limbs; finely inlaid paneling of ebony, tulip, or violetwood gave one an idea of what the decoration had once been.

The wind swept through the rooms, howling round the thick walls, rousing the echoes of the past, as though proclaiming itself the sole master of the ruined palace. I was seized with anguish; from the rafters, owls stared at me with their round eyes and seemed to say: "See what has become of your ancestral home."

I turned away with a heavy heart, thinking of the unpardonable errors which can be committed by those whose possessions are too great.

The author, in the uniform of the Gourevitch school

chapter IX

As a child, I was dreadfully spoiled by my mother; and as I grew older I became more and more unmanageable; I was wayward and extremely lazy. My brother, who was then twenty-one, had just entered the University of St. Petersburg. As for me, my parents wished to send me to a military college. I had an argument with the chaplain during the entrance examination. When he asked me for an example of one of the miracles performed by Christ, I replied that He had been able to feed five people with five thousand loaves of bread. Thinking this was a slip of the tongue, he repeated his question. I insisted that my answer was correct and began to prove that this was indeed a miracle. He gave me the lowest mark he could, and I was ignominiously flunked.

In desperation, my parents decided to send me to the Gourevitch Secondary School which had a reputation for strict discipline; it was called "the school for failures." The principal added to his educational gifts a particular skill in taming rebellious natures and, when I was told of my parents' decision, I made up my mind to fail in the entrance examination again as I had done before. The Gourevitch School, however, was my parents' last hope, and I was unable to carry out my plan as, at their request, the principal admitted me without an examination, which was most disappointing.

What anxiety I caused my poor parents! I was most undisciplined, and any kind of restraint was odious to me. I flung myself passionately into a life of pleasure, thinking only of satisfying my desires, and impatient of any restriction of my freedom. I would have liked to own a yacht and sail the world where fancy led me. I loved beauty, luxury, comfort, the color and scent of flowers, and at the same time I dreamed of a nomadic existence, like that led by my remote ancestors.

I had, however, a feeling that a world unknown to me existed—one for which I yearned in my heart of hearts. It was adversity and the saving influence of a noble woman that at last enabled me to enter that world.

After I went to the Secondary School, my brother recognized my existence and began to treat me like a grown man. Nicolas had a mistress named Polia, a woman of humble circumstances who adored him. She lived in a small flat near our house, and there we spent most of our evenings in the company of students, artists, and their girl friends. Nicolas taught me gypsy songs which we sang in harmony; at that time my voice had not broken, and I could still sing soprano. In Polia's flat we found an atmosphere of youth and spontaneous gaiety which was lacking at the Moïka. Our parents' circle of friends, who consisted chiefly of officers, mediocrities, and parasites, seemed deadly dull to us. The palatial dimensions of our house called for the pageantry of great receptions; the house had been designed for them. But the theater and state apartments were no longer opened save on rare occasions, and amidst sumptuous surroundings we led a dreary life confined to a few rooms. By contrast, Polia's humble dining room with its samovar, *zakouskis*, and bottles of vodka was for us the symbol of joy and liberty. I liked the bohemian way of living, for I knew neither its inconveniences nor its dangers.

During one of the parties at Polia's flat, when everyone had drunk a good deal more than was good for them, we decided to finish the evening by a visit to the gypsies. But as I was obliged to wear the school uniform, I knew I would not be allowed in any of the night clubs, especially those where the gypsies sang.

Polia had the bright idea of dressing me up as a woman, and by the time she had finished with me not even my best friends would have recognized me.

The gypsies lived in the suburbs of our great cities, in a locality called Novaïa Deresvnia in St. Petersburg and Grouzini in Moscow.

Nicolas Youssoupoff,
the author's brother (1907)

Novaïa Deresvnia was situated in a district known as The Islands, for the many canals of the Neva made it quite an archipelago.

The gypsies lived in an atmosphere of their own, as characteristic as their copper-colored skins, ebony hair, and blazing eyes. The men wore brightly-colored Russian blouses, long-sleeved black caftans embroidered in gold, baggy trousers over high top-boots, and wide-brimmed black hats. The women's dresses were always brightly colored; they wore very long, full, gathered skirts, shawls over their shoulders, and scarves on their heads tied at the nape of their necks. In the evening, when they appeared before the public, their costumes were the same but made of richer materials, with the addition of barbaric ornaments such as necklaces of sequins, and heavy gold or silver bracelets. All gypsies have a beautiful supple walk, and all their movements are extremely graceful. Some of the women are very beautiful, but they are fiercely proud and tolerate no liberties unless accompanied by a promise of marriage. The gypsies led a patriarchal life, faithful to their own traditions: no one visited them in search of a clandestine love affair; they only came to hear them sing.

They entertained their guests in a large room furnished with divans set around the walls; small tables, some armchairs, and a few rows of chairs occupied the center of the room. These were always brightly lit, for the gypsies did not care to sing in semi-darkness. The expressive mimicry which accompanied their singing and increased its charm needed a lot of light. Habitués ordered champagne and called for their favorite choruses and singers.

Most of the gypsy songs have been handed down by oral tradition; each generation has transmitted them to the next from remote times. Some are sad, sentimental, nostalgic; others are filled with a kind of frenzied gaiety. When a drinking song was sung, a gypsy woman passed through the audience bearing a silver tray on which were glasses of champagne, and each person present had to drain one.

Night and day, without interruption, chorus followed chorus, although occasionally a gypsy dance was performed as an interlude;

the clicking of heels that stressed the rhythm of the music added to its charm. The peculiar atmosphere created by the singing and dancing, and by the beautiful primitive women, stirred the soul as well as the senses. Everyone fell a victim to their spell. Some visitors who came for a few hours stayed for days and spent fabulous sums in the place.

The gypsy singing was a revelation to me, for I had never before heard it; although it had often been described to me, I had never expected it to be so fascinating. I realized that under its spell one could easily squander a fortune.

I also realized that my disguise allowed me to go wherever I chose, and from that moment I began to lead a double life: by day I was a schoolboy and by night an elegant woman. Polia dressed very well and all her clothes suited me to perfection.

Nicolas and I often spent our holidays abroad. In Paris we stayed at the Hôtel du Rhin, Place Vendôme, where we had a small flat on the ground floor. By stepping over the window sill we could go in and out without having to pass through the hotel lobby.

One evening there was a fancy-dress ball at the Opéra and we decided to go, Nicolas in a domino and I dressed as a woman. To while away the first part of the evening we went to the Théâtre des Capucines and sat in the front row of the stalls. After a while I noticed that an old gentleman in a stage box was eyeing me persistently. When the lights went up for the interval I recognized King Edward VII. My brother, who had been smoking a cigarette in the foyer, came back laughing; he told me that he had been accosted by a most dignified person with a message from His Majesty who wished to know the name of the lovely young woman he was escorting. I must confess that this conquest amused me enormously and greatly flattered my vanity!

I haunted *café-concerts* and knew most of the popular tunes of the time and could sing them in a soprano voice. Nicolas conceived the idea of turning this talent to account by getting an engagement for me at The Aquarium, at that time the smartest *café-concert* in St. Petersburg. He knew the manager personally, went to see him, and offered to let him hear a young French-woman who sang the latest Parisian songs.

On the appointed day, dressed in a gray tailored suit, fox fur, and large hat, I saw the manager of The Aquarium, and went through my repertoire. He was delighted and engaged me on the spot for two weeks.

Nicolas and Polia saw to my clothes. They ordered a dress of blue tulle embroidered with silver, and a headdress of ostrich feathers in several shades of blue. To complete the effect I wore my mother's well-known jewels.

Three stars took the place of my name on the program and this intrigued the public. When I came onto the stage, blinded by the spotlights, I was in such a panic that for a few moments I felt completely paralyzed. The orchestra struck up the first bars of "Paradis du Rêve," but the music seemed faraway and indistinct. A few kindly people among the audience on seeing my agitation tried to encourage me by applauding. I finally pulled myself together and sang my first number, which was received very coldly. However, the next two songs, "La Tonkinoise" and "Bébé d'Amour," had an enormous success. The last one roused such enthusiasm that I had to repeat it three times.

Nicolas and Polia waited for me in the wings, greatly excited. The manager suddenly appeared with a huge bouquet of flowers and warmly congratulated me. I found it difficult to keep a straight face, so I thanked him as best I could, gave him my hand to kiss, and dismissed him hastily.

Strict orders had been given that no one should enter my dressing room, but while Nicolas, Polia, and I rolled on the sofa in convulsions of laughter, flowers and love letters poured in. Officers whom I knew very well asked me to supper with them at The Bear. I longed to accept, but Nicolas expressly forbade it and took me, with all our friends, to finish the evening with the gypsies. My health was drunk at supper, and I was finally obliged to stand on a table and sing to the accompaniment of guitars.

I appeared six times at The Aquarium without a hitch, but on the seventh evening I saw some friends of my mother staring at me through opera glasses. They recognized me from my likeness to my mother, and also knew the jewels I was wearing.

And so the scandal came out. My parents made a terrific scene, but Nicolas loyally took the blame and said it was all his fault. My parents' friends and the companions of our bohemian life were sworn to secrecy. They kept their word and the affair was hushed up. My career as a cabaret singer was nipped in the bud, but I did not give up the disguises which provided me with such delightful amusement.

At that time, fancy dress balls were the rage in St. Petersburg. I excelled in the art of disguising myself, and owned a collection of very beautiful costumes, both men's and women's. For a fancy dress ball given at the Opéra, I had faithfully copied the portrait of Cardinal de Richelieu by Philippe de Champaigne. The cappa magna, its train carried by two little Negroes, won me a real triumph.

Another ball ended in a tragicomedy. I went as the Allegory of Night, in a sequined dress, and with a diamond star in my wig. On such occasions Nicolas, who distrusted my fertile imagination, always came with me or had me watched by reliable friends.

That evening, an officer in the Guards, who was a famous Don Juan, courted me assiduously. The officer and three of his friends offered to take me to supper at The Bear. I accepted in spite of the risk, or rather because of the risk, which thrilled me immensely. Seeing that my brother was flirting with a masked lady, I seized the opportunity to slip away.

I arrived at The Bear escorted by my four officers, who engaged a private room. Gypsies were sent for to create the right atmosphere; and under the influence of the music and the champagne, my companions became very enterprising. I was holding them off as best I could, when the boldest of them crept up behind me and tore off my mask. Realizing that disaster was imminent, I seized a bottle of champagne and hurled it at a mirror which was smashed to pieces. Taking advantage of the general shock caused by what I had done, I leapt to the door, switched off the lights, and fled. Once safely outside, I hailed a coachman and gave him Polia's address. Then I remembered that I had left my sable cape at The Bear.

On an icy winter night, a diamond-bedecked young woman in a ball dress passed rapidly through the streets of St. Petersburg in an open sleigh. Who could have identified this madwoman with a boy belonging to one of the most respectable families in town?

My pranks could not be concealed indefinitely from my parents. My father sent for me one day. As he never summoned me except for matters of great importance, I naturally had some misgivings. And, sure enough, when I entered the room he was livid with rage and his voice shook. He called me a guttersnipe and a scoundrel, adding that people like me were not fit to breathe the same air as honest folk. He declared that I was a disgrace to the family and that my place was not in his house but in a Siberian convict settlement. Finally he sent me out of his room. The door banged so violently that a picture on the wall crashed to the ground.

I stood still for a moment, aghast at this outburst. Then I went to my brother.

Seeing me so depressed, Nicolas tried to cheer me up. I took advantage of this to unburden my heart, and reminded him how vainly I had several times sought his support and advice, particularly after my encounter with the Argentinean at Contrexéville. I also reminded him that it was he and Polia who had first thought of disguising me as a woman, for their own amusement, and that this had been the beginning of my "double life." Nicolas had to admit that I was right.

Later on, when I was old enough to take an interest in women, life became even more complicated. Although I felt much attracted to them my numerous love affairs never lasted long because, being accustomed to adulation, I quickly tired of doing the courting and cared for no one but myself. The truth is I was a horrible little beast. I liked to be a star surrounded by admirers. It was all great fun, but I did enjoy being the center of attention and doing whatever I liked. I thought it quite natural to take my pleasure wherever I found it, without worrying about what others might think.

I have often been accused of disliking women. Nothing is further from the truth. I like them when they are nice. A few among them have played an important part in my life, and especially the one to whom I owe my happiness. But I must admit that I have met very few who answered to my ideal of womanhood. Generally speaking, I have found among men the loyalty and disinterestedness which I think most women lack.

The Youssoupoff villa at Tsarskoïe-Selo

chapter X

We often stayed at Tsarskoïe-Selo and lived in the pavilion which my grandmother had copied from the one offered her by Nicolas I. It was a Louis XV house, white inside and out; in the center of the building was a large room with six doors which led to the drawing rooms, to the dining room and to the garden. All the furniture was of the same period as the house, painted white and covered with flowered cretonne; long curtains of the same material were lined with buttercup-yellow silk, and the light that glimmered through them seemed full of sunshine. In this house everything was bright and gay. A profusion of flowers and plants scented the air and gave the illusion of perpetual spring. On my return from Oxford, I turned the attics into bachelor chambers with a private entrance.

Every thing at Tsarskoïe-Selo recalled Catherine the Great: the Great Palace designed and built by Rastrelli, the beautiful arrangement of the reception rooms, the "Amber Room" (the Czarina's private drawing room), the celebrated Cameron colonnade with its marble statues, the immense park with its pavilions and groves, lakes and fountains. One of the Great Catherine's happiest fancies, a charming red and gold Chinese theater, stood out against a background of pine trees.

The Imperial family did not live in the Great Palace, which was used only for official receptions. Nicolas II resided at the Alexander Palace which was built by Catherine the Great for her grandson Alexander I. In spite of its modest size, the Alexander Palace would not have lacked charm had it not been for the young Czarina's unfortunate "improvements." She replaced most of the paintings, stucco ornaments, and bas-reliefs by mahogany woodwork and cosy-corners in the worst possible taste. New furniture by Maple was sent from England, and the old furniture was banished to storerooms.

The fact that the Sovereign resided at Tsarskoïe-Selo meant that many other members of the Imperial family and of the aristocracy had homes there too. Picnics, suppers, and receptions followed in quick succession, and time passed happily in the unsophisticated atmosphere of semi-country life.

During 1912 and 1913 I saw a great deal of the Grand Duke Dimitri Pavlovitch, who had just joined the Horse Guards. The Emperor and Empress both loved him and looked upon him as a son; he lived at the Alexander Palace and went everywhere with the Czar. He spent all his free time with me; I saw him almost every day and we took long walks and rides together.

Dimitri was extremely attractive: tall, elegant, well-bred, with deep thoughtful eyes, he recalled the portraits of his ancestors. He was all impulses and contradictions; he was both romantic and mystical, and his mind was far from shallow. At the same time, he was very gay and always ready for the wildest escapades. His charm won the hearts of all, but the weakness of his character made him dangerously easy to influence. As I was a few years his senior, I had a certain prestige in his eyes. He was to a certain extent familiar with my "scandalous" life and considered me interesting and a trifle mysterious. He trusted me and valued my opinion, and he not only confided his innermost thoughts to me but used to tell me about everything that was happening around him. I thus heard about many grave and even sad events that took place in the Alexander Palace.

The Czar's preference for him aroused a good deal of jealousy and led to some intrigues. For a time, Dimitri's head was turned by success and he became terribly vain. As his senior, I had a good deal of influence over him and sometimes took advantage of this to express my opinion very bluntly. He bore me no grudge and continued to visit my little attic where we used to talk for hours in the friendliest way. Almost every night we took a car and drove to St. Petersburg to have a gay time at restaurants and night clubs and with the gypsies. We would invite artists and musicians to supper with us in a private

The Grand Duke Dimitri

room; the well-known ballerina Anna Pavlova was often our guest. These wonderful evenings slipped by like dreams and we never went home until dawn.

We were having supper in a restaurant one evening when an officer belonging to the Czar's escort came up to me. He was youngish, very handsome, and wore the tunic of a Tcherkess cavalryman with a dagger stuck through his belt. "You probably do not remember me," he said after giving me his name, "but perhaps you can recall the circumstances of our last meeting, for they were somewhat peculiar. I rode on horseback into the dining room at Arkhangelskoïe, and your father was so angry that he had me thrown out."

I remembered the occasion perfectly. I told him that I had been filled with admiration for him and had been furious at my father's attitude. He sat down at our table and spent part of the evening with us. He said very little but looked at me closely and finally exclaimed: "You are so like your mother!"

He seemed very much moved, abruptly rose, and took his leave.

The next day he rang me up at Tsarskoïe-Selo and asked whether he could come and see me. I told him that I lived with my parents and that in view of what had happened his presence in their house would be embarrassing, to say the least. He then proposed that we should spend an evening together in St. Petersburg. I agreed, and on the appointed day we went to hear the gypsies sing. He was very silent at first but, toward the end of the evening, what with the champagne and the singing, he became quite talkative. He confided to me that his feeling for my mother remained unchanged, and that my likeness to her had been a great shock. He would have liked to see me again, but in spite of my real liking for him I made it clear that we would have to remain casual acquaintances and could never be friends. That was our last meeting.

My relations with Dimitri underwent a temporary eclipse. The Czar and Czarina, who were aware of the scandalous rumors about my mode of living, disapproved of our friendship. They ended by forbidding the Grand Duke to see me, and I myself became the object of the most unpleasant supervision. Inspectors of the secret police prowled around our house and followed me like a shadow when I went to St. Petersburg. But Dimitri soon got back his independence. He left the Alexander Palace, went to live in his own palace in St. Petersburg, and asked me to help him with the redecoration of his new home.

Dimitri's sister, the Grand Duchess Marie, had married Prince William of Sweden. Later she divorced him to marry an officer in the Guards, Prince Poutiatin, whom she also divorced. I often saw Dimitri's half brother and his two half sisters, the children of his father, the Grand Duke Paul Alexandrovitch by his morganatic marriage to Madame Pistohlcors. They were near neighbors of ours in Tsarskoïe-Selo; the Grand Duke Paul's two daughters were talented amateur actresses. Their brother Wladimir was also extremely gifted. If he had not been brutally murdered in Siberia with several other members of the Imperial family, there is no doubt that he would have been one of the best poets of our time. Some of his works might be compared to those of Pushkin.

His beautiful and intelligent eldest sister Irene was very like her grandmother, the Empress Marie, wife of Czar Alexander II. She married my brother-in-law, Prince Theodore, and had two children by him, Michael and Irene. Wladimir's younger sister, Natalie, was radiantly pretty and had all the charming grace of a playful kitten. She married the French couturier Lucien Lelong, and afterward an American, Mr. J. C. Wilson.

The Grand Duke and the Grand Duchess Wladimir spent their summers at Tsarskoïe-Selo. The Grand Duchess had the graceful bearing of a great lady of the Renaissance. She was born a Princess of Mecklenburg-Schwerin, and ranked immediately after the two Empresses. She was very able and intelligent and carried out all the duties of her position with perfect tact. She was always very kind to me, and was much entertained by accounts of my adventures. For a long time I was in love with her daughter the Grand Duchess Helen Wladimirovna, later Princess Nicolas of Greece, whose beauty fascinated me. She had the loveliest eyes imaginable, and everyone fell under their charm.

About three miles from Tsarskoïe-Selo was Pavlovsk, the seat of

The Grand Duchess Helen,
Princess Nicolas of Greece

the Grand Duke Constantine Constantinovitch. No unfortunate improvements had marred this eighteenth-century masterpiece and it remained exactly as it had been when it belonged to Czar Paul I. The Grand Duke was a most cultured man, a musician, a poet, and an actor. Many people still remember his talented performance in one of his own dramas, *The King of Judea*. The Grand Duke and Grand Duchess and their eight children were all much attached to their beautiful home, and devoted much love and care to its upkeep.

Before going to the Crimea where we spent the autumn, we used to stop at Rakitnoïe, in the district of Kursk. This was one of our largest estates. On it were a sugar plantation, numerous sawmills, a brick factory, a wool-spinning mill, and several stock farms. The overseer's house and its outbuildings stood in the center of the estate. Each section of farm life was under separate management: studs, kennels, sheepfolds, barnyards, etc. Many a horse from our stables won races on the St. Petersburg and Moscow tracks.

Riding was my favorite sport, and for a time I was particularly interested in hunting. I liked to gallop through fields and woods with my borzois on a leash. The dogs often spotted game before I did, and gave such leaps and bounds that I had difficulty in keeping my seat. When hunting with these dogs, one end of the leash is tied to the rider's body; the other is slipped through the dogs' collars and held in the right hand. To free the dogs one releases this end, but if the borzois see their prey before the huntsman does he can easily be unseated unless he releases them in time.

My love for shooting did not last long. I once wounded a hare, and its piteous screams made me feel so guilty that from that day I gave it up.

Many of our friends joined us at Rakitnoïe for the shooting. Our old familiar friend General Bernoff always added a comic touch to the party. As he was short-sighted he often mistook cows for deer, or dogs for wolves. Once in my presence he killed a keeper's favorite cat which he had taken for a lynx. Seizing his victim by the tail, he threw it at my mother's feet with a theatrical gesture. He only realized his mistake when the keeper's wife arrived and threw herself weeping on the body of her pet. But when the general wounded a beater whom he had taken for some unknown species of game, my father took his gun away from him and would not allow him to shoot any more.

The Grand Duke Serge Alexandrovitch and the Grand Duchess Elisabeth Feodorovna were among our most frequent guests and always came accompanied by their own gay and youthful entourage.

I adored the Grand Duchess but had little liking for the Grand Duke. His manners seemed strange to me and I hated the way he stared at me. He wore corsets, and when he was in his summer uniform the bones could be clearly seen through his white linen tunic. As a child, it always amused me to touch them, and this of course annoyed him intensely.

Some of our shoots were a long way off, and to reach them one had to travel through interminable steppes and forests. We used special carriages, big brakes called *lineikis,* which were drawn by four or even six horses, and held some twenty people. To provide a little variety, for the journeys were monotonous, I was made to sing. The Grand Duke's favorite was an Italian song, "Eyes Filled with Tears"; I was obliged to sing it several times a day and ended by loathing it.

We had lunch in tents and did not return home until the evening. After supper the grown-ups played cards, and my brother and I had to go to bed. But nothing would have induced me to close my eyes until the Grand Duchess had come to say good night to me. She blessed me and kissed me and I was filled with a wonderful peace and went quietly to sleep.

My memories of our visits to Rakitnoïe are not very pleasant. When I lost interest in shooting I actually grew to loathe it, and finally I gave all my guns away and stopped going to Rakitnoïe with my parents.

chapter XI

Until the end of the eighteenth century the Crimea was an independent state ruled by a khan. The charming palace which belonged to its Tartar sovereigns can still be seen at Baktchisaraï, its former capital. When it was conquered by Catherine the Great in 1783, the Crimea was annexed to Russia and the khan was dethroned and replaced by a governor.

The country is enchanting, not unlike the Riviera but wilder. High, rocky mountains follow the coast, pine forests run down the slopes to the shores of the Black Sea, which is as capricious as a woman: sparkling gaily in fair weather, dark and fearsome when a storm sweeps over it. The climate is mild and the countryside a riot of flowers, mostly roses.

The Tartar population was lively, friendly, and picturesque. The women wore full Turkish trousers, a tight-fitting jacket of some bright shade, and a small embroidered cap to which a veil was attached. But only married women veiled their faces. Girls dressed their hair in a multitude of tiny plaits and all women, married or single, dyed their fingernails and hair with henna. Men wore an astrakhan cap, colored shirt, and baggy trousers which narrowed at the ankles. The Tartars were Moslems; above their flat-roofed, whitewashed houses towered the minarets of mosques from which the voice of a muezzin could be heard calling the faithful to prayer, night and morning.

The Crimea was the Imperial family's favorite holiday resort, and also that of a large portion of the Russian aristocracy. Most of the estates were grouped along the southern coast, between the ports of Sebastopol and Yalta. As they lay close together, neighborly relations were friendly and social gatherings frequent. We owned several estates in the Crimea. The two most important ones were Koreïz, on the Black Sea, and Kokoz in the heart of a valley surrounded by high mountains. We also had a house on the Bay of Balaklava, but we never lived in it.

Koreïz was a rather ugly gray stone house which would have looked better in a town than at the seaside. However, it was friendly and comfortable. Pavilions reserved for guests were scattered throughout the park. The air was filled with the fragrance of thousands of La France roses, whose delicious scent also invaded the house. The gardens and vineyards stretched terrace upon terrace down to the seashore.

My father had inherited Koreïz from his mother, and carried out his own ideas both in his management of the estate and in the alterations he made. For a time, he had been an ardent enthusiast of sculpture and bought an inconceivable number of statues. The park was overcrowded with them; nymphs, naiads, and goddesses peeped out of every shrub and thicket; it was most Olympian-looking. On the seashore he built a pavilion and a swimming pool where the water was kept at a medium temperature so that one could bathe at all seasons. Bronze groups representing scenes from Tartar legends stood on the shore, and a Minerva on the jetty recalled the Statue of Liberty brandishing her torch. There was even a water nymph on a rock; each time this statue was swept into the sea by a storm, it was immediately replaced.

My father's fancies sometimes took the most extravagant forms. I can still remember my mother's astonishment when he made her a birthday present of Aï-Petri, a mountain which towers above the southern coast of Crimea. It is a bare rocky peak, the highest on the peninsula, without a tree, or a shrub.

Each autumn, he organized a sort of fair called The Sheep Fair. Everyone was invited to it, from the members of the Imperial family down to the population of the neighboring villages. Herds of sheep and goats arrived from the Kokoz Mountains; a blue ribbon was tied around the neck of each sheep and a pink one around that of every

Koreïz, Youssoupoff estate in the Crimea

goat. Everyone could eat and drink as much as he pleased, and there was the added attraction of a free lottery. People wandered among the sheep and goats and the display of food, wondering what it was all about, and vaguely expecting some surprise. But nothing happened and everyone went home without the least idea of what they had come for. However, to avoid hurting my father's feelings, they faithfully came back the next year.

The buyers of our wines got the fruit from our orchards as a bonus, but the trees had been so skillfully grafted that it had become impossible to recognize the species of these hybrid products, as their taste no longer corresponded to their appearance!

My father loved the open air. He was fond of planning long excursions on horseback in the mountains. These sometimes lasted a whole day. He led the party and quietly went his own way without listening to the guides or paying any attention to his companions. His taste for fishing had an unexpected repercussion on my education. He went out at dawn one day and returned with a strange little man. He said to me: "This is your new tutor." He had found him standing on a rock, rod in hand, and had immediately invited him to fish from his boat and then brought him home to lunch.

My new tutor was a dirty, evil-smelling dwarf. The whole week through, he wore the same white shirt trimmed with scarlet tassels; on Sunday mornings he put on a dinner jacket, a colored cravat, and yellow shoes. My mother was horrified and protested vehemently, but my father was so delighted with his latest discovery that he refused to listen to her. As for me, I loathed the man from the moment I set eyes on him, and made his life such a burden that he soon gave notice.

My father then decided that I should have a spartan training. He began by removing from my room all the furniture that I had chosen with such loving care and replaced it with a camp bed and a stool. I watched the removal in a state of suppressed rebellion. Apprehension was added to my fury when I saw the servants bring in a suspicious-looking cupboard which they deposited in the middle of the room. I tried to open it but in vain, which made me still more apprehensive.

Next day my father's valet, who had apparently been given the role of chief torturer, pulled me out of bed, seized me in his muscular arms and locked me into the cupboard. I was immediately drenched in a shower of icy water. As I never could stand cold water, my feelings can be easily imagined. In spite of my screams and all my efforts to get out, the door of the cupboard remained closed till the supply of water came to an end. The shock I got was so great that when the cupboard was finally opened I fled naked through the passages like a madman, rushed out of the house and, without stopping to take a breath, climbed to the top of a tree. My yells roused the whole house. My parents ran out and ordered me to come down, which I only consented to do when they promised me faithfully that there would be no further cold showers. I even threatened to throw myself from my perch if they did not promise. My father had to give in, but I caught a severe cold and was ill for weeks.

Our departure for the Crimea was always a red-letter day for Nicolas and me and we eagerly looked forward to the moment when our private coach would be coupled to the Nord-Sud Express.

We left the train at Simferopol where we spent a few days with Aunt and Uncle Lazareff. My uncle was Governor of the Crimea. Everyone loved him because of his even temper and his great kindliness; his wife was no less popular. We adored our charming, gay aunt; she had a very pretty voice and was always ready to sing for us and get up amateur theatricals.

We went with the Lazareffs to Simferopol when my uncle took up his appointment. All the notables had gathered at the station to meet their new governor. My uncle looked very dignified in full uniform but, as he passed from one coach to the other in order to alight from the train, he slipped between the two cars and fell astride one of the buffers, and it was in this unconventional position that he took over his new duties.

From Simferopol we continued our journey in a big landau which held the whole family. Other carriages with the servants and our luggage followed in the rear. Our staff, although numerous, was small compared with that of some Russian families when they traveled.

Count Alexander Cheremeteff not only took all his servants and their families with him, but also his musicians, and even a few cows from his farms to be sure of having fresh milk during the journey.

Nicolas and I loved these expeditions. Everything amused us: the change of horses which took place twice on the way, the choice of a suitable spot for lunch, the meals eaten in tents. Above all, we were happy to be alone with our parents, for this happened all too seldom.

During one period, a surprise always awaited us on reaching Koreïz, which we owed to the overseer's fertile imagination. For instance, he once had the strange idea of inscribing in black ink on each object in the house what he considered to be its value; many of our things were irreparably damaged. Another time, he had the whole house painted red with white lines imitating bricks. My father's beloved statues had not been spared: they were painted flesh-color to give them a lifelike appearance. This was the last time the overseer was able to exercise his imagination at the expense of our possessions, for my father dismissed him. It took a whole year to scrape the paint off the house and the statues.

Among our retainers at Koreïz was a poor halfwit, a strapping great fellow of Tartar origin called Missioud. He was colossally tall and afflicted with a large goiter. This innocent giant adored his master and followed him like a shadow. My father was bored to death by his slavelike devotion but did not want to hurt his feelings, so invented an occupation for him: dressed as the keeper of the seraglio, in a black caftan embroidered in gold, equipped with a gun and hunting horn, his job was to guard a fountain in front of the house. Each time a visitor arrived, Missioud would sound his horn, fire off his gun, and shout, "Hurrah!" Sometimes, however, he got flustered and did his act at the departure, instead of at the arrival, of guests, which was not so well received.

We were in St. Petersburg when my father received a telegram from the Crimea which read: "Missioud informs His Highness that he is dead." Poor Missioud, on falling seriously ill, had composed the telegram himself, asking that it be sent off after his death.

Koreïz was truly a Promised Land for our friends; they could come there with their entire family and servants and live exactly as they liked. And life was charming in that country full of fruit and flowers, among a friendly, kindly population.

My brother and I always looked forward eagerly to the arrival of our cousins. We used to go bathing with them, and took baskets of fruit to eat on the beach. We went for long rides on our tireless little Tartar ponies, and when in Yalta we never failed to pay a visit to Florin, the French pastry shop where the cakes were delicious.

On the day after our arrival at Koreïz, an endless procession of neighbors would call on us. Field Marshal Miliutin, who was over eighty, walked the five miles between his estate and ours. Baroness Pilar was a friend of my grandmother or, more precisely, was her devoted slave. Small and fat, her face covered with hairy warts, she managed to be pleasant and amusing in spite of her incredible ugliness. She lent herself to all my grandmother's whims, and the latter entrusted her with her silkworms and made her collect snails.

Prince Galitzin's leonine appearance—he was a giant with a tousled mane of hair—justified his Christian name, Leo. Always half tipsy, he never missed a chance of creating a scandal and, not content with drinking himself, tried to intoxicate all his friends with the wine from his vineyards. He always brought a number of cases of wine and champagne with him. No sooner had his barouche entered the courtyard than he would start to bellow in his stentorian voice: "The guests have arrived!" Alighting from his carriage, he immediately began juggling with bottles of wine and would break into a drinking song:

Drink to the dregs,
Drink to the dregs.

I would rush out to meet him, hoping to get a first taste of his excellent wines, but before so much as greeting anyone he ordered the servants to unload and open the cases. Then he invited the whole household, masters and servants, to join him in a wild carouse till most of them were completely drunk. On one occasion he so pestered my grandmother, who was then over seventy, that she threw the contents of her glass in his face. He pounced on her and carried her off in a wild dance, with the result that the poor old lady had to take to her bed for several days.

My mother dreaded Prince Galitzin's visits. She once locked herself in her rooms for twenty-four hours on account of this madman's frantic outbursts which no one could control. When all the servants were intoxicated, he would totter to a sofa and fall asleep for the night. It was the most difficult thing in the world to get rid of him next day.

Count Serge Orloff Davidoff lived alone at Selame, his estate on the sea. He was feeble-minded, and physically was a monster with tousled hair, gaping nostrils, and a lower lip drooping to the chin. Always a fop, he sported an eyeglass and white gaiters, and scented himself with chypre, which did not prevent him smelling like a goat. He was very good-natured and even rather likable and his favorite pastime was playing with matches. A generous supply of these was always placed near him, and he spent hours lighting them and blowing them out; after which he would go away without having said a single word. One of the happiest days of his life was when I brought him a box of matches a yard long which I had found in a shop on the boulevards in Paris.

His ugliness and feeble-mindedness did not prevent his taking an interest in women. He once caused a scandal during a religious ceremony celebrated at the Winter Palace in the presence of the Imperial family. According to etiquette, the ladies were in court dress; Count Orloff put on his eyeglass and inspected their décolletages with such loud chuckles that he was asked to leave the church. Gossip credited him with several love affairs; be that as it may, he was certainly very sentimental and touchingly faithful. He never forgot my mother's birthday, and whether she happened to be at Koreïz or not would always bring her a huge bouquet of roses.

One of our near neighbors, Countess Kleinmichel, owned a considerable library, mostly composed of works on Freemasonry. One day a parchment document in Hebrew was discovered there and sent to St. Petersburg to be translated into Russian. This translation was published in the form of a pamphlet entitled *The Protocols of Zion*;

most of the copies disappeared mysteriously the day they were published. They were probably destroyed, but in any case it is a fact that during the Bolshevik Revolution anybody found with this pamphlet in his possession was shot on the spot. A copy found its way to England, and is now in the British Museum; it was translated into English under the title of *The Jewish Peril* and into French under that of *Les Protocoles de Sion*.

Countess Panine was a highly intelligent woman with very advanced opinions. She lived in a sort of feudal castle where she received politicians, artists, and writers. It was at her house that I met Leo Tolstoï, Chekov, and also a charming couple: the well-known singer Yan-Rouban and her husband, Pohl, a talented composer and painter. Madame Yan-Rouban gave me singing lessons and often came to our house. I don't know when I have met a singer with more flawless elocution, or one who rendered Schumann, Schubert, and Brahms more sensitively.

Among the estates that lay near Sebastopol, one of the finest was Aloupka, belonging to the Worontzoff family. Walls and statues were smothered in wisteria, and beautiful fountains graced the park. Unfortunately, the interior of the house was in a state of sad neglect, for its owners came there very rarely. It was rumored that a huge serpent lived in the ivy which covered the wall that surrounded the estate, and that this animal was sometimes seen to glide to the shore and disappear into the sea. This legend terrified me as a child, and I could never be induced to go walking in the neighborhood.

All these estates were situated on the coast of the Black Sea, not far from the little port of Yalta which was made so famous by the "Big Three" Conference in 1945. Yalta was a center for excursions, and was the home port of the Imperial Yacht *Standart*.

All the estates belonging to the Imperial family lay by the seaside. The Czar himself lived in Livadia, a modern palace in the Italian style with large bright rooms, which was built in place of the former dark, damp, comfortless building. The Grand Duke Alexander Mikhaïlovitch's estate, Aï-Todor, was near ours, and the memories it evokes are particularly dear. The old house was smothered in

The Grand Duke Alexander, the Grand Duchess Xenia, and their children

flowers, its walls were covered with roses and wisteria; everything about the place was infinitely pleasing, but most delightful of all was the lady of the house, the Grand Duchess Xenia Alexandrovna. Her chief attraction lay not in her beauty but in the rare, delicate charm which she had inherited from her mother, the Empress Marie Feodorovna. Her wonderful gray eyes seemed to penetrate one's innermost soul, and everyone who came near her fell a slave to her grace, modesty, and kindness of heart. From early childhood I looked forward to her visits and, when she left, I would wander about the rooms, rapturously sniffing a delicious odor of lilies of the valley which still lingered in the air.

The Grand Duke Alexander was "tall, dark, and handsome," with a strong personality. His marriage to the Grand Duchess Xenia, the Czar's eldest sister, was a departure from the time-honored tradition by which members of the Imperial family married foreigners. He entered the Naval College of his own free will and remained strongly attached to the sea all his life. He was convinced that Russia needed a powerful navy, and succeeded in convincing the Czar of this, but he ran up against the opposition of high naval authorities, the very ones who were responsible for the disastrous war with Japan. The Grand Duke took an active part in the development of the merchant marine, and it was at his instigation that a special Ministry of the Merchant Marine was created of which he remained in charge until the Czar signed the proclamation convening the first Duma. When he resigned, however, he accepted the command of the Baltic destroyer flotillas, delighted to find himself at sea again. He was cruising in Finnish waters when he received a telegram calling him to Gatchina, where the Grand Duchess and her children were staying; his son Theodore was dangerously ill with scarlet fever. Three days later he learned from his manservant, who had remained on board the flagship, that the crew was about to mutiny and awaited his return to hold him as a hostage. Overcome with grief, he heard the verdict of his brother-in-law, the Emperor: "The Government cannot risk leaving a member of the Imperial family in the hands of the revolutionaries." Sick at heart, the Grand Duke made the delicate health of his children an excuse for going abroad.

He rented a villa at Biarritz and spent some months there with his family, and returned there regularly several years running. He was at Biarritz when Blériot flew the Channel.

The Grand Duke had been one of the first to take a keen interest in aviation. He immediately realized the significance of Blériot's exploit, and decided to do all he could to get Russia equipped with an air force. He made contact with Blériot and Voisin, and returned to Russia with his plans all complete. He was received with sarcastic smiles.

"If I understand Your Imperial Highness rightly," said General Soukhomlinoff, Minister of War, "you propose to introduce Blériot's toys into the Army? May I ask whether our officers must leave the Army to go soaring over the Straits of Dover or whether the fantasia will take place in St. Petersburg?"

The fantasia took place in St. Petersburg, for the city had its first aviation week in the spring of 1910. General Soukhomlinoff judged it "prodigiously diverting but without the least interest for national defense." Nevertheless, three months later, the Grand Duke laid the first stone of the Aviation School which supplied most of our pilots and observers in 1914.

In his early youth the Grand Duke began to collect books for a naval library; on the eve of the Revolution, this library comprised more than 20,000 volumes. These priceless works were destroyed during the Revolution by a fire which broke out in the Grand Duke's palace, then used as a club for young Communists.

One day when I was out riding, I met a very beautiful girl accompanied by an elderly lady. Our eyes met and she made such an impression on me that I reined in my horse to gaze at her as she walked on.

Every day I went riding on the same road, at the same hour, hoping to meet the lovely stranger again. I waited in vain and then wended my sad way home. But one afternoon the Grand Duke and the Grand Duchess Alexander called on us accompanied by their daughter, the Princess Irina. To my surprise and delight I recognized the girl I had met on my ride. This time I had plenty of time to admire the wondrous beauty of the girl who was eventually to become my wife and lifelong companion. She had beautiful features, clear-cut as a cameo, and looked very like her father.

A little later I made the acquaintance of her brothers, the Princes Andrew, Theodore, Nikita, Dimitri, Rostislav, and Basil.* None of them looked at all alike, but they had all inherited their mother's charm.

Our estate of Kokoz, which in Tartar means "blue eye," lay in the heart of a valley, near a small Tartar village of white, flat-roofed houses. It was a corner of fairyland, especially in the spring when the apple and cherry trees were in bloom. As the old house was falling to pieces, my mother had a new one built in the style of the country. From the small hunting lodge which had first been planned, it soon developed into a large and beautiful house reminiscent of the Khan Palace at Baktchisaraï. It was white, with a roof of old glazed tiles which time had turned to soft shades of green. An orchard surrounded the house, a little stream ran by the gate; one could fish trout from a balcony. Inside, the furniture painted red, blue, and bright green had been copied from old Tartar furniture. Oriental fabrics covered the divans and walls. The light in the large dining room filtered through Persian stained-glass windows built just below the ceiling. At night, lights placed outside the windows gave out a soft and delicate glow which blended exquisitely with that of the candles on the table. From a marble fountain on one of the walls, water ran drop by drop, with a cool and plaintive murmur, into a number of small shallow basins. The fountain was an exact copy of one in the Khan Palace. According to the legend, a young and beautiful European girl had been abducted by the Khan and held prisoner in his harem. The damsel wept so continuously that her tears became a gushing spring known as The Fountain of Tears.

The "blue eye" was everywhere in evidence: in the stained glass of

*To reduce the expenses of the Civil List, Alexander III had issued a decree by which only children of the Czar and his grandchildren in the male line would have the right to the title of Grand Duke or Grand Duchess. All other members of the Imperial family were to bear the title of Prince and Princess of Russia.

TOP: *Kokoz, another Youssoupoff estate in the Crimea*
ABOVE: *The dining room of Kokoz*

the windows, upon the fountain in the cypress grove, in the oriental pattern of the dinner service.

I often brought friends to Kokoz, which was only about thirty miles from Koreïz. Oriental robes were at the guests' disposal and everyone was costumed for dinner. King Manuel of Portugal once came to spend the day, and was so enchanted by Kokoz that he said he would like to stay forever. We often entertained the Czar and Czarina there, and they too had a great affection for the place.

The surrounding mountains were covered with forests and were full of elk. We used to go for long walks, and would stop and lunch in one of the numerous hunting lodges we had built on the estate. One of these lodges, called "The Eagles' Nest," stood on the edge of a cliff; we used to throw stones and put the eagles to flight and watch them as they wheeled majestically over our heads.

My father once invited the Emir of Bokhara and his suite for a day's shooting. After a very gay picnic lunch served in The Eagles' Nest, the butler handed round a tray of cigarettes with the coffee and liqueurs. With the Emir's permission everybody lit one. Then hell broke loose in the form of a magnificent display of fireworks, which caused such a panic among the guests that they rushed outside, thinking that an attempt had been made upon their lives! I was in fits of laughter at the success of the fake cigarettes I had bought in Paris. My laughter gave me away, and I was severely reprimanded by my father. A few days later, however, to everyone's astonishment, the Emir returned and pinned a diamond and ruby star on my breast. It was one of his country's most exalted decorations. He also asked to be photographed with me. He alone had appreciated the joke!

chapter XII

In 1906 my father was given the command of the Chevalier-Gardes, and we had to leave our house on the Moïka for a suite of rooms in the regimental quarters on the Zaharievskaïa. Nicolas and I were in despair at having to leave our own home in St. Petersburg and to miss our holidays at Arkhangelskoïe. We had a villa in Krasnoïe-Selo, where we now spent the summer, as my father's new regiment was stationed there. Our parents kept open house for the officers of the regiment and their wives; some of these were very nice, but neither my brother nor I liked the life, and our one idea was to escape it by going abroad or to Arkhangelskoïe. We were inseparable at that time. When the holidays were over, Nicolas resumed his studies at the University and I went back to the Gourevitch School. In winter, although we lived with our parents, all our free time was spent at the Moïka where our friends joined us in the evening.

Among these was Prince Michael Gortchakoff, known to all his friends as Mika; he was a very intelligent boy, hot-headed, but with a heart of gold and very good-looking in rather an oriental way. Knowing how much my conduct distressed my parents, he decided to try to reform me. In this he did not succeed, and in fact I led him such a life that he had a nervous breakdown and was obliged to go abroad for treatment. He bore me no grudge, however, and we have always remained very good friends. He later married Countess Steinbock Fermor, a charming woman with a very sweet nature.

Until I was sixteen, I used often to talk in my sleep. One evening before leaving for Moscow, my parents came into my bedroom and heard me say distinctly and repeatedly: "The train has run off the lines . . . the train has run off the lines." This struck them so forcibly that they put off their journey and, by a curious coincidence, the train they were to have taken *did* run off the lines and many lives were lost. This was sufficient to establish my reputation as a prophet, and I naturally exploited this for my personal ends. My parents allowed themselves to be guided by my so-called revelations until the day came when the fraud was discovered and my career as a prophet came to a sudden and distinctly disagreeable end.

My brother and I took a great interest in spiritualism. We witnessed some rather surprising things at the séances which we held with a few friends. But when a marble statue broke and fell off its pedestal at our feet, we resolved to give them up. I none the less continued to take a deep interest in everything connected with the mystery of life after death.

It was at this time that Nicolas and I promised each other that the first of us to die would appear to the survivor. The Almighty God, the afterlife, and self-perfection were constantly on my mind. A priest with whom I talked freely on these matters told me: "Don't try and find an answer to all these questions. Don't philosophize too much. Just believe in God." But this wise advice did not satisfy my craving for knowledge. I immersed myself in the study of occult sciences and theosophy. I had difficulty in believing that it was possible, during the course of our brief sojourn on earth, to earn the right to eternal life, as the Christian doctrine teaches us. The theory of reincarnation seemed, to my mind, a much better solution of the problems which preoccupied me. I learned that certain exercises of bodily and spiritual discipline could little by little develop in one a superhuman power which enabled one to master one's own weaknesses and dominate other people. With the conviction that I was inspired by a divine truth, I devoted myself to the practice of Yoga exercises. Every day I took a special course of gymnastics and did an incalculable number of breathing exercises; at the same time, I tried to concentrate and develop my will power. I soon noticed a change in myself: my mind became clearer, my memory improved, and my strength of will increased. Several people told me that even my expression had changed. I myself noticed that some people could not look me in the eye, and I concluded that I had acquired a sort of hypnotic power. To test my capacity for bearing pain, I held my hand over a lighted candle. I suffered the most excruciating pain, but it was not till the smell of roast flesh filled the room that I withdrew my hand. Having to undergo a particularly painful dental operation, I amazed the dentist by refusing an anesthetic. I felt proud of having acquired so much control over myself and I no longer doubted that I could also control other people.

Nicolas and I had met a young actor of great talent, Blumenthal Tamarine, known to his friends as Vova. Gorki's *The Underworld* was then being given at the Alexander Theater, and Vova advised us to see this play in which Gorki paints the life of St. Petersburg's tramps in the Wiasemskaïa-Lavra quarter. After seeing the play, I was seized with a longing to visit this "Beggars' Market" and asked Vova to help me set about it. He knew a great many theatrical people and easily found the kind of clothes we needed.

On the appointed day, we all three went off disguised as beggars, slinking through deserted alleys to avoid the police. We were obliged to pass by the Bouffes Theater just as the play ended and the audience came pouring out. I played my part in good earnest, as I was curious to know how it felt to beg; taking up my stand at the street corner, I held out my hand and asked for alms. Although I was only a fake beggar, I was indignant when grand ladies covered with jewels and costly furs, and fine gentlemen smoking big cigars, passed me without so much as a glance. I understood how the real poor must feel.

When we reached the Lavra gates, Vova advised us to keep silent to avoid giving ourselves away. At the night shelter we hired three sordid pallets and lay down on them, pretending to sleep, but furtively examining our surroundings. What we saw was frightful. All around us the dregs of humanity, both men and women, lay half-naked, drunk, and filthy. The popping of corks could be heard as they drained bottles of vodka at a gulp and threw the empty bottles at their neighbors. The unfortunate wretches quarreled, copulated, used the filthiest language, and vomited all over each other. The stench of the place was beyond description. Sickened by the revolting spectacle, we fled.

Once outside, I drew a deep breath of fresh night air. It was difficult to believe that what I had just seen was real. How, in our times, could a government allow human beings to be reduced to such abject misery? I was haunted for a long time by memories of the horrible sights I had seen.

We must have looked the parts to perfection, because we had the greatest difficulty in persuading the porter of our house to let us in.

During a trip we made to Paris in the summer of 1907, Nicolas met Manon Loti, one of the great courtesans of the time, and fell madly in love with her. She was a very pretty and very well-dressed woman who lived in the greatest luxury: she had a house of her own, magnificent carriages, sumptuous jewelry, and even a dwarf whom she looked upon as a mascot. She went everywhere with an ex-cocotte called Bibi. Bibi had grown old and infirm but was still proud of her former liaison with the Grand Duke Alexis Alexandrovitch.

Nicolas had completely lost his head, and spent all his days and nights with Manon. From time to time he deigned to remember my existence and invited me to accompany Manon and himself to a cabaret. But three is not company and I soon had a liaison of my own with a charming young girl, less showy than Manon but most attractive. She smoked opium and one evening offered to initiate me into the delight of an artificial paradise! She took me to a Chinese opium den at Montmartre where we were received by an old Chinaman who led us to the basement. I was struck by the peculiar odor of the drug, and also by the deathlike silence that reigned in the place. Half-dressed people lay on rush mats apparently plunged in deep sleep. A small oil lamp burned in front of each smoker.

Nobody took any notice of us. We stretched ourselves out on a vacant mat and a young Chinaman brought lamps and prepared pipes. I had already smoked several pipes and was beginning to feel dizzy when suddenly a bell rang and someone cried: "Police!"

All the sleepers leapt to their feet and hurriedly started to tidy themselves. My companion, who was familiar with the premises, led me out through a secret exit and we left the building unmolested. She had, however, great difficulty in getting me to her apartment, where I collapsed on her bed. The next day I woke with a racking headache and swore never to smoke opium again; it goes without saying that I broke my word at the first opportunity.

Soon after this adventure, I left for Russia with my brother.

We resumed our gay, carefree life in St. Petersburg and Nicolas soon forgot his Parisian love affair. As happens to all rich young men, he was constantly pursued by matchmaking mothers, but Nicolas was far too fond of his freedom to think of marriage.

But, as ill luck would have it, he met a most beautiful and attractive girl and fell passionately in love with her. She and her mother led a very worldly life. They entertained a lot and their parties were always very gay.

When my brother met this girl she was engaged to an officer in one of the Guards regiments. This, however, did not deter Nicolas, and he made up his mind to marry her himself. Our parents refused their consent to a match of which they thoroughly disapproved. Personally, I knew the young woman too well not to share their point of view, but I had to conceal my feelings in order to keep my brother's affection and confidence, for I still hoped to induce him to change his mind.

Meanwhile the date of the wedding was continually being postponed. Wearying of these repeated delays, the fiancé finally insisted upon a day being fixed. Nicolas was in despair; the girl wept and declared that she would rather die than marry a man she did not love. I found out that she had asked Nicolas to have supper with her for the last time on the evening before the wedding. Having failed to persuade Nicolas not to go, I decided to go with him to the party. Vova was among the guests and, after he had drunk a good deal, he launched into an impassioned speech and exhorted the lovers to place their love above any other consideration . . . When the weeping fiancée begged Nicolas to elope with her, I rushed off to fetch her mother, but it was only with the greatest difficulty that I persuaded her to come back with me. When we got to the restaurant where the party was being held, mother and daughter fell into each other's arms. I took advantage of this to get Nicolas away. I practically had to drag him home.

The marriage took place on the following day and the couple left for Paris on their honeymoon. This, to my parents' great relief, seemed to put an end to the whole affair. Nicolas resumed his normal way of living, which completely reassured my mother, but I, for one, was not deceived by his apparent indifference.

The Russian opera company, with Chaliapin, was then giving a series of performances in Paris. My brother suddenly decided to attend these performances. Our parents, suspecting that Chaliapin was merely an excuse, tried to dissuade him. But nothing could hold Nicolas back.

They then sent me to Paris so that I could keep an eye on him. When I heard that he had been meeting the young woman again, I telegraphed my parents asking them to join me.

Nicolas remained hidden away and gave no sign of life. I decided to consult two of the best-known clairvoyants of the period: Madame de Thèbes and Madame Freya. The first warned me that a member of my family was in serious danger of being killed in a duel. The second said much the same thing, and added a prophecy about myself: "In a few years you will take part in a political assassination and will go through a terrible ordeal which will end in a complete victory for you."

Contradictory reports reached us. There was no possible doubt that the husband was aware of his wife's relations with Nicolas, but, while some people claimed that a duel was inevitable, others believed that he would merely ask for a divorce. Finally, we heard that he had actually challenged my brother, but that the seconds pronounced the motives insufficient.

Then one day to our surprise the husband came round to see us. He told us that he and Nicolas had been reconciled; he said that he considered his wife mainly responsible for what had occurred, and that he was going to apply for a divorce.

We were greatly relieved to know that a duel had been avoided, but we were still very anxious about the outcome of the divorce proceedings.

Soon alarming news called us back to St. Petersburg: the husband, probably urged on by his brother officers, was again considering a duel.

Not a word could be got out of Nicolas, who remained obstinately silent. However, one day he told me that the duel was to take place very soon. I immediately warned my parents and they sent for him. He managed to reassure them by stating quite positively that nothing would happen.

That same evening, I found two notes on my desk: one from my mother, asking me to come to her as soon as possible, the other from Nicolas inviting me to supper at Contant's. I thought the invitation a good omen, for this was the first time since our return to Russia that he had asked me to spend the evening with him.

I first went to see my mother and found her seated before the mirror while her maid brushed her hair for the night. I can still see the expression of radiant happiness in her eyes.

"I had a talk with your brother this evening," she said; "all the rumors of a duel are pure inventions; everything has been arranged. You can't imagine how happy I am. I dreaded the duel, because Nicolas will be twenty-six in a few days."

It was then that I heard of the strange fate which it appears has pursued the Youssoupoff family since its earliest days: in each generation all the heirs but one die before reaching the age of twenty-six. My mother had had four sons, of whom only Nicolas and I survived. She had never ceased to fear for each of us in turn. The threat of a duel coinciding with the approach of my brother's twenty-sixth birthday had made her anxiety almost unbearable.

I kissed my mother, who was weeping for joy, and went off to the restaurant where I was to meet Nicolas. As I did not find him there, I searched the whole town for him and returned home, more anxious than ever. What with the clairvoyants' predictions and my mother's revelations, Nicolas' disappearance drove me wild with anxiety. He himself had told me that the duel would be taking place soon. He had probably wished to spend this last evening with me. What unforeseen circumstances could have prevented this? A prey to the gloomiest thoughts, I finally fell into a fitful sleep.

I was awakened by my valet, Ivan, who gasped: "Come quickly, something terrible has happened . . ." Gripped by a dreadful foreboding, I jumped out of bed and rushed to my mother's rooms. I met several of the servants on the staircase; their faces were distorted with grief; none of them would answer my questions. Heartbreaking sobs came from my father's dressing room. I entered it, to find my father standing pale as death before a stretcher on which my brother's body lay. My mother was kneeling beside the body and seemed to have completely lost her reason. . . .

We dragged her away with the greatest difficulty and laid her on her bed. She called for me when she grew calmer, but when she saw me she took me for Nicolas. This dreadful scene left me dazed with horror and grief. My mother finally fell into a sort of coma. When she came to, she would not allow me to leave her side.

My brother's body was placed in the chapel; then came the long exhausting services for the dead, followed by an endless procession of relations and friends. Two days later, we left for Arkhangelskoïe where the burial was to take place in our family vault.

The Grand Duchess Elisabeth Feodorovna was among the friends waiting for us at Moscow station, and she came with us to Arkhangelskoïe.

A number of our peasants were present at the burial services. Most of them were in tears; every one of them showed in the most touching way how deeply they felt for us.

The Grand Duchess stayed with us for some time. Her kindly presence was a help to us all, especially to my mother in her extreme despair. My father was very reserved and concealed his grief, but the blow had told on him. As for myself, I was obsessed by a desire for revenge which would certainly have driven me to some desperate act if the Grand Duchess had not managed to calm me.

By then I knew the facts about the duel: it had taken place in the early morning on Prince Belosselsky's estate, on the Island of Krestovsky. It had been agreed that the weapons would be revolvers, and the distance thirty paces. The signal was given, Nicolas fired in the air; his adversary fired at him and missed him. He then insisted that the distance be reduced to fifteen paces. Nicolas agreed, and again fired in the air; the officer took careful aim and killed him instantly. Thus ended an encounter which was not a duel but a murder. Later, when going through my brother's papers, I found a letter proving that a certain Chinsky, a very well-known occultist, had played a sinister part in this affair. They showed clearly that Nicolas was completely under his influence. He told my brother that he was his guardian angel, directed by God's will; Chinsky made out that it was my brother's duty to marry the girl, and he encouraged him to follow her to Paris. All his letters sang her praises, and her mother's as well. Chinsky also warned Nicolas against revealing his intentions to his parents or to me.

Before leaving Arkhangelskoïe, the Grand Duchess made me promise that as soon as my mother was a little better I would come to see her in Moscow, to talk about my future. Some time passed before I could do this. My mother's health improved slowly but she never fully recovered from my brother's death.

When I was coming back from a walk one day, I paused to gaze at the vast park, its statues and lawns and the splendid house which contained such priceless collections. I realized that all this would some day be mine and that it was only an infinitesimal part of my fortune. The idea that I would one day be one of the richest men in Russia went like wine to my head. I remembered how I used to slip into the theater and play at being my ancestor, the great eighteenth-century patron of the arts. Once again I saw the Moorish room at the Moïka, where I lay on cushions of spun gold, draped in silks from the Orient, glittering with my mother's diamonds, lording it over my slaves. Wealth, splendor, power: I could not imagine life without them. Mediocrity and ugliness filled me with horror. . . . But what would happen if a war or a revolution deprived me of my fortune? I recalled the miserable wretches I had seen at the Wiasemskaïa-Lavra. Could I ever, by a turn of Fortune's wheel, sink to their level? The very thought was horrible. I quickly went into the house. As I passed my portrait by Seroff, I stopped to examine it carefully. Seroff was a remarkable psychologist and excelled in bringing out the character of his models. On the face of the young man before me I could read vanity, pride, and selfishness. How could it be that I had changed so little after the terrible ordeal we had all been through? How could I still be the same heartless egotist? I was seized with such loathing for myself that for a moment I thought of committing suicide. It was only the knowledge that I would bring further grief to my parents that stopped me.

Remembering that I had promised the Grand Duchess that as soon as my mother was better I would go and see her in Moscow, I took advantage of the improvement in my mother's health to do so.

The Grand Duchess Elisabeth

chapter XIII

I do not claim to reveal any new facts about the Grand Duchess Elisabeth Feodorovna. Those who have read the many books on the last years of the czarist régime are familiar with this courageous and noble figure. However, I cannot, in telling the story of my life, omit to mention the woman who played such an important and helpful part in it; one whom, since childhood, I had loved and revered as a second mother.

All those who knew her paid tribute to the extraordinary beauty and generous nature of this exceptional woman. Tall and slender, with serene gray eyes, a sweet and gentle expression and delicate clear-cut features, she added to these physical qualities a keen intellect and great kindness of heart. She was the sister of the Czarina Alexandra and of the reigning Prince Ernest of Hesse-Darmstadt, and the daughter of Princess Alice of Great Britain; she was thus the granddaughter of Queen Victoria. Her other sisters were Princess Victoria of Battenberg, later Marchioness of Milford Haven, and Princess Henry of Prussia. She had married the Grand Duke Serge Alexandrovitch, fourth son of Czar Alexander II.

The first years of her married life were spent in St. Petersburg, where she entertained a great deal in her palace on the Nevsky Prospect and led the brilliant life which her position called for, although, even then, she cared very little for pomp and ceremony. In 1891 the Grand Duke was made Governor General of Moscow, and the Grand Duchess was soon as much loved in Moscow as she was in St. Petersburg. She led the same active life, and divided her time between her social obligations and her numerous charitable works.

On the 17th of February, 1905, as the Grand Duke was driving across the Senate Square in the Kremlin, a terrorist threw a bomb at him which blew him and his carriage to pieces.

This was during the Japanese war, and the Grand Duchess had organized a workroom in the Kremlin where clothes were made for the troops in Manchuria. She was working there when she heard the explosion and she ran out without even putting on a coat. In the square, she saw the wounded coachman and the two dead horses. The Grand Duke's body had been literally blown to pieces and parts of it were scattered over the snow. The Grand Duchess gathered these precious remains with her own hands and had them taken to the chapel in her palace. The violence of the explosion was such that some of the Grand Duke's fingers, with his rings still on, were found on the roof of a neighboring house. All these gruesome details were given us by the Grand Duchess herself. We were at St. Petersburg when the tragic news arrived and we immediately left for Moscow.

Everyone admired the fortitude and calm with which the Grand Duchess met this blow. She spent the days before the funeral in prayer; her deep Christian faith gave her the courage to take a step which amazed her immediate circle of friends: she went to the prison where the assassin was confined and asked to be taken to his cell:

"Who are you?" he inquired.

"I am the widow of the man you killed. What led you to commit this crime?"

The rest of their conversation was never divulged, but more or less fantastic versions of it were put about. Some said that after his visitor left, the murderer broke down and wept.

One thing is certain: that the Grand Duchess wrote to the Czar, asking that the man's life should be spared. Nicolas II would have agreed to this if the assassin had not obstinately refused to ask for it. He even wrote to the Grand Duchess, denying that he had ever felt the least remorse for his act, and refusing in advance the pardon she had solicited for him.

The Grand Duchess visited the coachman, who had been dreadfully wounded. On seeing her by his bedside the unfortunate man, not knowing of his master's death, asked: "How is His Imperial

Highness?" The Grand Duchess replied: "He sent me to see how you were getting on."

After her husband's death she continued to live in Moscow, but retired from the world and gave herself up entirely to pious and charitable works. She gave some of her jewelry to her close relations and sold the rest. My mother bought a magnificent pear-shaped pearl from her, a gift from Czar Nicolas II. The day he gave it to his sister-in-law the Czar had remarked: "Now you own a pearl almost as beautiful as Zenaïde Youssoupoff's 'Peregrina.' "

After disposing of all her possessions, the Grand Duchess bought a piece of land in the Ordinka quarter of Moscow, on the right-hand side of the river. In 1912 she built the Convent of Martha and Mary of which she became the Mother Superior. With a last touch of worldliness, for she had been a woman of extreme elegance and great taste, she had the dress of her order designed by Nesterov, a Muscovite painter: a long pearl-gray robe of fine wool, a lawn wimple which framed the face, and a white woolen veil that fell in long classical folds. The nuns were not cloistered, but dedicated their lives to visiting the poor and caring for the sick. They also traveled through the provinces, founding new centers. The institution developed rapidly; in a few years all large Russian cities had similar establishments. The Ordinka Convent had to be enlarged: a church, a hospital, workshops, and schools were added. The mother superior lived in a small, simply furnished three-room house; her wooden bed had no mattress and her pillow was stuffed with hay. The Grand Duchess slept little, a few hours at most, when she was not spending the whole night by a sickbed, or praying over a coffin in the chapel. Hospitals and nursing homes sent her their worst cases, and she nursed them herself. On one occasion, a woman who had overturned a lighted oil stove was brought in; her clothes had caught fire and her body was a mass of burns. Gangrene had set in and the doctors despaired of saving her. With a gentle but obstinate courage, the Grand Duchess nursed her back to life. It took two hours each day to dress her wounds, and the stench was such that several of the nurses fainted. The patient recovered within a few weeks and this was considered a miracle at the time.

The Grand Duchess Elisabeth

The Grand Duchess thought it wrong not to tell patients when they were about to die; she considered, on the contrary, that it was her duty to prepare them for death and to inspire them with faith in eternal life.

During the first World War, she widened the scope of her charitable activities by centralizing all donations to the wounded, and creating new organizations. Although she was fully aware of what was going on, she was never interested in politics, being too much absorbed in her work to think of anything else. She was beloved by all; whenever she left the convent a crowd knelt as she passed by, and, making the sign of the cross, kissed her hand or her garments as she alighted from her carriage.

Although she did so much good, many people criticized her way of living. Some even went so far as to say that by leaving her palace and giving all she had to the poor she, as the Czarina's sister, had lowered the dignity of the throne. The Czarina herself was of this opinion; the two sisters did not get on at all well. Both were converts to the Orthodox Church, both were fervent believers, but each understood our religion in a different way. The Czarina was inclined to follow a complicated, dangerous road to perfection: she dipped into mysticism and was led astray. The Grand Duchess chose the true and narrow path, that of humility and love; her faith was simple as a child's. But the chief reason for their disagreement was the Czarina's blind confidence in Rasputin. The Grand Duchess considered him a fiend and an impostor, and did not conceal her opinion from her sister. They met at longer and longer intervals, and finally ceased to meet at all.

The revolution of 1917 did not shake the Grand Duchess' strong spirit. On March 1st, a troop of revolutionary soldiers surrounded the convent, shouting: "Where is the German spy?" The Grand Duchess came forward and replied very calmly: "There is no German spy; this is a convent, of which I am the Mother Superior."

When they stated their intentions of taking her away with them, she said that she was ready to follow them but that first she wished to say farewell to her nuns and receive the priest's blessing in the chapel. The soldiers consented, provided that a delegation of their men were present at the ceremony.

When the Mother Superior entered the chapel, surrounded by armed soldiers, everyone knelt, weeping. After kissing the cross that the priest held out to her, she turned to the soldiers and asked them to do the same. Not one of them refused. Impressed by the Grand Duchess' calm, and the veneration shown her, they filed out in silence, entered their trucks, and drove away, leaving her free. A few hours later, members of the Provisional Government called on the Grand Duchess and apologized; they admitted that they were unable to curb the lawlessness which was spreading over the country and begged her to return to the Kremlin where she would be in safety. She replied that having left the Kremlin of her own free will, she would not go back to it because of a revolution: that she was determined, God willing, to remain with her nuns and share their fate. The Kaiser offered several times, through the agency of the Swedish Embassy, to give her shelter in Prussia, as he feared that Russia was on the eve of terrible happenings. None knew this better than he, as he was one of those responsible for them. But the Grand Duchess sent him word that she would never leave her convent, or Russia, of her own free will.

After this alarm, the community had a respite for a short time. When the Bolsheviks assumed power, they granted all persons at the Ordinka Convent the right to live there as before; they even sent food to the convent.

But in June 1918 the Grand Duchess was arrested along with her faithful servant Varvara and taken to an unknown destination. Patriarch Tikhon tried in vain to trace her and have her set free. Finally, it became known that she was a prisoner in the small town of Alapaïesk, in the district of Perm, along with her cousin the Grand Duke Serge Mikhaïlovitch, Princes John, Constantine and Igor, sons of the Grand Duke Constantine Constantinovitch, and Prince Wladimir Paley, son of the Grand Duke Paul Alexandrovitch.

On the night of July 18, twenty-four hours after the assassination of the Czar and his family, they were thrown alive into a mine shaft. Inhabitants of the neighboring town witnessed the massacre from afar. They went to the mine after the Bolsheviks had gone, and claimed to have heard groans and hymns. But no one dared to help the victims.

A few weeks later, the White Army entered the town. By order of Admiral Koltchak, the bodies of the martyrs were taken from the pit and placed in coffins. Strips of a nun's veil were found to have been used to dress the wounds of the victims. Later, the coffins were sent to Harbin and from there to Pekin. The Marchioness of Milford Haven subsequently had the remains of the Grand Duchess and her servant Varvara removed to Jerusalem. They were buried in the crypt of St. Mary Magdalene, the Russian church which stands near the Mount of Olives. The Grand Duchess' coffin split during its transfer from Pekin to Jerusalem, and a clear, fragrant fluid flowed from it; her body had escaped decomposition, and several miraculous cures took place at her tomb. One of our archbishops related that during a stay in Jerusalem, as he prayed before the Grand Duchess' tomb, he saw the door of the church open and a woman in white draperies cross the nave and stop before an icon of the Archangel Michael. He recognized the Grand Duchess when she turned and pointed to the icon; then the vision disappeared.

The only relics I have of the Grand Duchess Elisabeth are a few beads from her rosary and a fragment of wood from her coffin. This wood at times exudes a delicious odor of flowers.

I am firmly convinced that the name of "saint" by which she was known to the Russian people will one day be recognized by the Church.

But to return to my narrative where I left it at the death of my brother: I had now made up my mind to go and see the Grand Duchess Elisabeth, and set out for the Kremlin which I reached in a state of great mental distress. At the Nicolas Palace, I was at once shown in to the Grand Duchess' presence and found her seated at her desk. I broke down completely and threw myself at her feet. She gently stroked my hair and waited until I had calmed down. When I had recovered my self-control, I confided all my troubles to her: my spiritual turmoil and the conflicting emotions that were torturing me. To confess was in itself a relief. The Grand Duchess listened most attentively: "You were right to come to me," she said; "with God's aid, I am certain I can help you. No matter what trials He sends us, if we have faith in Him and confidence in our prayers, He will give us the strength to bear them. When doubt assails you, do not despair—kneel before an icon of the Savior and pray; you will feel better at once. The tears you have just shed came from your heart. Always be guided by your heart rather than by your head, and your life will be transformed. Happiness does not consist in living in a palace or enjoying a large fortune; these can be lost. True happiness is something that neither men nor events can take from you. You will find it in Faith, in Hope, and in Charity. Try to make those around you happy, and you will be happy yourself."

The Grand Duchess then talked of my parents; she reminded me that I was their only remaining son and urged me to be as considerate and loving as I could and not to neglect my invalid mother. She asked me to help her in her charitable work. She had recently opened a hospital for tuberculous women, and suggested that I should visit the poverty-stricken slums, where this dreadful disease was widespread.

I returned to Arkhangelskoïe, soothed and comforted. The Grand Duchess' words were an answer to everything that had worried me for such a long time. I again remembered the advice the priest had given me: "Do not philosophize too much . . . just believe in God." I had taken too little heed of it at the time, and had turned to occultism instead. I had succeeded in developing my will power, but had failed to find peace of mind. The strength and self-confidence of which I was so proud had crumbled the first time they were tested, leaving me wretched and bewildered. I realized that I could find relief and spiritual comfort only in the simple faith I had been taught as a child.

A few days later, I returned to Moscow and began my work among the poor. I started off by visiting slums where the squalor and destitution were indescribable. Most of the hovels never saw the sun; whole families were crowded into tiny rooms, and slept on the bare ground in dampness, filth, and cold.

An unknown world was revealed to me, a world of suffering more horrible than anything I had seen at the Wiasemskaïa-Lavra. I longed to snatch these poor creatures from their pitiful conditions, and I was staggered by the immensity of the task. I thought of the incalculable sums spent on wars and on scientific research which resulted in the destruction of humanity, while so many wretched men and women were reduced to subhuman conditions.

I had of course a great many disappointments. . . . I had realized a large sum of money by selling some personal belongings, but it melted away in a few days. I found that people took advantage of my lack of experience and imposed upon my good will. It was not till later that I understood that financial help must be given with great discrimination and without any thought of return. The Grand Duchess' example proved to me that one's only reward was in the giving. Almost every day I visited the sick at the Moscow Hospital. These poor people were touchingly grateful to me for the little I did for them. In reality it was I who was indebted to them, because of all they unconsciously taught me. I envied the doctors and nurses who were able to help them far more effectively.

I was most grateful to the Grand Duchess for understanding the desperate emptiness of my life and for giving me a new interest, but I was tormented by the idea that there was much she did not know, and that she might still be cherishing some illusions about me.

Finding her alone one day, I confessed to her all the facts of my private life of which I supposed her to know nothing. She heard me in silence, and when I had finished she kissed me.

"Don't worry," she said, "I know more about you than you think. That is why I am so much interested in you. Anyone who is capable of doing much evil is also capable of doing much good, if he sets about it in the right way. No matter how serious the offense, it is redeemed by sincere repentance. Remember, the only thing that defiles the soul is spiritual sin; it can remain pure in spite of carnal weaknesses. It is your soul that I am thinking of, and I want to lay it open to you. Fate has given you everything that a man could wish; you have received much, and much will be asked of you. Do not forget your responsibilities; you must set an example and earn the respect of others. The trials you are going through will teach you that life is not just a pastime. Think of all the good you can do! And all the evil! I have prayed much for you, and believe that Our Lord will hear me and help you."

Her words filled me with a new hope and gave me strength to face the future.

My mother, knowing that I was busy in Moscow all day and in the Grand Duchess' kindly care, stayed on at Arkhangelskoïe. We lived quite alone there. My mother spent most of her time at my brother's grave, my father had a great deal to do, and we seldom saw him. My work in Moscow absorbed me, and I stayed in the city all day and only came home for dinner. In the evening, after my father had retired to his rooms, I often stayed with my mother late into the night. Our common sorrow drew us even closer together than before, but her nervous state prevented my talking as freely as I would have wished, and I suffered on account of this. When I went to my room it was more often to think than to sleep. The religious books given me by my mother and the Grand Duchess were laid aside: the profound but simple words I had heard had sunk into my heart and were sufficient food for thought. Until then I had lived only for pleasure, avoiding the sight of suffering in any form; I had not grasped the fact that there were any more essential values than money and the power that goes with it. I now felt the vanity of all this. In discarding my thirst for power and my love for worldly possessions I had at last found freedom.

I then decided to change my way of living. My head was filled with plans for the future, which I would certainly have carried out had I not been driven into exile. I longed to turn Arkhangelskoïe into an art center and build close to it a number of houses for painters, musicians, writers, and craftsmen in the same style as the main building. They should have an academy, a school of music, and a theater. I wanted to turn the château itself into a museum, reserving a few rooms for exhibitions. I planned to make the park still more beautiful by damming the river and flooding the surrounding fields, thus turning them into an immense lake; the terraces would then be extended to the water's edge.

My plans were not confined to Arkhangelskoïe. We owned houses in St. Petersburg and Moscow which we never lived in; these I intended to turn into hospitals, clinics, and homes for old people. The Moïka house and Ivan the Terrible's palace would become museums, where the finest specimens from our collections would be exhibited. I further planned to build sanatoria on our Crimean and Caucasian estates. I meant to reserve a room or two for my personal use in all these different places. I would present the land to the peasants, the factories and workshops would be converted into joint stock companies. The sale of all jewelry and valuables which had no artistic or historical interest, plus the money in the banks, would give me a capital sum, the interest on which would be ample to carry out all these plans.

These were merely dreams for the future, but they haunted me. I was always on the lookout for new ideas, and was so obsessed by my projects that I even saw Arkhangelskoïe in my dreams just as I hoped it would be one day.

I told my mother and the Grand Duchess of my plans. The latter understood and approved of them, but I had to face my mother's opposition, for she did not see eye to eye with me on the question of my future. I was the last of the Youssoupoffs, and she considered that my first duty was to marry. I told her that I did not feel fitted for family life, and that children would entail obligations which would prevent me from disposing freely of my fortune. I added that, in times when revolutionary passions were so rife, it was no longer possible to live as one did during the time of Catherine the Great. As to leading a shabby, bourgeois existence in a setting of such pomp and ostentation—that was, to my mind, completely out of the question. The quality that I wanted to preserve in Arkhangelskoïe could only be retained if its luxury and splendor ceased to be enjoyed by a privileged few: it should be placed at the disposal of the greatest possible number of people chosen from among those who were capable of appreciating it and deriving benefit from it.

When I realized that I could never convince my mother, and that these discussions upset her, I gave them up.

chapter XIV

In the autumn the Grand Duchess came with us to the Crimea. Her company, the new interests provided by the journey, the beautiful landscapes and splendid weather, all had an excellent effect on my mother's health. But soon after we arrived the improvement in her condition was checked by the streams of visitors who came to offer their condolences. As my mother was always very sweet and kindly, she saw them all. The result was a nervous breakdown, and she was once more obliged to stay in bed.

The Grand Duke Dimitri also came to stay in the Crimea, and hardly a day went by without his coming to see me. We used to talk together for hours and I was deeply touched by his friendliness. He asked me to regard him as a brother, and assured me that he would do everything in his power to replace Nicolas—which he faithfully did for many years.

But I soon tired of this monotonous existence, and resolved to take up my work in Moscow again. When I spoke to the Grand Duchess about this, she advised me not to leave my mother until she had completely recovered. The doctors, alas, gave me little hope of that. They said that her condition might improve, but that she would never regain her health entirely.

I could not make up my mind what to do: on the one hand, I felt I ought to stay with my mother at Koreïz and, on the other, I knew that the life I was leading was not only purposeless but unhealthy. I was still undecided, when I discovered that the Grand Duchess and my mother had made up their minds it was high time I was married; what was more, they had even chosen a wife for me. But in thus disposing of me they had not reckoned with my independent spirit; they already saw the young wolf turned into a lamb. In many respects, however, I was a wolf in sheep's clothing. Come what might, I intended, if I married, to choose my own wife. The idea that they wished to keep me under their thumb, so to speak, roused all my rebellious instincts and I longed to break away from it all. I definitely decided to go to Moscow to resume the work which interested me so much.

I never regretted this decision; in caring for the poor, I gradually recovered my peace of mind.

A few weeks later, my parents, the Grand Duchess, and Dimitri returned from the Crimea, and I went with them to St. Petersburg and to Tsarskoïe-Selo where we spent the winter.

The Grand Duke Alexis Alexandrovitch, the Czar's uncle, died that year and the count went into mourning. The Grand Duke Wladimir made this the excuse for asking the Czar to allow his son, the Grand Duke Cyril, to return to Russia so that he might attend his uncle's funeral. The Grand Duke Cyril had been exiled when he married his first cousin, Princess Victoria of Great Britain, who was the divorced wife of the Grand Duke of Hesse, the Czarina's brother.

I knew the Grand Duke of Hesse very well, for he had often stayed with us at Arkhangelskoïe. He was a very good-looking fellow, gay and attractive. He had a passionate love of beauty and boundless imagination. Having taken it into his head one day that his white pigeons were not in keeping with the old stones of his palace, he had their feathers dyed sky blue. His marriage was not a happy one, and the Grand Duchess divorced him and married her cousin Cyril. This created a great scandal at court where neither divorces nor marriages between first cousins were tolerated. The Czarina was very bitter, as she considered the marriage a personal affront to her brother; she urged the Czar to forbid the Grand Duke Cyril's return to Russia, and to deprive him of his title and the privileges that went with it. The exiled couple finally won their way back to favor, but always bore a grudge against the Czarina.

A short time after the Grand Duke Alexis' death, that of Father

John of Kronstadt saddened all Russia. During his lifetime Father John had already been considered a saint. Ordained at twenty-six, at the Cathedral of St. Andrew of Kronstadt, he very quickly won the love and veneration of the faithful. Nearly all his time was spent in visiting the poor and the sick; he gave them everything he possessed, to his last penny, and often walked home barefoot, having given his shoes to some beggar he had met on the way. Innumerable pilgrims flocked to him from all parts, including even Moslems and Buddhists who begged for his intercession on behalf of their sick ones. His prayers often brought about cures which were considered miraculous.

After the birth of one of my brothers, my mother was in such a serious condition that the doctors despaired of saving her life. Father John was sent for when she was already in a coma, but as he entered the room my mother was seen to open her eyes and stretch out her arms to him. Father John knelt by her bed, and began to pray; when he rose, he blessed my mother and said simply: "God will help her and she will recover." And she was indeed soon out of danger.

As he found it impossible to hear the confessions of such large numbers of people, Father John instituted mass confessions. Several witnesses told me that on such occasions the noise in the church was unbelievable, as each person wanted to be heard above the others. Women's voices, being the shrillest, always drowned those of the men. A sect of women calling themselves the *Janites* caused Father John a great deal of trouble. They were convinced that he was the reincarnation of Christ, and often made hysterical scenes, flinging themselves on him and even biting him until the blood flowed. He generally refused to give them Holy Communion.

He had retained a deep feeling for my mother and often came to see her when I was a child. I shall never forget his clear, penetrating gaze and kindly smile. I saw him for the last time in the Crimea, shortly before his death, and shall never forget what he said to me then: "Divine inspiration is for the soul what respiration is for the body: just as a man cannot exist without air, the soul cannot live without the breath of the Holy Spirit."

Father John was seventy-eight when, while on his way to visit a dying man, he was lured into a trap and set upon by ruffians. He owed his life to his coachman, who succeeded in rescuing him and brought him home, half dead. Father John, who never entirely recovered from the effects of this assault, died several years later without having revealed the names of his aggressors. His death was a great misfortune for Russia, and particularly for the Czar and Czarina who lost in him a wise and faithful counselor.

During the course of that same winter, a mysterious event reminded me of the promise I had exchanged with my brother, that the first of us to die would appear to the other. I was staying at the Moïka in St. Petersburg for a few days. I awoke one night and, driven by some irresistible force, I rose, crossed my bedroom and went toward my brother's room. It had been kept locked since his death. Suddenly I saw his door open, and Nicolas appeared on the threshold. His face was radiant, he stretched out his arms to me . . . I was about to leap toward him when the door closed gently and I saw no more.

Our life at Tsarskoïe-Selo was very monotonous. With the exception of Dimitri I scarcely saw a soul. Several times in the course of the winter the Czarina, who was at the Alexander Palace, sent for me. She wished to talk to me about my future and offered to become my spiritual guide. But while it was easy for me to talk freely with her sister I never felt at ease with the Czarina: Rasputin's shadow always seemed to come between us.

"Any self-respecting, honest man," she said to me once, "should serve in the Army or take up a position at court. I am surprised that you do neither."

I replied that as I had a horror of war I was naturally strongly averse to a military career, and that, as far as a position at court was concerned, I was too independent and too fond of plain-speaking ever to make a good courtier. I could not imagine myself as a civil servant of any kind. I would some day have an enormous fortune and all the responsibilities that went with it. I would have to look after my estates and my factories, and see to the well-being of my peasants. This task, if well done, would be my way of serving my country and therefore of serving my Emperor.

The Empress noticed that I had put the name of Russia before that of the Czar:

"But the Czar is Russia!" she exclaimed.

At that moment, the door opened and Nicolas II entered the room.

"Felix's ideas are absolutely revolutionary," said the Empress to him.

The Emperor opened his eyes in astonishment and turned his kindly gaze on me, but remained silent.

My mother, whose health was improving, was able gradually to take up some of her activities again and attend to her many charities. My father was seldom at home and spent most of his evenings at his club. I stayed with my mother night after night reading aloud to her while she knitted, but such a monotonous and practically idle life could not last indefinitely. In the spring, I decided to take a long journey through Russia to visit our estates and various undertakings. This idea had the full approval of my parents; my father put his railway coach at my disposal and I set out with our chief agent, my father's secretary, and several other friends.

The journey lasted over two months; I was full of my own importance, and felt like a young king visiting his states. I was enchanted by the beauty and variety of the regions I visited, and was greatly touched by the welcome I was given everywhere. The peasants in their national costumes greeted me with songs and dances; many of them knelt before me. Our coach in the train was filled with flowers and presents of all sorts: chickens, geese, ducks, and pigs in such quantities that a second car had to be coupled to ours, and when the journey ended in the Crimea, where my parents had arrived for the autumn, I felt like a conquering hero returning with the spoils of war.

But after that the monotony and idleness of the life I led became again unbearable. I was then twenty-one and felt the urgent need of a change. I thought of going abroad. I remembered that one of my friends, a former naval officer, Basil Soldatenkoff who lived in Paris, had advised me to go to Oxford. I decided to do so. When I told the Grand Duchess she tried at first to dissuade me, but at last she gave way and promised to do her best to get my parents' consent. This proved to be a long and difficult task. However, without doubting for an instant that my parents would in the end agree, I wrote Basil announcing my impending arrival in Paris, where I expected to spend a few days on my way to England.

My parents finally consented, on the condition that I would not stay away more than a month. That was already a victory.

A few days before I left, the Czarina sent for me in Livadia; I found her seated on the terrace, embroidering. She told me that she was much surprised that I was leaving my sick mother, and tried for a long time to dissuade me from going. She pointed out that many young men who, like myself, left Russia, found themselves so much out of their element when they returned home that they ended by settling down abroad. I had no right, she said, to run the risk of following their example. My duty was to stay in Russia and serve the Czar.

I assured her that I had no intention of remaining abroad, for I loved my country more than anything in the world, and that my purpose in going to Oxford was to fit myself to be of greater use to Russia and my Emperor on my return.

My reply apparently displeased the Empress, for she changed the subject. On dismissing me, she asked me to call on her sister Princess Victoria of Battenberg, who lived in London, and gave me a letter for her. She wished me a happy journey and expressed the hope of seeing me that winter at Tsarskoïe-Selo.

The day I left, a religious service was held in our chapel to ask for the protection of Heaven on me. It was both touching and funny; everybody cried, kissed, and blessed me. One would have thought that I was starting out on a dangerous expedition to the North Pole or to Tibet rather than on a short journey to England.

Finally I left, accompanied by my faithful Ivan, and reached Paris without incident except for the loss of my passport at the German frontier.

Basil Soldatenkoff met me at the station. He was a fine fellow: intelligent, athletic, attractive, extremely headstrong, and dynamic. He called his racing car "Lina," after the beautiful Lina Cavalieri with whom he was very much in love. Women doted on this great, strapping, handsome youth who ran his life as he did his car, at top speed. He had married a charming woman, Princess Helen Gortchakoff, but the marriage was not a happy one.

After a few days in Paris, I left for England with Basil.

chapter XV

In London I stayed at the Carlton.

Autumn had already set in—the wrong season for a first visit to England. However, my first impression was a very good one. I found the English attractive, hospitable, self-possessed and, above all, quite frankly imbued with a sense of their own superiority. The day after my arrival I lunched at the Russian Embassy and noticed with surprise that our ambassador, Count Benckendorff, hardly knew a word of Russian.

The next day I was asked to lunch with Prince and Princess Louis of Battenberg. The Princess questioned me at great length about Rasputin; all she had heard about his influence over her sister had alarmed her. She was too intelligent not to foresee the catastrophe that threatened my country. When I told her that I intended to enter an English university, she advised me to see her cousin, Princess Marie Louise of Schleswig-Holstein, and also the Bishop of London, as they might both be useful to me. I followed her advice at once. Both the Princess and the Bishop welcomed me most cordially and advised me strongly to go to Oxford. Later, when I was an undergraduate there, these two kindly counselors often came to visit me. The Bishop introduced me to a young Englishman, Eric Hamilton; we went up to Oxford together and studied at the same college. We have remained friends ever since, and he is now Dean of Windsor.

Taking my letters of introduction with me, I called on the master of University College, the oldest college in Oxford. The master received me most kindly and told me a great deal about the life and customs of the University. I learned that I would have a three weeks' holiday every two months, and that the summer vacations lasted three months; this would allow me to go to Russia quite often. The master showed me through the college and undergraduates' rooms, which were small but fairly comfortably furnished. One suite on the ground floor was vacant; it consisted of a large room with a grilled window looking onto the street, and a tiny room next to it. The master told me that the large room was called the "Club," because, no matter who had it, the other undergraduates were in the habit of meeting there to drink their whisky. He also told me that in my first year I would have to live in the college, but that during the two following years I could rent a house or flat in the town. I asked him if I could have these two rooms next winter.

This matter satisfactorily settled, I strolled through the town. Oxford, with all its ancient colleges surrounded by lovely gardens hidden behind high walls, won my heart. Innumerable generations of undergraduates had lived for centuries behind these ancient walls, a fit setting for the spirit of eternal youth. I would have hated to leave Oxford had I not been certain of returning.

Before returning home via Paris, I went to see the Grand Duke Michael Mikhaïlovitch, the brother of my future father-in-law; he lived with his family at Kenwood, a lovely house on the outskirts of London. The Grand Duke had been in exile since his morganatic marriage to Countess Merenberg, Pushkin's granddaughter. She had been given the title of Countess Torby, and was a most delightful woman, very popular in London society. Her husband's cantankerous nature was a great trial to her; he never ceased thundering out abuse against his Russian family. Owing to his odd temperament, the Grand Duke could not be held responsible for his actions, but everyone was sorry for his wife. They had three children: a son they called "Boy" and two very pretty daughters, Zia and Nada. I saw a great deal of them during my years at Oxford.

I brought back from England quite a collection of animals for Arkhangelskoïe: a bull, four cows, six pigs, and a large number of roosters, hens, and rabbits. The larger animals were sent direct to Dover to be shipped to Russia, but I took the crates containing the fowls and rabbits with me, and had them placed in the basement of the

Carlton. I simply could not resist the temptation of opening the crates and letting the animals loose in the hotel. The result was marvelous! In the twinkling of an eye, they had scattered in all directions; cocks and hens fluttered and cackled, the rabbits messed the whole place up. What a pandemonium! The staff entered into the spirit of the thing and started to chase them all over the hotel, but the manager was furious and so were the guests. In short, it was a great success.

I stayed in Paris for a few days to see some friends, among them the musician Reynaldo Hahn and Francis de Croisset. We had several pleasant musical evenings together; Reynaldo was very fond of hearing me sing, and taught me some of his lovely songs.

I arrived in Russia in excellent spirits and full of energy. My parents were then at Tsarskoïe-Selo. I found my mother much calmer and more resigned. The Grand Duke Dimitri was eager for a detailed description of my journey, and the Czarina, who at that time was still on friendly terms with my mother and often came to see her, also questioned me about my stay in England and about her sister Princess Victoria. I refrained from telling her how anxious her sister was about Rasputin's influence on her! I soon left for Moscow, and resumed my visits to the hospital for tubercular cases. Many of the old patients had been replaced by others, but the staff remained the same, and I was happy to find myself among them once again. I often saw the Grand Duchess Elisabeth and had long talks with her.

I spent the summer at Arkhangelskoïe where I saw the animals I had bought in England. My father was delighted with my purchases and asked me to send for a second bull and three more cows. Accordingly I sent off the following telegram, which will give an idea of my knowledge of English: "Please send me one man cow and three Jersey women." The order was rightly interpreted, as the arrival of the animals testified, but a facetious journalist got hold of my telegram and it appeared in the English papers, to the joy of all my English friends.

This was 1909; and the year in which I met Rasputin for the first time.

We were back in St. Petersburg where I was spending Christmas with my parents before returning to England. For a long time I had been on friendly terms with the G. family, and more particularly with the youngest daughter, who was a fervent admirer of the *starets*. She was too innocent a girl to understand his ignominious nature, and too guileless to form an unbiased opinion as to his motives. He was, according to her, a man of exceptional spiritual power who had been sent into the world to purify and heal our souls, and to guide our thoughts and actions. This extravagant description left me skeptical, and although at that time I knew nothing definite about Rasputin something inside me made me suspicious of him. However, Mlle G.'s enthusiasm roused my curiosity and I questioned her in detail about the man she so much admired. She looked upon him as an apostle come straight from Heaven; he had no human weaknesses, no vices; he was an ascetic whose whole life was devoted to prayer. I heard so much about him that I felt I ought to judge him for myself, and I accepted an invitation to meet the starets a few days later at the G.s' house.

The G.s lived on the Winter Canal. When I entered the drawing room, mother and daughter were seated at the tea table, wearing the solemn expression of persons awaiting the arrival of a miraculous icon which was to bring a divine blessing on the house. In a little while the door opened and Rasputin came in with short quick steps. He walked up to me, said "Good evening, my dear boy," and attempted to kiss me. I drew back instinctively. He smiled maliciously and, going up to Mlle G. and then to her mother, he calmly put his arms around them and gave each of them a resounding kiss. From the very first his self-assurance irritated me, and there was something about him which disgusted me. He was of middle height, muscular and thin. His arms were disproportionately long, and just where his untidy crop of hair began to grow there was a great scar, which I found out later was the mark of a wound received during one of his highway robberies in Siberia. He seemed to be about forty, and with his caftan, baggy breeches, and great top-boots he looked exactly what he was—a peasant. He had a low, common face framed by a shaggy beard, coarse features and a long nose, with small shifty gray eyes sunken under heavy eyebrows. The strangeness of his manner was disconcerting, and although he affected a free and easy demeanor one felt him to be ill at ease and suspicious. He seemed to be constantly watching the person he was talking to.

Rasputin remained seated for a few moments, then began to pace up and down the room with his short quick steps, mumbling under his breath. His voice sounded hollow, his pronunciation indistinct. We drank tea in silence as we watched him, Mlle G. with enthusiastic attention, I with great curiosity.

Soon he sat down and gave me a searching look. We began to talk. He spoke volubly in the tone of a preacher inspired from above, quoting the Old and New Testaments at random, often distorting their real meaning, which was a trifle confusing.

As he talked I studied his features closely. There was something really extraordinary about his peasant face. He was not in the least like a holy man; on the contrary he looked like a lascivious, malicious satyr. I was particularly struck by the revolting expression in his eyes, which were very small, set close together, and so deep-sunk in their sockets that at a distance they were invisible. But even at close quarters it was sometimes difficult to know whether they were open or shut, and the impression one had was that of being pierced with needles rather than of merely being looked at. His glance was both piercing and sullen; his sweet and insipid smile was almost as revolting as the expression of his eyes. There was something base in his unctuous countenance; something wicked, crafty, and sensual. Mlle G. and her mother never took their eyes off him, and seemed to drink in every word he spoke.

After a little while Rasputin rose, and giving me a soft, hypocritical glance pointed to Mlle G. and said: "What a faithful friend you have in her! You should listen to her, she will be your spiritual spouse. Yes, she has spoken very well of you, and I too now see that both of you are good and well suited to each other. As for you, my dear boy, you will go far, very far."

With these words he left the room. When I went away, my mind was filled with the strange impression he had made on me.

A few days later I met Mlle G. again; she told me that Rasputin liked me very much and wanted to see me again.

Shortly after, I left for England where a very different life awaited me.

After an atrocious crossing, I spent the night in London. The manager of the Carlton, who had not forgotten my practical joke with the fowls, eyed me askance. I reached Oxford early the next morning and the first person I met was Eric Hamilton. He came with me to my rooms and promised to fetch me for lunch in the great dining hall, where I would see all my fellow undergraduates. Before lunch a manservant brought me my student's cap and gown. I liked the "togs," especially the mortarboard, but the luncheon was awful. Not that I minded, as I had other things to think about. In the afternoon I set about arranging my rooms. I turned the small one into a bedroom; my icons and their night light hanging in a corner over my bed reminded me of Russia. The large room became my living room. I placed my books on shelves, my knickknacks and photographs on tables, hired a piano, bought a few flowers, and managed to make my rather cold and impersonal quarters look quite cosy and pleasant. That same evening, the "Club" was filled with undergraduates who sang, drank, and chattered until dawn. Within a few days I knew almost everyone in college. I was not a scholar; what interested me most was meeting people from different countries, talking to them, and trying to understand their ideas, morals, and customs. I could not have found a better place for this than Oxford, which was a meeting ground for the youth of all nations; I felt as though I were taking a trip around the world. I also liked the outdoor life there; not the violent games, but I got a lot of hunting, polo, and swimming, which I enjoyed very much.

All the undergraduates who lived in the college had to be in by midnight, and this rule was very strictly applied. Anyone breaking it three times in one term was expelled. The culprit was always given a funeral; all the undergraduates escorted him to the station in a solemn procession, singing dirges. To help my friends, I had the idea of making a rope out of knotted sheets which could be attached to the roof and let down to the street. Anyone who was late had only to knock at my window and I immediately climbed up to the roof and threw down the rope. One night, hearing a tap at the window, up I went, let down the rope and caught a policeman!

Without the personal intervention of the Bishop of London, I would certainly have been expelled.

I almost met the same fate on another occasion and on my own account. I was returning from London where I had dined with a fellow undergraduate. In spite of a heavy fog, we were driving at top speed, and we were anxious to be on time as I had already been late twice during the term, and a third offense would have automatically led to my expulsion.

Blinded by the fog, my friend who was driving crashed into the closed gates of a level crossing. The violent collision smashed the gate and I was thrown on the track. I must have lost consciousness, and, as I came to, I saw a light through the fog which grew larger and larger at terrifying speed. I was still too dizzy to realize what was happening, and was only saved by instinctively turning and rolling off the track. The London express thundered by, and the blast sent me head over heels into the ditch. I picked myself up without a scratch, but my friend, though alive, was in very bad shape, with several broken limbs. As to the car, needless to say very little of it remained after the express had gone by. I telephoned from the gatekeeper's cottage for an ambulance, and after taking my friend to the Oxford Hospital I reached my college two hours late. However, in view of the circumstances, I was not expelled.

Every morning, after a cold shower which I hated, and a hearty breakfast, the only decent meal of the day, I attended lectures until lunchtime. The afternoon was given up to sports, and after tea each of us worked in his rooms. We spent the evenings at the "Club." Sometimes we had music, and there was always much conversation and lots of whiskey.

In this pleasant and healthy atmosphere I spent my first year at Oxford, but I suffered terribly from the cold. There was no means of heating my bedroom, and its temperature was much the same as out of doors. Water froze in my washbasin, and when I rose in the morning the carpet was so damp that I felt as though I were walking through a marsh.

The following year, availing myself of the right accorded to second-year men to live outside college, I rented a very ordinary and unattractive little house in the town, which I quickly furnished to suit me. Two of my fellow undergraduates, Jacques de Beistegui and Luigi Franchetti, came to live with me. The latter played the piano beautifully and we loved to listen to him till all hours of the night. I had brought a good chef from Russia. The rest of my staff was composed of a French chauffeur, an excellent English valet, Arthur Keeping, a housekeeper, and her husband who looked after my three horses. I had bought a hunter and two polo ponies; a bulldog and a macaw completed my menagerie. Mary, the macaw, was blue, yellow, and red; the bulldog answered to the name of Punch. Like all of his kind, he was most eccentric. I soon noticed that checks on linoleum or on any kind of material drove him wild.

One day when I was at Davies my tailor's, a very smartly dressed old gentleman, wearing a checked suit, came in. Before I could stop him, Punch rushed at him and tore a huge piece out of his trousers. On another occasion I went with a friend to her furrier's; Punch noticed a sable muff encircled by a black and white checked scarf. He immediately seized it and rushed out of the shop with it. I, and everyone else at the furrier's, ran after him halfway down Bond Street, and it was only with the greatest difficulty that we managed to catch him and retrieve the muff, happily almost intact. When the holidays came, I took Punch to Russia, not thinking of the stringent law governing the entry of dogs into England. As six months in quarantine was out of the question, I decided to evade the law. On my way to Oxford in the autumn, I passed through Paris and went to see an old Russian ex-cocotte whom I knew. I asked her to come to London with me; she would have to dress as a nurse and carry Punch, disguised as a baby. The old lady agreed at once, as the idea amused her immensely, although at the same time it frightened her to death. The next day, we left for London after giving "Baby" a sleeping draught so as to keep him quiet during the journey. Everything went smoothly and not a soul suspected the fraud.

During one of my holidays in Russia I had the opportunity of seeing a most impressive sight: the glorification of the relics of Blessed Yossaf, which took place at the Kremlin in the Cathedral of the Assumption. The Grand Duchess Elisabeth had asked me to go with her, and the seats which had been reserved for her gave us an excellent view of the ceremony. A vast crowd filled the cathedral. The shrine containing the remains of the Blessed Yossaf was placed in front of the chancel, and sick people carried on stretchers, or in the arms of relations, were brought to kiss the relics. Cases of people "possessed by the Devil" were particularly gruesome; the inhuman screams and contortions of the victims grew more and more violent as they approached the shrine, and it sometimes took several people to hold them. Their shrieks drowned the magnificent religious chants as though Satan himself were blaspheming through their mouths; but their cries calmed down the moment they were made to touch the shrine. I saw several miraculous cures.

On September 14, 1911, Prime Minister Stolypin was assassinated at Kiev. He was a great statesman, deeply devoted to his country and to the throne. He was a bitter enemy of Rasputin and never ceased to oppose him, thus earning the antagonism of the Czarina, for she considered that an enemy of the starets must also be an enemy of the Czar.

The attempt on Stolypin's life in 1906 had already been mentioned in a previous chapter. He had restored order in Russia by a series of wise measures. At the time of his death he was preparing a new law for the expansion of peasant land-ownership and the suppression of communal village property. He was killed by a revolver shot, during a gala performance at which the Czar was present. As Stolypin lay dying on the ground, he raised himself in a last effort and, turning toward the Imperial box, made a gesture as though to bless its occupants. The assassin was a revolutionary Jew by the name of Bagroff who, strange as it may seem, worked in the Secret Service and was a friend of Rasputin's. An investigation was started but was quickly stopped, as though for fear of embarrassing disclosures.

Stolypin's death was a triumph for the enemies of Russia and of the throne; there was no one now to stand in the way of their criminal plans. Dimitri told me how indignant he was at the Emperor's indifference; both he and the Empress seemed to be quite unconscious of the seriousness of what had happened. The Czarina made this curious remark to Dimitri: "Those who have offended God in the person of our friend, may no longer count on divine protection. Only the prayers of the 'starets,' which go straight to Heaven, have the power to protect them."

I spent some time in Paris toward the end of the holidays; I saw Jacques de Beistegui again, and we had a very good time before returning to Oxford. The *Bal des Quat'z Arts* was about to take place. I had heard so much about it that I was most anxious to see it, and Beistegui and I decided we would go. The question of costumes was simplified by the fact that prehistoric dress was de rigueur that year. A leopard skin was all that was needed. Beistegui, who never liked to waste money, bought an imitation skin and rigged himself out in a blond wig with two braids, which made him look more like a valkyrie than a cave-dweller. As for myself, Diaghilev lent me the costume worn by Nijinsky in *Daphnis et Chloé*: a leopard skin and the big straw hat worn by Arcadian shepherds, tied round the neck and hanging over the shoulders.

The ball was a great disappointment. Never in my life have I seen anything so disgusting. A crowd of half-naked people rushing about excitedly in an overheated atmosphere heavy with the odor of perspiring bodies. Nakedness, which can be so chaste when associated with youth and beauty, is obscene in the old and the ugly. Most of the people at the ball were hideous, and all of them were drunk; they had lost all sense of decency and gave free play to their bestiality. Sickened by this revolting spectacle, we left early. Our leopard skins had been torn from us; nothing remained of our costumes but Jacques's blond wig and my Arcadian hat.

It was about this time that I met the famous *demi-mondaine*, Émilienne d'Alençon, who was as lovely as she was intelligent. She had a subtle, caustic wit which was most entertaining, and I became a frequent guest at her fine house in the Avenue Victor Hugo. In her garden was a Chinese pavilion which she had furnished and decorated with the greatest taste. Subdued lighting added to the voluptuous charm of a retreat where she spent most of her time reading, smoking opium, and composing poems which she was fond of reading to me. She was clever enough to surround herself with interesting people, and entertained admirably, always with the most perfect poise which, indeed, was characteristic of most of the great *demi-mondaines* of the period. Their distinction of mind and manner might well serve as a model to many so-called society women of today.

Apart from my regular holidays, a telegram sometimes summoned me to my mother, for her health was still very precarious. She had a particularly violent attack of nerves during a stay in Berlin with my father, and he, knowing that I alone could soothe her, sent for me and I came at once.

Although the heat in Berlin was stifling, I found my mother in bed, buried under furs, windows closed, and refusing all nourishment. She was in great pain and her cries were heartbreaking.

We had long known that there was nothing organic the matter with her and that her sufferings were purely nervous, so we sent for a psychiatrist, one of the greatest specialists in Berlin. As soon as he arrived I took him to my mother's room and let them alone together.

Suddenly a peal of laughter was heard through the door. It was so long since I had heard my mother laugh that I was dumbfounded. I opened her door: there was no mistake, it was my mother's charming, infectious laughter. Professor X sat stiffly on his chair looking very embarrassed, and obviously disconcerted by his patient's gaiety.

"Please take him away," she said as soon as I went in. "I can't bear it, he'll make me die of laughter!"

I showed the bewildered professor to the door. When I went back to my mother's room, she gave me no time to ask questions.

"Your precious professor is in far worse shape than I am," she said. "He looked at the watch by my bed, and seeing that it had stopped, what do you think he said? 'How curious! Have you noticed that your watch has stopped at the very hour when Frederick the Great died?' "

All things considered, this eminent practitioner's visit was not without value, but he had certainly never expected to cure his patient by appealing to her sense of humor, even if unconsciously.

When I went away a few days later my mother was much better.

A curious incident, which has remained unexplained, marked my brief visit; every night, when I went to bed, I found a red rose on my pillow. As no one could enter my room without a key, I was forced to conclude that one of the maids in the hotel had a soft spot in her heart for me!

Shortly after my return to England, I received an invitation to a big fancy-dress ball at the Albert Hall. As I had plenty of time, and I was in Russia on a holiday, I ordered a Russian costume in St. Petersburg. I had found some sixteenth-century gold brocade embroidered with red flowers, and the costume was magnificent: studded with precious stones, edged with sable, with a toque to match. It caused a sensation. I met all London at the ball, and the next day my photograph was in every paper. It was there that I met Jack Gordon, a young Scotsman, an Oxford undergraduate like myself, but at another college. He was extremely good-looking and rather like a Hindu prince, and was very popular in London society. As we both liked to lead a gay social life, we rented two connecting flats at 4 Curzon Street. I engaged the Misses Frith, two most pleasant elderly spinsters who looked as if they had stepped out of one of Dickens' novels, to decorate them. All went well until I ordered a black carpet. They must have thought me the devil in person for, from that day, whenever I entered their shop, they disappeared behind a screen, and nothing could be seen of them but two quivering little lace caps. My carpet set a fashion in London—it even became the cause of a divorce. An Englishwoman ordered one against her husband's wish. He considered it funereal: "Either me or the carpet," he said, which was rash, for she chose the carpet.

One afternoon I had a telephone call from a well-known hostess asking me if I would preside at a big dinner she was giving at the Ritz. I accepted, and did my best to help her to receive her guests, who were the cream of London society. The fare was excellent, the wines were choice, and the surroundings delightful. In fact, it was all a great success. Next day, to my intense surprise I received the bill, which amounted to a fabulous sum!

Diaghilev was then in town with the Russian ballet; Pavlova, Karsavina, and Nijinsky were having a triumphant season at Covent Garden. I knew most of these artists, but I was particularly fond of Anna Pavlova. I had seen her in St. Petersburg, but I was then too young really to appreciate her. When I saw her in London in *The Swan*, she moved me profoundly. I forgot Oxford, my studies, and my friends. Night and day, I could think of nothing but the ethereal being who held whole audiences under her spell, fascinated by the quivering of the swan's snow-white feathers on which a huge ruby blazed like a great drop of blood. In my eyes, Anna Pavlova was not just a great artist and as beautiful as an angel: she brought the world a message from Heaven! She lived in Hampstead at Ivy House, a charming place, and I often went to see her there. She had a genius for friendship, which she rightly held to be the noblest of all sentiments. She gave me more than one proof of this during the years when I was lucky enough to see her often. She knew me inside out: "You have God in one eye and the devil in the other," she used to say to me sometimes.

A delegation of Oxford undergraduates asked her to dance in the University theater. As she was going on tour, she had not a single free evening and at first she refused; but on learning that the students were friends of mine she agreed, thereby throwing her impresario into a panic. On the day of the performance she came to my rooms with the entire *corp de ballet*. As she wanted to rest, I left her there and took her company around Oxford.

When we returned from our walk, a car belonging to the parents of a girl whom certain misinformed persons alleged to be my fiancée was standing at my door. I met the whole family coming down the stairs, looking most embarrassed: not finding me in the drawing room, they had opened my bedroom door and seen Anna Pavlova asleep on my bed.

That evening Pavlova received a delirious ovation from Oxford's undergraduates.

It was about this time that what I took to be eye trouble, but turned out to be something quite different, first made its appearance. In theaters, drawing rooms, in the street, people suddenly seemed to be enveloped in a cloud. After this had happened several times, I

Anna Pavlova in The Dying Swan

consulted an oculist. He examined me very thoroughly and then assured me that there was nothing wrong with my eyesight. I stopped worrying about this phenomenon until the day when it took on a new and terrible meaning for me.

We rode to hounds once a week, and my friends used to come and have breakfast with me before going to the meet. It was during one of these meets that I first had a sinister foreboding when I saw this curious cloud creep over one of my friends who was sitting opposite me. A few hours later, on jumping a hurdle, he fell and was so severely injured that his life hung in the balance for several days.

Shortly afterward, a friend of my parents who was passing through Oxford came to lunch with me. During the meal, I suddenly saw him through the cloud. In writing to my mother, I mentioned this, adding that I was convinced that some danger threatened our friend. A few days later, a letter from her announced his death.

When I happened to meet an occultist at a friend's house in London, I told him the story. He said that he was not surprised, that it was a form of second sight, and that he had heard of several similar cases, notably in Scotland.

For a whole year, I lived in dread lest this horrible cloud should hide the face of someone I loved. Fortunately these visions ended as suddenly as they had begun.

London society was split into several sets. I preferred the more unconventional ones, where I could meet artists and where a certain amount of informality was permitted. The Duchess of Rutland was the leader of one such set. She had a son and three daughters; I was particularly friendly with two of the latter, Margery and Diana. One was dark, the other fair; both were lovely, witty, and full of imagination. It would be hard to say which was the more attractive of the two; I was under the spell of both. Lady Ripon, a celebrated beauty of the Edwardian era, was a woman of great breeding, and still very attractive in a very English way. Extremely intelligent, shrewd and astute, she could carry on a brilliant conversation on topics which she knew nothing about. Her sparkling wit had sometimes a touch of malice, concealed under her deceptively angelic air of innocence.

She entertained a great deal at Coomb Court, her magnificent house near London, and she possessed the unique gift of giving her receptions the right atmosphere. The King and Queen were received with pomp and ceremony; politicians and men of learning found themselves in a correct if rather solemn atmosphere, and artists in a *vie de Bohème* that was free from all vulgarity yet easy and unconventional. Lord Ripon was a racing man with little taste for society, and put in brief and infrequent appearances at his wife's receptions. Sometimes his head could be seen peering over a screen, behind which it almost immediately disappeared.

In spite of the disparity in our ages, Lady Ripon had a great liking for me; she often telephoned, asking me to help her with her receptions and week-end parties.

One day she had invited Queen Alexandra and several other members of the royal family to lunch, and arranged a party for the same evening at which Diaghilev, Nijinsky, Karsavina, and the entire Russian ballet were to appear. The weather was very fine and the Queen gave no signs of leaving. At five, tea was served; six o'clock, seven o'clock came and still the Queen did not go. For some unknown reason Lady Ripon did not wish the Queen to know that she was having the Russian ballet at her house that evening. She begged me to help her avoid a "collision"—a somewhat tricky task. So when Diaghilev and his artists arrived I took them straight to the ballroom where an array of bottles of champagne had been put on ice. I locked the door and entertained them until the Queen left—when we all staggered out.

Lady Ripon's daughter, Lady Juliet Duff, was very like her mother in many ways. She had the same charm and spontaneous kindliness that made her so popular with all her friends.

It was at Lady Ripon's that I met Adelina Patti, Melba, Puccini, and countless other artists. I also met King Manuel of Portugal there, and we remained fast friends until his death.

Although I went on studying at Oxford, I became more and more absorbed in the amusing and frivolous life I led in London. My flat in Curzon Street was too small, and I rented a larger one overlooking

Hyde Park. I took a great deal of trouble over the decoration of this flat, and the result was most satisfactory.

I kept Mary, my macaw, and several other birds in the entrance hall, which I furnished with plants and wicker chairs and tables. To the right of the hall was a white dining room decorated with blue Delft pottery; the carpet was black, the curtains of orange silk, the chairs were covered with toile de Jouy in the same shade as the pottery. The room was lit by a blue glass bowl hanging from the ceiling, and by silver candlesticks on the table with orange shades. This effect of double lighting was very becoming to women, and gave to their faces the delicate semi-transparency of porcelain. To the left of the hall was a large drawing room divided by a recess. It contained a grand piano and mahogany furniture covered with chintz of a Chinese design in the same shade of green as the walls. On these I hung English colored prints. A white bearskin was stretched on the black carpet in front of the fireplace. The room was lit entirely by table lamps.

Next door was a smaller drawing room; it was modern, the color scheme green and blue, the furniture by Martine.

The walls of my bedroom were hung in two shades of gray cretonne, and blue curtains formed a sort of alcove; my icons were placed on either side of the bed in glass cases, and were dimly lit by night lights. The furniture was lacquered gray, and the carpet was black with a design of flowers.

My third year at Oxford was almost up, and I had to abandon my frivolous life for a few months to prepare for the final examinations. How I succeeded in passing them is still a mystery to me.

I was very sorry to leave Oxford and all my friends, and I felt quite melancholy when I got into my car, with my parrot and my bulldog, and set out for London.

I had taken such a fancy to life in England that I decided to prolong my stay there until the following autumn. Two of my cousins, Maya Koutouzoff and Irina Rodzianko, came to stay with me. Both were very beautiful women and I enjoyed going about with them.

For a performance at Covent Garden they wore, at my suggestion, tulle turbans with a big bow which made a perfect frame for their lovely faces. The whole audience stood up to stare at them, and during the interval all my friends flocked to our box, asking to be introduced. A handsome young Italian diplomat, known as "Bambino," instantly fell in love with Maya. He never left us from that moment, spent all his time at my flat, and had himself invited wherever we went. He continued coming round to the flat after my cousins left, and we remained excellent friends.

Prince Paul Karageorgevitch, later Regent of Yugoslavia, was then in London and stayed with me for some time. He was a very pleasant fellow, a good musician, and excellent company. He, King Manuel, Prince Serge Obolensky, Jack Gordon, and I were inseparable and went everywhere together.

I was asked to take part in a charity performance organized at Earls Court. This included a pantomime in which ambassadors from various countries were to make a formal *entrée* before the queen of an imaginary country. The period chosen was the sixteenth century, and the beautiful Lady Curzon, seated on a throne and surrounded by courtiers, was to be the queen.... I was to impersonate a Russian ambassador from the Court of Moscow and made my entrance on horseback, followed by a retinue. My Russian costume was exactly right for the part, and a circus supplied a magnificent full-blooded, snow-white Arab horse. The first entrance was that of Prince Christopher, dressed as a king, his ermine-lined mantle trailing on the ground, a crown on his head and ... a monocle! I came next. To my astonishment, as I entered the ring, my horse on hearing the music began to dance. Everyone thought this was part of the program and when my horse had finished his act I was greeted with loud applause. But was I embarrassed! After the performance a number of friends had supper with me. Prince Christopher draped in his royal mantle, crown on head and monocle in eye, sat astride the hood of my car as I drove home, to the delight of the crowd. We drank so much that night that not one of my guests was in a fit condition to go home. The next day at about twelve o'clock I was awakened by the arrival of a chamberlain of the Greek Court in search of his Prince. He had looked everywhere for him, and had even sent an SOS to

Scotland Yard. He searched among the bodies lying in armchairs, on sofas, and even on the floor, but there was no Prince Christopher. I was becoming quite alarmed, when I suddenly heard snores which seemed to come from out of the piano. I lifted the silk cover and there was the Prince, rolled in his royal mantle, his crown by his side, his eyeglass in his eye, sound asleep.

My last year in London was the gayest of all. Fancy-dress balls were the rage and there was one almost every night. I had a wide range of costumes but my Russian one was always the greatest success.

I was to be Louis XIV at a ball given at the Albert Hall, and even went to Paris to have my outfit made. But, at the last minute, the costume struck me as being altogether too ostentatious, so I passed it on to the Duke of Mecklenburg-Schwerin, and attended the ball, not as the King of France, but as the humblest of his subjects, a simple French sailor. The German prince looked magnificent: gold brocade, precious stones, and feathers galore.

I was on very friendly terms with dear old Mrs. Hwfa Williams. "Madame," as we all called her, was almost completely deaf; but in spite of this and of her age, she was full of joie de vivre and was as popular as many younger and prettier women. King Edward VII took her with him wherever he went; she amused him so much that he could not do without her. Her country house, Coomb Spring, was named after a fountain to which Mrs. Williams attributed rejuvenating powers; she used to bottle the water from the so-called Fountain of Youth and sell it to her friends for fabulous sums. Weekends at her house were always extremely gay. Her friends were all free-and-easy, and sometimes a trifle questionable. They would turn up unexpectedly, and were always sure of a warm welcome at any time of the day or night, or might even find her ready to set off with them for an evening jaunt to London.

Once I spent a few days in Jersey and, as I was always interested in livestock, I stopped by a meadow to admire a magnificent herd of cows. One cow came up to my car, and looked at me so touchingly with her great eyes, that I was seized with an irresistible desire to buy her. Her owner at first demurred, but ended by agreeing.

As soon as I reached London, I entrusted my cow to the care of "Madame," who welcomed her with enthusiasm. She put a ribbon and a bell around her neck and called her Felicita.

Felicita became as tame as a dog; she went walking with us, and all but followed us into the house. In the autumn, when the time came to me to return to Russia, I wanted to take my cow back with me to Arkhangelskoïe. But "Madame" grew deafer and deafer. She couldn't hear a word I said. I wrote on a piece of paper: "The cow belongs to me." She tore the paper up under my nose, tossed the pieces in the air, and looked at me with a mocking smile. Faced by such treachery, I resolved to kidnap Felicita.

I got a few friends together, and one night we all drove to Coomb Spring wearing masks. Unfortunately the noise of the engine woke the lodgekeeper who, thinking we were gangsters, gave the alarm. "Madame" jumped from bed, seized a revolver, and began firing at us from her window. It was impossible to make her hear or understand who we were. When all the servants had been roused by the uproar, she at last recognized us. The cunning old lady served us a magnificent supper, and such heady wines that we completely forgot what we had come for.

On the eve of my departure for Russia, I gave a big farewell party at the Berkeley. The dinner, which was in fancy dress, was followed by a ball at the studio of one of my friends, a painter. The next day I left London, taking with me the most wonderful and lasting memories of my life in England.

It is sometimes said on the Continent that England is everyone's enemy, and *La perfide Albion* is often blamed for her selfish and insular policy. For myself, having a horror of politics, I prefer to regard the English from another angle. I have known them in their own country: hospitable, great gentlemen, and faithful friends. The three years that I spent among them were perhaps the happiest of my youth.

chapter XVI

I was sad at leaving England where I had made so many friends. I felt that one chapter of my life was over forever.

I spent a few days in Paris seeing my French friends, and then left for Russia with Basil Soldatenkoff who had offered to drive me in his racing car "Lina." Basil always drove at full speed, and when I begged him to go a little slower he merely laughed and stepped on the accelerator.

On reaching Tsarskoïe-Selo, to my great delight I found my mother in much better health. We had long talks, mostly about my future. The Czarina asked me to come to see her and questioned me at great length about my life in England. She too wished to discuss my future, and insisted that I should get married.

It was a great joy to meet all my friends again, especially the Grand Duke Dimitri; to be back in my own country, in my home, to be once again in St. Petersburg with its beauty and its gaiety. We resumed our merry parties in the company of artists and musicians and, of course, of the gypsies, with whom we sometimes stayed till dawn. How happy I felt in Russia! And, above all, how much I felt at home!

I went several times to see the Grand Duchess Elisabeth in Moscow. The question of my marriage came up in all our conversations, but no specific name was ever mentioned and it was difficult for me to object on principle. However, there was no question; everybody had decided it was time I got married.

I was dining with the Grand Duchess Wladimir one evening at Tsarskoïe-Selo when someone mentioned the festivities in connection with the centenary of the battle of Borodino. Everyone criticized the Czarina for having forbidden the Grand Duchesses to be present at this ceremony. I urged the Grand Duchess Helen and the Grand Duchess Victoria, the daughter and daughter-in-law of my hostess, to disregard this arbitrary veto and go to Borodino incognito. I offered to take them there myself and invited them to spend a few days at Arkhangelskoïe on the way.

My proposal was greeted with enthusiasm. The Grand Duchess Marie approved but refused to join us. When I told my mother she also gave her approval, but warned me that we would probably get into trouble.

I left for Moscow the very next day with Basil Soldatenkoff and my valet Ivan, so as to arrange a fitting reception for my guests. I asked Nastia Poliakowa, the famous gypsy singer, to come to Arkhangelskoïe with her chorus, and also sent for Stefanesco, the cymbal player, who happened to be in Moscow at the time.

Basil and I went to meet my guests at the station. The Grand Duchesses were accompanied by several members of their suite; we were ten in all, full of gaiety and high spirits.

Arkhangelskoïe was looking glorious and the roses in the garden filled the house with their delicious perfume. The charm and beauty of the Grand Duchess Helen made Arkhangelskoïe seem still more wonderful than usual. We spent our days out of doors, and our nights listening to Stefanesco and the gypsies. Time sped by so pleasantly that we almost forgot the Borodino celebrations, and we were so sorry to leave that we put off our departure till the last moment.

On our way we were to spend the night in a village with a tradesman who had placed two rooms in his house at our disposal. The larger room was given to the ladies, and the men had to make the best of the other and bed down on the floor on mattresses. As I did not feel sleepy, I went for a walk in the warm, starlit night. When I returned, I found the house in darkness and my companions busy table-turning. The Grand Duchess Helen told me that a spirit had materialized who claimed to have commanded, in 1812, the regiment of which she herself was the honorary colonel. Mortally wounded during the battle in a village some four miles from Borodino, he had been carried to a house with a red roof, the fourth on the right on entering the village; this he described in detail. He asked the Grand Duchess to pray for the peace of his soul beside the bed in which he had died.

We passed through this very village the next day on our way to Borodino. There was the red-roofed house exactly as he had described it. The Grand Duchess asked the kindly old peasant-woman who opened the door to allow her to rest for a while. We could see into a room in the corner of which stood a bed. While I talked to the old woman, the Grand Duchess went into the room and, kneeling by the bed, offered up a short prayer. Then, feeling very much impressed, we got into the car and drove away under the astonished eyes of the peasant-woman.

The review had just begun when we reached Borodino. Police officials, on recognizing the Grand Duchesses, wished to lead them to the Imperial box; to their astonishment, the Grand Duchesses asked for seats in the public stand. This, as we discovered to our dismay, was next to the Imperial box. The Czarina saw us and cast very cold glances in our direction.

It was a magnificent review, and ended with the blessing of the troops. We were all very much moved when the miraculous icon of the Blessed Virgin of Smolensk was held aloft for the Benediction.

That same evening we returned to Arkhangelskoïe, where Stefanesco and the gypsies were waiting for us; but soon my charming guests left, and our delightful little holiday was over.

Shortly afterward, I myself left for the Crimea. I found a letter there from King Emanuel of Portugal, announcing his arrival. I was delighted to see him again and to renew the friendship we had formed in England. I appreciated his keen mind, his delicate wit, and his natural kindliness; he was very fond of music and often asked me to sing gypsy songs which reminded him of the songs of his own country. King Emanuel had a mania for letter-writing, and he once showed me part of his correspondence with the Kaiser and with King Alfonso XIII of Spain. He tried to add me to the list of his victims, but our exchange of letters was brief. I have always hated writing letters. Besides which, I felt quite incapable of sending suitable replies to his, which were as admirable in style as they were edifying in thought. I finally bought a *Manual for the Perfect Correspondent* from which I copied, haphazard, regardless of the context. When he received, signed by me, a letter from a little girl lost in a big city describing her adventures and her emotions, the King must have understood, for he ceased writing to me.

During the summer of 1912 the Czar went to Port-Baltic to meet the Emperor of Germany. This was no pleasure trip, as neither the Czar nor the Czarina liked the Kaiser. "He thinks he is a superman," the Czarina once said in my hearing, "and he's really nothing but a clown. He has no real worth. His only virtues are his strict morals and his conjugal fidelity. His reported love affairs are a myth."

When giving me an account of the Port-Baltic meeting, Dimitri said that it had been completely lacking in cordiality. The absence of sincerity on both sides had created an atmosphere of constraint which was felt by all.

The marriage of the Grand Duke Michael Alexandrovitch and Madame Woulfert, which took place in the autumn, distressed the whole Imperial family and particularly the Dowager Empress. The Grand Duke Michael was the Czar's only brother and, after the Czarevitch, heir to the throne. After his marriage he was obliged to leave Russia and live abroad with his wife who was given the title of Countess Brassoff. Their only son was killed in an automobile accident, soon after the Revolution. Morganatic marriages such as this did great harm to the prestige of the Imperial family. The private lives of those who may be called upon to reign should be governed by the interests of their country and by the duties incumbent upon their rank. Noblesse oblige.

I spent the winter of 1913 in St. Petersburg with my parents. This was to be a red-letter year for me.

The Grand Duke Alexander Mikhaïlovitch called on my mother one day to discuss the possibility of a marriage between his daughter Irina and myself, thereby bringing about the realization of my ardent

Princess Irina

Prince Theodore,
the author's brother-in-law

wishes. I had never forgotten the young girl, practically a child, whom I had met one day while out riding in the Crimea. The child had grown into a girl of dazzling beauty. She was very shy and reserved, which added a certain mystery to her charm. The deep feeling for her which was born in my heart made me realize the unworthiness and the triviality of my conduct in the past. There existed between Irina and myself the perfect harmony which is the basis of all true happiness.

Little by little, Irina became less timid. At first her eyes were more eloquent than her conversation but, as she became more expansive, I learned to admire the keenness of her intelligence and her sound judgment. I concealed nothing in my past life from her, and, far from being perturbed by what I told her, she showed great tolerance and comprehension. She fully understood the qualities in women which "put me off" and made me prefer the company of men. She disliked as much as I did the pettiness of some women, and their general lack of frankness. Irina was an only daughter, with six brothers, and had none of these feminine failings.

My future brothers-in-law adored their sister, and were inclined to look askance at the man who was about to take her from them. Prince Theodore in particular was very hostile to me. This fifteen-year-old boy was tall for his age; his wild and curly chestnut hair framed a handsome, typically nordic face with very mobile features. His expression could be as ferocious as a wild beast's, or as gentle as a child's. He had a keen sense of humor and an unexpected turn of mind. The hostility which he had shown me at first soon changed into a deep and lasting friendship. When I married his sister, he made his home with us; in fact he could not live without us, and only left us in 1924 when he married Princess Irene Paley, daughter of the Grand Duke Paul Alexandrovitch.

Before my engagement to Irina had been officially announced, Dimitri came to see me to ask whether there was any truth in the rumor that I was to marry his cousin. I replied that there was some question of it but that nothing, so far, had been settled. "Because," he went on, "I too intend to marry her." I thought at first that he was joking, but not at all; he assured me that he had never been more serious in his life. Princess Irina would have to choose between us. We made a mutual promise not to say or do anything that might influence her. But, when I repeated this conversation to Irina, she said that she had made up her mind to marry me and that nothing and no one would induce her to change her mind.

Dimitri bowed before a decision which he realized was final, but our friendship was to suffer and our relations were never the same afterward.

chapter XVII

In 1913, *Russia celebrated with great pomp* the tercentenary of the Romanoff dynasty. I went abroad at the beginning of the summer. Irina and her parents had to remain in Russia for the festivities, but joined me later in England. After a brief stay in London, they spent the rest of the season at Le Tréport, in France. I stayed with them for some time before returning to Russia.

Shortly after my return, the Grand Duchess Elisabeth invited me to go with her on a pilgrimage to the Solovetz Monastery. This monastery was founded in the beginning of the fifteenth century by St. Zavvati and St. Zosima, and is situated in the extreme north of Russia, on an island in the White Sea. We were to sail from Archangel, and as the Grand Duchess wished to visit some churches it was agreed that I should meet her at the ship. However, I lost all sense of time as I strolled about the town and reached the quay to find that the ship had left. I chartered a motorboat, but only caught up with the ship as it reached Solovetz, where I landed at the same time as the Grand Duchess, feeling very sheepish.

The entire community, headed by its superior, came to meet the Grand Duchess, and we were immediately surrounded by a swarm of monks, who stared at us with much curiosity.

The monastery had beautiful crenelated fifteenth-century walls made from oval blocks of red and gray granite, and surmounted by numerous bell turrets. The surrounding country was extremely beautiful; countless lakes linked by canals turned the island into a sort of archipelago on which grew great forests of fir trees.

Our cells were pleasant and clean; on the whitewashed walls hung numerous icons, and before each of them a night light flickered. The food, on the other hand, was atrocious; during the whole of our stay, which lasted two weeks, we lived on holy bread and tea.

Most of the monks had long hair and beards. Some of them were filthy and unkempt; I have often wondered why uncleanliness seems to be the rule in most monasteries, as though it were necessary to smell bad to please God.

The Grand Duchess attended all the services. So did I at first, but after a couple of days I felt so holy that I begged to be excused from further attendance as I had no intention of becoming a monk. But one of the services I attended made a deep impression on me owing to four anchorites who were there. Their hoods were pulled over their faces, giving only a glimpse of their emaciated features. Crossbones and skulls embroidered in white on their black frocks were particularly gruesome.

We went one day to visit one of these hermits, who lived in a cavern in the heart of the forest. It was reached through an underground passage so small that it could only be entered by crawling on all fours. I managed to take a snapshot of the Grand Duchess in this position, which I showed her to her great amusement. Our anchorite slept on a stone, and the sole ornament of his cell was an icon of Our Saviour before which a night light flickered. He gave us his blessing without saying a single word.

I spent a great part of my days going from one island to the other, often accompanied by young monks who sang in chorus; at twilight their fine voices, echoing over the water, were very moving. Sometimes I went alone, landing at any place I liked the look of. When I returned to the monastery, I joined the Grand Duchess and a few monks with whom I had made friends, and we had long talks together. Once back in my cell, I would remain for hours at a time before the open window, gazing at the immensity of the night sky. In the silence of the night, the beauty and mystery of nature seemed to draw me closer to the Creator. My prayers were wordless, but my heart was lifted up toward Him in simple trust.

He is everywhere, I thought, in everything that lives and

breathes. Invisible, inconceivable. He is the alpha and omega of all things, the Infinite and the Truth.

In the past, I had been worried by many questions to which I could find no answer; I was tortured by the mystery of life. Very often, in the midst of the luxury that surrounded me, I had felt its vanity and emptiness. Human misery, as I had seen it in the slums of St. Petersburg, filled me with horror. The philosophers whose books I had read had, for the most part, greatly disappointed me. Their theories sometimes seemed to me dangerous. Speculation such as theirs often ends by drying up the heart. I had an intense and instinctive dislike for destructive theories, and could not understand the stubborn pride of those who refused to accept with simple faith the things that were beyond their comprehension. On the other hand, the teachings of the Church had not enlightened me. To my mind, even the Holy Scriptures savored too much of man.

As I gazed out of the window of my cell into the starry night I found a peace that no theories had ever brought me. I even came to wonder whether monastic life was not the only true one. Yet had God himself not shown me the path that I should follow? When I spoke about this to the Grand Duchess, she replied without hesitation that I should marry the woman I loved and who loved me. "You will remain in the world and of the world," she said, "and wherever you go, you must always try to love and help your neighbor. Let yourself be guided by the only true teaching, that of Christ. It answers to all that is best in the heart of man and kindles the flame of Charity, which is Love."

The whole of my life has been the brighter for the radiance cast over it by this remarkable woman, whom I have regarded as a saint since my early youth.

On our return, we stopped again at Archangel. While the Grand Duchess visited churches and convents, I spent two hours before the train left in strolling around the town. In the main street my attention was attracted to a poster announcing the sale by auction of a white bear. I went into the auction room and bought the bear, which was as vicious as it was big. I could imagine the reception he would give intruders in the courtyard of our house on the Moïka. I gave instructions that he should be sent at once to the station, and saw to it myself that he was put in a cattle truck which the terrified stationmaster promised to have coupled to the Grand Duchess' train. Having made these arrangements, I joined the latter in her saloon carriage where she was having tea with a few ecclesiastics who had come to see her off. All of a sudden, we heard furious grunts outside. A crowd gathered on the platform; our visitors exchanged anxious glances. The only person who kept calm was the Grand Duchess, and she was convulsed with laughter when she heard what it was all about. "You are quite mad," she said to me in English. "What will these poor bishops think?" I had no idea what they thought, but I knew what they would have liked to do to me from the sour looks they gave me and from their icy good-bys.

The train moved off to the cheers of the crowd, although no one knew whether their enthusiasm was for the Grand Duchess or the bear. We spent a very bad night, being awakened at each stop by bloodcurdling snarls. A large number of people, including court officials, awaited the Grand Duchess at St. Petersburg. One can imagine their stupefaction when they saw her return from a pilgrimage with a huge white bear!

In August, hearing that Irina had fallen and sprained her ankle very severely and that she had gone to see a doctor in Paris, I left immediately to join her. During her treatment, which was long and painful, I went to see her every day at the Ritz Hotel where she was staying with her parents. My future father-in-law's sister, the Grand Duchess Anastasia Mikhaïlovna of Mecklenburg-Schwerin, was in town. Although she was well over forty, she had lost none of her high spirits; she was kind and affectionate, but her eccentric and despotic nature made her rather formidable. When she heard that I was going to marry her niece, she took me in hand. From that day my life was no longer my own. She was an early riser and she used to telephone me at eight in the morning. Sometimes she came to the Hôtel du Rhin, where I was staying, and sat reading the papers in my room while I dressed. If I happened to be out, she sent her servants all over Paris to look for me and sometimes took part in the search herself. I never had a moment's peace. I had to lunch, dine, go to the theater, and supper with her almost every day. She usually slept through the first act of a play, and then woke up with a start to declare that the performance was stupid and that she wished to go somewhere else. We often changed theaters two or three times in one evening. As she felt the cold, she made her footman sit on a chair at the door of her box, holding a small traveling bag filled with shawls, scarves, and furs. All these objects were numbered. If by chance, she was awake and felt a draft, she would ask me to bring her such or such a number. I could have put up with all this but unfortunately she had a passion for dancing. At midnight, now wide awake, she would drag me to a night club where she danced till dawn.

Fortunately, toward the end of September, Irina had recovered and we all left for the Crimea.

The Dowager Empress, Marie Feodorovna, formerly Princess Marie Dagmar of Denmark

chapter XVIII

Shortly after our arrival in the Crimea, our engagement was at last made public. Some of the letters and telegrams that poured in gave me a good deal to think about. I had never dreamed that any of my friends could be so much affected by my marriage.

Soon afterward, Irina again went abroad with her parents: first to Paris to order her trousseau, and then to Denmark to visit her grandmother. I was to join them in Paris and accompany Irina and her mother to Copenhagen to be presented to the Dowager Empress.

When I arrived at the Gare du Nord, I found Count Mordvinoff waiting for me on the platform, and was amazed to hear that he had been sent by the Grand Duke Alexander to tell me that our engagement had been broken off: I was not even to attempt to see Irina or her parents again. I questioned the Grand Duke's emissary in vain; he could tell me nothing more.

I was shocked beyond words by this message, but I was not going to allow anyone to treat me so offhandedly. No one had the right to condemn me unheard. I was determined to plead my cause and defend my happiness, so I went to the hotel where the Grand Duke and Grand Duchess were staying and walked straight to their rooms unannounced. Our conversation must have been as disagreeable for them as it was for me. But by the end of it I had persuaded them to reverse their decision and give their definite consent to our marriage. Feeling relieved, but bewildered, I then went to see Irina who again assured me that she was more than ever determined to marry me. Later on I was grieved to find that the people who had tried so hard to damage me in the eyes of her parents were the very ones I had thought to be my real friends. I knew that my coming marriage had upset some of them, but I now saw to what lengths they were prepared to go to prevent it. Still, that degree of affection, wherever it came from and however mistakenly it was expressed, touched me deeply.

I know that in writing all this I may appear to be absurdly, or even odiously, conceited. But I must be objective if I want my narrative to be a truthful one. It remains a fact that the power I have always had of attracting people, though quite out of proportion to my own merits, has had far-reaching consequences for myself and for others. I admit that for a time this both flattered and amused me; but it soon palled, because it was too easy, and there was too much of it. When I felt myself being carried forward on a wave of destiny, I did not bother much about the friends I left behind. But I now realized that I could not cast them off so easily; I could not feel indifferent to pain that I had been responsible for causing, even unconsciously. I felt a certain moral responsibility. I would have liked to do something for them, were it only to substitute for the love I could not give them the more precious gift of friendship.

It now remained for me to overcome the Dowager Empress' opposition, for she too had been influenced against me.

Irina and her mother had already left for Denmark, and a few days later I received a telegram inviting me to Copenhagen.

I had never had any contact with the Dowager Empress since my early childhood. It was only in 1913 that I had the honor of being presented to this great lady who, in spite of her voluntary retirement and the modesty of her bearing, was certainly one of the most striking personalities of our time.

Princess Marie was the daughter of King Christian IX and Queen Louise of Denmark. Her features were less regular than those of her sister, Queen Alexandra of England, but she had extraordinary charm, which her children and grandchildren have inherited from her. Although she was of small stature, her bearing was so majestic that when she entered a room one noticed no one else. When she married Czar Alexander III, Russia immediately took her to its heart. She was a model wife and a loving mother, yet she was able to devote much time and energy to charitable works. Her intelligence and political flair enabled her to play an important part in domestic and foreign affairs. A bitter enemy of Germany, she exerted all her influence in favor of the Franco-Russian alliance. Russian public opinion was divided on this subject; many people thought that only a triple alliance, Franco-Russo-German, could safeguard peace.

Alexander III died at Livadia on October 20, 1894, aged forty-nine. Six years before, when his train was derailed by the nihilists, he had saved his family by propping up the shattered roof of the dining car with his shoulders. The effect of this effort and the strain of continually fighting a threatened revolution exhausted him prematurely. After his death the Empress Marie continued to live at the Anichkoff Palace, St. Petersburg. She spent her summers at Gatchina, and frequently went to stay with her family in Denmark.

At the beginning of his reign, Emperor Nicolas II was under the good influence of his mother, but owing to the ill feeling which existed between the two Empresses this unfortunately did not last. The young Empress' morbid mysticism did not fit in well with Empress Marie's frank, well-balanced nature. In 1915 the latter, after giving repeated but vain warnings of the approaching catastrophe, left the capital and settled down in Kiev. From there she helplessly watched the collapse of the Empire.

Having been told of the disagreeable rumors that were being circulated about me, the Dowager Empress expressed the wish to see me. Irina was her favorite grandchild, and all her thoughts were for her happiness. I knew that our fate was in her hands.

As soon as I reached Copenhagen, I telephoned to the Amalienborg Palace to inquire when Her Majesty would receive me. I was told that I was expected for lunch. I was shown into the drawing room, where I found the Grand Duchess Xenia and her daughter. The joy that Irina and I felt on meeting again must have shown in our faces.

Several times during lunch, I felt the Empress' observant eyes on me. She afterward expressed the wish to see me alone. During the conversation that followed, I had the impression that, little by little, I was winning her over to my side. At the end, she rose and said kindly: "Do not worry, I will do what I can for your happiness."

It was decided that our marriage should take place on February 22, 1914, in the chapel of the Anichkoff Palace, the residence of the Dowager Empress.

Irina and I were to live in the Moïka house and my parents gave us the ground floor of the left wing. This, by the way, was really an *entresol,* as it was considerably above the ground level. I had a private entrance made, and a lot of other necessary alterations carried out.

The entrance hall was reached by a short flight of white marble steps lined with statues. To the right were the reception rooms which looked out onto the Moïka Canal. First came a ballroom with yellow marble columns, ending in great arcades opening onto the winter garden. Next was the large drawing room, hung in ivory silk and decorated with paintings of the eighteenth-century French School. The French Restoration furniture of gold and white wood was covered with the same ivory silk, embroidered with bouquets of flowers. The furniture in my private sitting room was of mahogany, covered in bright green with an embroidered center design. The walls were of sapphire blue on which hung Gobelin tapestries and Dutch paintings. The color scheme of the dining room was amethyst; large glass-fronted cabinets which could be lighted up at night contained a collection of Arkhangelskoïe porcelain. The library was paneled with Karelian birch and had emerald-green hangings. All the ceilings were painted in gray monochrome, and decorated with perfect stucco work. Aubusson carpets, objets d'art, chandeliers, and girandoles of rock crystal completed the decoration. The general scheme ranged in style from Louis XVI to Empire, which had always been my favorite period.

Facing onto the formal courtyard were our small chapel and our private apartments: our bedroom and Irina's boudoir facing south, a mosaic swimming pool, and a small steel-lined strong room with glass cases for Irina's jewels.

To the left of the entrance hall, I had a *pied-à-terre* arranged for my

The author and Princess Irina
at the time of their engagement (1914)

own use, in case I ever came to St. Petersburg alone. The drawing room was divided into two unequal parts by pillars and a curtain; the smaller part was slightly raised, and was to be my bedroom. The furniture was of mahogany, and the Holland linen hangings enhanced the beauty of the old paintings on the walls. Next door was a small octagonal dining room lit by a high window. The doors of this room were so skillfully concealed that when they were closed there seemed to be no exit. One of these doors led to a secret staircase which went down to the basement, which I intended to turn into a Renaissance drawing room. Halfway down the staircase, a concealed door opened onto the courtyard. It was through this door that Rasputin attempted to escape, two years later.

The work was barely finished when the Revolution broke out. We were never able to enjoy the home which we had taken so much trouble to arrange.

The Grand Duchess Elisabeth was not present at our marriage. She considered that a nun would be out of place at such a worldly ceremony. However, I went to see her in Moscow a few days before; she welcomed me with her usual graciousness, and when I left she gave me her blessing.

The Czar inquired through my future father-in-law what I would like for a wedding present. He thought of offering me an office at court, but I replied that His Majesty would gratify my wishes to the full by granting me the privilege of using the Imperial box at the theater. On receiving my reply, Nicolas II laughingly agreed.

We were overwhelmed with gifts: the most gorgeous jewels as well as the simplest and most touching presents from our peasants.

Irina's wedding dress was magnificent; it was of white satin embroidered in silver, with a long train. Her face veil, which had belonged to Marie Antoinette, was held by a tiara of rock crystal and diamonds.

The question of what I should wear gave rise to lively discussions. I firmly refused to appear in a tail coat in the daytime, but all the suggestions made raised a storm of protest. Finally the uniform of the nobility—a black frock coat with collar and lapels embroidered in gold, and white broadcloth trousers—was decided on.

All members of the dynasty who married someone not of royal blood were obliged to sign a document renouncing their rights to the throne. Although Irina was very distant in the line of succession, she had to comply with this regulation before marrying me; but it did not seem to worry her very much.

On the wedding day, a coach drawn by four white horses brought my fiancée and her parents to the Anichkoff Palace. My own entrance was much less impressive. The fusty old lift stopped halfway up to the chapel, and the whole Imperial family, including the Czar, had to help to liberate the wretched bride-groom. Then, accompanied by my parents, I walked through several rooms already filled with people to the chapel where I awaited the arrival of Irina.

The bride entered on the Czar's arm; he led her to her place next to mine and the service began.

It is customary at Russian marriages for one of the priests to spread a carpet of pink silk before the bridal couple across which, in the course of the ceremony, they have to walk. Tradition has it that whoever first sets foot on this carpet will rule the household; Irina had made up her mind to do this, but she caught her foot in her train and I took advantage of this to forestall her.

When the service was over we walked in procession to one of the reception rooms to receive the customary congratulations. For two hours the guests filed past us; Irina was worn out. We then went to the Moïka, preceded by our parents, who waited for us at the foot of the staircase to offer us the traditional bread and salt. We were then congratulated by all our servants. After this the same ceremony took place all over again at the Grand Duke Alexander's palace.

The time for our departure arrived at last; a crowd of relatives and friends were waiting at the station. Once more we had to shake hands and be congratulated. After the last demonstrations of affection were over, we entered our coach; a black nose suddenly emerged from a profusion of flowers; and there was my Punch triumphantly ensconced among the roses.

As the train moved out, I saw Dimitri standing on the platform, by himself—a lonely figure.

chapter XIX

We stayed in Paris at the Hôtel du Rhin, where I had booked the rooms I usually occupied, as I wanted Irina to see them. The day after our arrival, we were awakened at nine o'clock by the Grand Duchess Anastasia Mikhaïlovna who turned up followed by three grooms carrying her wedding present: twelve wastepaper baskets!

Irina had brought all her jewelry with her, as she wanted to have it reset; we had long discussions with Chaumet, the jeweler who was to modernize it.

We did not care to stay long in Paris as we knew too many people there, so as soon as we had done our shopping we left for Egypt; but as all our movements were reported in the papers we never had much peace. In Cairo, the Russian Consul insisted on following us like a shadow and reading us sentimental poems of his own composition of which he was extremely proud.

One evening, as we wandered through the narrow streets of the old quarter, we came to a small square and there we saw a magnificent Arab, dressed in gorgeous robes and wearing a profusion of necklaces, rings, and bracelets, reclining on velvet cushions on the steps of a house and sipping his coffee. A continuous stream of women and children passed before him and threw coins into a bag which lay on the ground beside him. From the houses nearby, heavily painted women sitting cross-legged behind their latticed windows displayed their somewhat faded charms. As we left this questionable quarter we met our consul, who was horrified to find us in such a disreputable neighborhood.

He told us that the Arab who had aroused our curiosity owed his affluence to the peculiar interest taken in him by a certain person of very high rank. Thus, he had become the owner of several streets full of brothels, from which he derived an enormous income.

From Cairo we went on to Luxor. The modern town is built on the site of ancient Thebes which was buried, in the course of centuries, under alluvial deposits from the Nile. Nothing, alas, remains of the old city except a number of temples erected by successive dynasties of Pharaohs, which have been brought to light by excavations. It is said that the ancient Egyptians lived in mud or adobe homes, and that their more elaborate handiwork was reserved exclusively for tombs and temples, the symbols of life to come. The Valley of Kings is an immense, irregularly-shaped circus in the desert on the left bank of the Nile. The tombs are a series of galleries and rooms hollowed out of the rock, decorated with paintings which have remained amazingly fresh.

Although the splendors of Upper Egypt were most interesting, I suffered so much from the heat that I refused to go any further. On our return to Cairo I had an attack of jaundice and was obliged to remain in bed for the rest of our stay. From Cairo we left for Jerusalem, where we wanted to spend Holy Week and Easter Day. We were sorry to leave Egypt, for we had fallen under its spell.

When we arrived at Jaffa, we found the chief of the local police waiting for us: an incredibly fat man, covered with decorations. He offered to take us to a house where we could rest for a few hours before taking the train to Jerusalem. He showed us into a carriage drawn by a couple of fine Arab horses, while he himself sat on the box beside the coachman. When Punch saw his enormous bottom jutting out from the box, the temptation was too great. The wretched police officer was stoic, but I had the greatest trouble in making my dog let go.

When we reached the house, our guide, still rather shaky from Punch's onslaught, showed us into a room sparsely furnished with a few chairs and a sofa, where he left us.

We were just settling down to have a good rest, when the door opened and in came the Governor of Jaffa, escorted by our guide and an imposing retinue, and they stayed and stayed and stayed. . . . We were saved by our Chief of Police, who warned us that it was time to leave for the station.

The Russian Consul joined our train before we arrived in Jerusalem, so as to warn my wife of the reception in store for her there. When she saw the number of officials waiting for us on the platform, Irina refused to leave the train and I had practically to force her to get down. After much shaking of hands, we were taken straight to the Orthodox cathedral. More than 5,000 Russian pilgrims lined the road leading to it, and cheered the Emperor's niece. They had come from all parts of Russia to spend Holy Week in Jerusalem.

The Greek Patriarch, Damian, and his clergy, were waiting for us in the cathedral. When we arrived he rose and gave us his blessing. After a Te Deum had been sung, we entered our carriage again and drove to the hotel of the Russian Mission, where a suite of rooms had been reserved for us.

The next day we were received in private audience by the Patriarch. We found the audience long and rather tiresome. Irina and I sat on either side of the primate, while the clergy lined the walls. Coffee, sweetmeats, and champagne were served. But as the Patriarch knew only a few words of Russian and the others spoke not a word of either French or English, conversation languished, in spite of the interpreter. The Patriarch was, as a matter of fact, a man of great distinction, and during our stay in Jerusalem we had several opportunities of meeting him in less formal circumstances. On his first visit to us, Punch made a dash for him, and the venerable old gentleman very nearly shared the fate of the Chief of Police.

We visited all the holy places in Jerusalem in great detail; within the walls and in the outskirts of the city, every stone seemed alive with memories of Jesus Christ. During a walk which we took outside the town, we passed some poor wretches dressed in rags, begging by the roadside. Their faces and bodies were covered with sores and scabs. Their limbs were rotting away and their eyes hung out of their sockets; the women were carrying children who looked quite healthy. When we went up to them to give them alms, we were sickened by their overpowering stench. Later we discovered that they were lepers.

During Holy Week, we went to several services in the Basilica of the Holy Sepulcher. On Holy Saturday, as Irina was not feeling well, I went alone. I had a seat in the gallery where I could follow the unusual ceremony being celebrated that day in the chapel of the Holy Sepulcher. The day before, the civil authorities had put seals on the door of this chapel, which is in the center of the Basilica. The faithful believe that the thirty-three candles held by the Patriarchs are lighted by a flame which comes down from Heaven on Holy Saturday. In order that the faithful may be sure that the Greek and Armenian Patriarchs have neither matches nor lighters concealed on their persons, and that no trickery is possible, these high ecclesiastical dignitaries are searched by Mohammedan soldiers before they enter the church, where the pilgrims await them each holding a bunch of thirty-three tiny candles. The Patriarchs approach the Holy Sepulcher, open the door after breaking the seals, and enter the sanctuary. A second later, lighted candles can be seen through the small windows on either side of the chapel. Then follows a rush of the faithful, pressing forward to light their own tapers from the miraculous flame. During the scuffle, priests hustle the Patriarchs out, to protect them from the crowd's fanatical enthusiasm.

It was an amazing sight: lighted by thousands of glittering tapers, the whole church was like an ocean of flame. The congregation behaved like maniacs, tearing off their clothes, burning their bodies with lighted candles to such a point that the smell of roasting flesh became unbearable. It was a scene of mob hysteria; I felt far indeed from the tomb of Christ.

On Easter evening, after the solemn Resurrection Mass, all the Russian pilgrims in Jerusalem were invited to the Mission for the traditional supper. They came bearing small lanterns, lit from the holy flame in Christ's tomb, which they were going to carry reverently back to Russia. On the long tables set in the garden, all these multicolored glass lanterns illuminating the night made an enchanting spectacle. Before the pilgrims' departure, they were again our guests in the Mission garden. Surrounded by so great a number of our compatriots, we had the feeling that we were back in Russia.

A few days later the pilgrims, who had heard that we were to attend a service at the Orthodox cathedral, determined to be present. The result was a terrible stampede; the doors had to be closed, but they managed to break down one of them and invaded the church. We barely had time to escape through a side exit.

Shortly before we left Jerusalem, during one of our last drives, a young Abyssinian Negro in a white tunic ran up to us and threw an envelope into our barouche. It was a petition asking us to take him into our service. He came to the Mission that evening for our answer. I liked his looks and engaged him on the spot, to Irina's great displeasure as well as that of our European servants. He was called Tesphé and had fled to Jerusalem from Abyssinia where he had committed some crime or other. He was practically a savage, but a very intelligent one; he learned Russian very quickly and was completely devoted to us. However, I must admit that he very soon began to make difficulties for us. We had left Palestine for Italy. At Naples I had to put up with a good deal of protest from the manager of the hotel when Tesphé made trouble with the maids. He thoroughly upset two elderly Englishwomen who complained of never being able to use the lavatory. Tesphé had established himself in it and was engrossed in the supreme pleasure of pulling the chain to hear the water run. For a long time it was impossible to make him sleep in a bed: he insisted on lying on the floor in the hall, outside our door.

Our car was waiting for us at Naples; accompanied by Tesphé and Punch, we took a short trip through Italy. We had sent our servants to Rome to await us there, and Irina herself was obliged to admit that on this occasion Tesphé proved to be an excellent lady's maid.

After spending a few days in Rome, we left for Florence where I knew a good many people. I saw little of them, for I wanted to be alone with Irina in a city which we both loved more than any other.

The evening before we left, I saw a familiar figure standing before the Loggia dei Lanzi. It was that of the Italian prince of whom I had seen a good deal in London when my two lovely cousins were staying with me and whom we used to call "Bambino." I introduced him to Irina and we asked him to dinner. I found him very much changed; he had lost his high spirits and youthful gaiety. He came back the next day to see us off and said that he would meet us soon in Paris and London. A few weeks later, we heard that he had committed suicide. He wrote me a farewell letter which touched me deeply.

When we passed through Paris, old Chaumet brought us Irina's jewels, which he had reset during our absence. He had not wasted his time: the five sets he had designed in diamonds, pearls, rubies, emeralds, and sapphires seemed each more beautiful than the other. They were much admired in London, but no jewels were needed to add to Irina's beauty.

I had kept my bachelor's flat in London, and it was there that we stayed. I was delighted to be, so to speak, at home, and to meet all my English friends again. No sooner had we arrived than we were caught in a whirl of social obligations which left us little time for anything else. My family-in-law were also in London, as well as the Dowager Empress, who was staying with her sister Queen Alexandra at Marlborough House, where we often went to see them.

One morning we were wakened by the sound of voices in argument in the hall. Slipping on a dressing gown, I went to see what was happening. I found Queen Alexandra and the Empress trying to persuade Tesphé to let them in. The Empress had run short of words and gone on to deeds, and was threatening him with her umbrella. After apologizing for my attire, I explained that Tesphé never disobeyed an order, and that as we had gone to bed very late we had given him strict orders not to admit anyone.

It was in the midst of the gaieties of the London season that we learned of the assassination of Archduke Francis Ferdinand of Austria.

Soon after, we had a letter from my parents asking us to join them at Kissingen, where my father was taking a cure.

The author, his wife, and their child (1915)

chapter XX

We arrived at Kissingen in July, where we found things most unpleasant. The Germans were all gloating over ridiculous stories about Rasputin which had been published in the newspapers and tended to throw discredit on the Czar and the Czarina.

My father was extremely optimistic, but the news grew more alarming every day. Shortly after our arrival we had a telegram from the Grand Duchess Anastasia Nicolaïevna, the wife of our future commander-in-chief, urging us to return home as quickly as possible if we wished to avoid being held up in Germany. On July 30, Russia answered the Austro-Hungarian attack on Serbia by decreeing a general mobilization. All Kissingen seethed with excitement. Crowds in the streets yelled and shouted insults at the Russians. The police had to be called in to restore order. It was clear that it was high time for us to leave, and we decided to go to Berlin. My mother was ill and had to be carried to the station on a stretcher.

Berlin was in a state of chaos. At the Continental Hotel where we were staying, the greatest confusion reigned. The morning after we arrived we were wakened at eight o'clock by the police, who had come to arrest us, together with our doctor, my father's secretary, and all our male servants. My father telephoned at once to the Russian Embassy, and was informed that everyone there was busy and that no one could be spared to attend to us.

Meanwhile, about fifty of us were shut up in a hotel bedroom just about large enough to hold fifteen. We remained standing there for two hours, so tightly packed that we could not move. Finally we were taken to the police station where, after our papers had been examined and we had been addressed as "dirty Russian pigs," we were warned that any of us who had not left Berlin by six o'clock would be arrested. It was past five when I returned to the hotel. My family were in a frenzy, convinced that they would never see me again. Time pressed, a decision had to be made. Irina telephoned to her cousin, Crown Princess Cecilie, who promised to speak to the Kaiser at once and give us an immediate answer. On his side, my father appealed for help to Sverbeeff, our ambassador: "Alas, my role here is over," said the latter. "I don't see what I can do for you, but come back to see me in the evening."

As time was so short and we expected to be arrested at any moment, my father applied to the Spanish Ambassador, who had taken over the protection of Russian interests in Germany, and asked him to send one of his secretaries to see him.

In the meantime, the Crown Princess telephoned to say that she was in despair, but could do nothing for us. She promised to come to see us, but warned us that the Kaiser considered us his prisoners and that his aide-de-camp would call on us, bringing a paper which we would have to sign. The German Emperor gave us the choice of three places of residence, and guaranteed that we would be treated with consideration. Upon which an official of the Spanish Embassy arrived, and we barely had time to explain the situation to him when the Kaiser's envoy was shown in. He solemnly drew a large sheet of paper covered with red seals from his briefcase, and handed it to us with a flourish. This paper stated that we promised to refrain from all political action and agreed to remain in Germany "for ever." My poor mother nearly had a fit. She wanted to go and see the Kaiser in person. I gave the paper to the Spanish diplomat to read.

"How can you be expected to sign such a piece of idiocy!" he exclaimed. "Surely, there's some mistake. The clause should read 'for the duration of hostilities' not 'for ever.' "

After a short discussion, we requested the aide-de-camp to return with the corrected text next morning at eleven. My father went with the Spanish diplomat to see Sverbeeff. It was agreed that the former would ask the Minister of Foreign Affairs, von Jagow, to place a special train at the disposal of the Russian Ambassador, for members of the embassy and any of his compatriots who wished to leave the country. A list of the passengers would be sent him immediately. Sverbeeff assured my father that our names and those of our staff would be included in the list. He also told my father that the Dowager Empress of Russia and my mother-in-law, the Grand Duchess Xenia, had passed through Berlin that very day. On hearing that we were at the Continental Hotel, they had tried to get in touch with us, hoping that we could return to Russia with them. But it was too late; their own position had become critical, and the Imperial train was obliged to leave Berlin at once to escape the hostile demonstrations of a crowd which broke the windowpanes and tore down the blinds of the car in which Her Majesty sat.

Early next morning we went to the Russian Embassy and from there to the station, where we were to take the train for Copenhagen. No military or even police guard was detailed to accompany us, as is customary on the official departure of an ambassador, so that we were entirely at the mercy of a frenzied crowd who threw stones at us all the way to the station. It was a wonder we were not lynched. Several of the embassy staff, some of whom had their wives and children with them, were struck over the head with sticks; they were covered with blood, while others had had half their clothes torn off them. As our car was the last, we were luckily taken for servants and escaped unmolested. Our servants managed to join us a few moments before the train left; they had gone to the wrong station and in their panic had lost all our luggage on the way. My English valet, Arthur, who had remained at the hotel to give the impression that we were still there, remained a prisoner in Germany until the end of the war.

We heaved a sigh of relief when the train moved out. Later we heard that the Kaiser's emissary reached the hotel shortly after our departure, and that when Emperor William learned that we had fled he gave orders that we should be arrested at the frontier. Fortunately the order arrived too late, and we crossed the frontier without further trouble. As for the unlucky aide-de-camp, he paid for his failure in the trenches.

On reaching Copenhagen we went straight to the Hôtel d'Angleterre where we arrived without even a toothbrush. A number of people called on us at once: the King and Queen of Denmark and their whole family, the Dowager Empress of Russia, my mother-in-law, and a great many other people who happened to be passing through the Danish capital. They were all extremely agitated by what had happened. The Dowager Empress asked that several trains should be placed at the disposal of those who lacked the means to return home and this was immediately done.

We left Denmark the following day. From the deck of the ferry boat which took us to Sweden, the Dowager Empress watched with visible emotion her native shores growing fainter and fainter; but her duty lay with the Russian people.

The Imperial train was waiting for us when we reached Finland. All along the way, Her Majesty received enthusiastic ovations from the Finns. These friendly demonstrations gave the lie to the rumors of a Finnish insurrection which had reached us in Denmark.

The general aspect of St. Petersburg was much the same as ever. Nothing suggested that we were at war.

The Empress Marie, who was going to Peterhoff, invited us to stay with her for a time.

Peterhoff is some distance from St. Petersburg, on the shores of the Baltic Sea. The pinkish-golden palace, its terraces, and formal French park adorned with a series of marvelous fountains, have earned it the name of the Russian Versailles. A long canal, bordered by high trees and fountains, ran down to the sea. It was preceded by a water stairway and a large ornamental lake in the center of which was a group representing Samson and the lion; an immense spray of water shot up from the lion's open jaws. Two of the innumerable fountains in the Peterhoff park caused an incident which amused the Dowager Empress' entourage for a long time. Among Her Majesty's ladies-in-waiting were two old spinsters well known for their punctuality. So when they arrived half an hour late for lunch one day, everyone was surprised. Plied with questions, the good ladies blushingly admitted that they had arranged to meet at the entrance of the park in front of the statue of Adam. But as they could not tell Adam from Eve, one waited in front of Adam and the other in front of Eve, hence the confusion.

The palace of Peterhoff, built in the eighteenth century by the Empress Elisabeth, was destroyed by shellfire during the last war. It was never lived in, but only used for receptions. The Czar had a house in the park, close to the seaside. A little further up was the Dowager Empress' "Cottage," and then "The Farm" where my family-in-law lived. Irina was born there.

After spending a few weeks at Peterhoff, we went with the Empress Marie to the Elaguine Palace, an Imperial residence situated on one of the islands in the estuary of the river Neva. Irina fell ill with measles there, which made us quite anxious, as she was expecting a baby. As soon as she recovered we settled in our own house, in the Moïka. As our rooms were not ready for us, we occupied the ones I used to share with my brother.

As an only son, I was not called up for military service, and I immediately began converting our various houses into hospitals. The Empress Marie was president of the Red Cross, which of course made things easy for me, and soon the first hospital for serious cases was opened in my Liteïnaia house. I put my whole heart into this work, feeling that it was better to allay pain than to inflict it. I had a picked staff: doctors and nurses were all the best I could find.

The military campaign had opened brilliantly by a deep breakthrough into East Prussia; the offensive was launched prematurely at the demand of the Allies to relieve the congested western front. At the end of August, through lack of ordnance, General Samsonoff's army corps was surrounded near Tannenberg. The General, not wishing to survive the loss of his army, shot himself. The offensive was successfully renewed on the Austrian front, but in February 1915 a further offensive in East Prussia ended in the disaster of Augustovo. On May 2, the Austro-German Army broke through the Southwestern Russian front. Our troops were underfed, ill-equipped, and had no ammunition, yet under these appalling conditions they fought against the best-equipped army in the world. Whole regiments were taken prisoner without having had a chance to resist, owing to the lack of equipment which failed to arrive in time. The heroism of our soldiers could not make up for the incapacity of those in command, for the total disorganization of transport facilities, and for the shortage of ammunition; the retreat became a rout. Behind the front, public opinion was roused. There was talk of treason in which the Czarina and Rasputin were implicated, and the weakness of the Czar caused much indignation.

At that time, and particularly in Moscow which was essentially a commercial town, big business was mostly in the hands of Germans, whose arrogance passed all bounds. A great many high-ranking officers in the Army and important court officials bore German names. Most of them came of Baltic stock, and had nothing in common with our enemy, but the effect upon the masses was none the less deplorable. The people firmly believed the absurd stories that were rife, for instance that the Czar, out of pure kindness of heart, had given captured German generals appointments in his suite. But it was a matter of general astonishment that important posts should have been given to men whose names and origins were not one hundred per cent Russian. German propaganda exploited this state of things, and attempted to stir up the people against the Imperial family by reminding them that the Czarina and most of the Grand Duchesses were of German extraction. The fact that the Empress hated Prussia in general, and the Hohenzollerns in particular, did not seem to matter. One day my mother drew the attention of the Czar to the bad impression made by having so many German names among court officials: "Dear Princess," he answered, "what can I do about it? They are all so attached to me, and so devoted. True, some of them are old, and even a bit feeble-minded, like my poor Friedrichs* who, the other day, came up to me, clapped me on the shoulder and said: "Well, well, there you are. Were you invited to lunch too?"

On March 21, 1915, my wife gave birth to a girl who was named Irina after her mother. I shall never forget my happiness when I heard the child's first cry. The midwife, Mme Günst, was a good creature but very garrulous. Her patients mostly belonged to European court cir-

*Then Minister of the Court.

cles, so she knew a vast amount of court gossip and when on the subject would talk away for hours. I must say that her stories were most entertaining, and that I took as much pleasure in listening as she did in telling them, sometimes forgetting that the young mother needed her services.

The christening took place in our chapel, in the presence of the Imperial family. The Czar was godfather and the Dowager Empress godmother. Like her father, my daughter was almost drowned in the baptismal font.

In 1915 the Czar sent my father on a mission abroad. Knowing his eccentric and rather whimsical nature, my mother was worried when she heard of this; she was afraid to let him go without her. Her fears turned out to be groundless; my father carried out his mission very successfully. His first visit was to Rumania, whose king and queen he knew personally. At that time Rumania was not ready for war, and hesitated as to whose side to take. In the course of a long interview with King Carol at which his Prime Minister Bratianu was present, my father made a frank exposé of the Russian point of view, and was given the formal assurance that when the time came Rumania would side with the Allies. The Sinaïa Palace impressed him greatly, particularly the Queen's apartments which were full of large stone crosses, skins of wild animals, magnificent furs, and human skulls.

During his visit to Paris, my father met President Poincaré, General Joffre, and several other leading personalities. At Joffre's headquarters in Chantilly my father decorated the French commander-in-chief with the Cross of St. George which the Czar had sent him.

My father's visit to the trenches filled him with admiration for the courage and high spirits of the troops. Amusing inscriptions over the entrances to dugouts gave an idea of the French soldier's happy disposition: *"In Memory of Marie, Lisette," "Good-by Adelaide," "My love-nest without a Rose."* When dining the same evening at the Ritz, he was surprised to see the room filled with British officers. They were perfectly groomed, although they had only left the trenches that same afternoon, and would return there the next morning after dining in Paris and sleeping all night in their cars for the sake of economy. To see them smoking their pipes, so cool and unconcerned, it was difficult to believe that within a few hours they would be deep in the mud again.

In London, life was more austere and orderly. My father was received by King George V and Queen Mary the day after his arrival. He thought they both looked tired and worried as if the whole responsibility for the war lay on their shoulders. He talked with Lord Kitchener, whose fine, penetrating intellect he admired even more than his commanding presence.

Lord Kitchener was very well informed on Russian affairs, and thought they would give cause for great anxiety in the future.

On returning to the Continent my father paid a visit to the King and Queen of the Belgians, whose noble, courageous attitude had enhanced their prestige in the eyes of their own people and their allies. He also met the Prince of Wales (the future King Edward VIII), the Duke of Connaught, and General French, who was extremely active in spite of his age.

Before leaving France my father had a last meeting at Chantilly with General Joffre, to pass on to him the impressions he had gathered in England from the talks he had had in that country.

His mission ended, my father returned to Russia. The Czar made him Governor General of Moscow but he did not hold that office long. One man could not fight the German faction singlehanded, for it held all the important posts. My father found treason and espionage everywhere, and he used the sternest measures to try to rid Moscow of the enemy's secret domination. But, as most of the ministers of state owed their positions to Rasputin's influence and were pro-German, they proved resolutely hostile to the new Governor General and thwarted all his plans. My father was disgusted by the systematic opposition of the Government, and went to General Headquarters where he had a conference with the Czar, the Commander-in-Chief, the General Staff, and the Cabinet. Bluntly and without mincing his words, he explained the situation as he found it in Moscow, and openly named the culprits. His violent diatribe had a tremendous effect. No one, until that moment, had dared to raise his voice publicly to the Czar against men in positions of authority. Unfortunately it all came to nothing. The pro-German party that surrounded the Czar was powerful enough to counteract rapidly the effect of the Governor General's plain speaking. On returning to Moscow, my father was informed that he had been relieved of his office.

All patriotic Russians were indignant at this measure, and at the Czar's weakness in tolerating it. It proved impossible to fight against the German camarilla. My father, much discouraged, retired to the Crimea with my mother, while I remained in St. Petersburg to continue my hospital work. But I soon found it impossible to go on leading a life of ease when all the men of my age were at the front. I decided to enter the Corps des Pages and take an officer's training course. The year I spent in a military school was not easy but it certainly did me a lot of good, and the discipline was excellent for my independent spirit which was so unamenable to any form of discipline.

At the end of August 1915, it was officially announced that the Grand Duke Nicolas had been relieved of his post as commander-in-chief and appointed to the Caucasus; the Czar was taking command of the armies in person. The news was, on the whole, badly received, for everyone knew that pressure had been brought to bear on him by Rasputin, and that this important step had been taken at his instigation. To overcome the Sovereign's irresolution the starets had appealed to his religious feeling. Although the Czar's opposition was feeble, it was in Rasputin's interest to remove him as far from St. Petersburg as possible. With the Czar at the front, he had a clear field. From then on, he made almost daily visits to Tsarskoïe-Selo. His opinions and advice amounted to orders, and were immediately transmitted to General Headquarters. Not a single important measure was taken at the front without his being consulted. The blind confidence which the Czarina placed in him caused her unwisely to refer the most important, and even the most secret, matters to him. Through her, Rasputin governed Russia.

A plot was hatched by the Grand Dukes and several members of the aristocracy to remove the Czarina from power and force her to retire to a convent. Rasputin was to be sent back to Siberia, the Czar deposed, and the Czarevitch placed on the throne. Everyone plotted, even the generals. As for the British Ambassador, Sir George Buchanan, his dealings with radical elements caused him to be accused by many Russians of secretly working for the Revolution.

Some of the people closest to the Czar and Czarina attempted to open their eyes to the fact that Rasputin's influence was a danger to Russia and to the dynasty. They always received the same reply: "This is all slander; saints have always been slandered." When photographs of the starets taking part in an orgy were shown to the Czarina, she indignantly ordered the police to find the wretch who had dared to impersonate the "holy man" and disgrace him in the eyes of the Emperor. The Dowager Empress wrote to her son, begging him to send Rasputin away and to forbid the Czarina to interfere in affairs of state. Many others did the same. The Empress was informed of this by the Emperor himself, who concealed nothing from her, and she broke off all relations with those who dared to criticize her.

My mother had been among the first to protest against the "starets." After a long conversation with the Czarina, she thought she had succeeded in shaking her confidence in her "miracle worker." But Rasputin's clique was on the watch. A thousand pretexts to keep my mother away were found very quickly. She had had no contact with the Empress for some time when, in the summer of 1916, she resolved to make a last attempt, and asked to be received at the Alexander Palace. Her Majesty greeted her very coldly and, on hearing the object of her visit, requested her to leave. My mother said that she would not do so until she had spoken her mind. She talked at great length. When she had finished, the Empress, who had listened in silence, rose and dismissed her with the words: "I hope never to see you again."

Later, the Grand Duchess Elisabeth, who appeared very rarely at Tsarskoïe-Selo, made a last attempt to convince her sister. She promised to come and see us on leaving the Alexander Palace. We all waited eagerly for her arrival, anxious to hear the result of the interview. She entered the room trembling and in tears: "She drove me away like a dog!" she cried. "Poor Nicky, poor Russia!"

Meanwhile, Germany was fully aware of the situation at the

Court of Russia, and placed spies among the starets' entourage. Rasputin, made garrulous by alcohol, gave away plenty of information, more or less deliberately. I have reason to believe that it was through these channels that Germany found out the exact date of Lord Kitchener's departure for Russia. He had been entrusted with the task of convincing the Czar that Rasputin should go, and the Czarina be deprived of all possibility of interfering in affairs of state. His ship was torpedoed on June 6, 1916.

The situation at the front became more and more serious, and the Czar grew weaker and weaker under the influence of drugs administered to him daily by order of Rasputin whose power had reached its zenith. Not content with dismissing and appointing ministers and generals, and attacking the highest dignitaries of the Church, he had formed a plan to remove the Czar from the throne, replace him by the sick little Czarevitch, proclaim the Czarina regent, and sign a separate peace with Germany.

All hope of opening the eyes of the Czar being given up, what means remained of ridding Russia of her evil genius? The Grand Duke Dimitri and Pourichkevitch, a member of the Duma, had come to the same conclusion as I had. Before even discussing the matter among ourselves, all three of us knew that Rasputin must go, even if that meant destroying him.

Rasputin

chapter XXI

Our memories are sometimes full of light and sometimes dark with shadow. In an eventful life some are sad and some are gay, some are pleasant, while others are so tragic that one's sole desire is never to recall them.

I wrote *The End of Rasputin* in 1927 because it was necessary to put an end to the garbled versions, entirely devoid of truth, which were being circulated about the Imperial family. I would not return to the subject now were it possible for me to omit it from my story. But in view of the importance and seriousness of the matter, I must pause for a moment before going on with my narrative. Let me recall the essential facts.

The political role played by Rasputin has been much discussed; his personality and the secret which lay behind his scandalous power are less well known. Before going over the principal episodes of a tragedy which had its epilogue in the cellars of my house, I think I should give a description of the man whom the Grand Duke Dimitri, Pourichkevitch, and I had decided to destroy.

Born in 1871 at Pokrovskoïe, a village on the Western Siberian border, Gregory Efimovitch Rasputin was the son of a drunken horse-thieving *moujik*, called Efim Novy. Gregory was a horse-thief like his father, a *varnak* they call it in Siberia, which is a deadly insult. In early youth his companions had nicknamed him *Raspoutnik* (i.e. profligate, rake)—and the name stuck to him. He received many a thrashing at the hands of the peasants and had often been publicly whipped by order of the county magistrate, but this only seemed to make him tougher.

He came under the influence of a priest who awakened the mystic in him; but his conversion lacked sincerity. Owing to his brutal, sensual nature he was soon drawn to the sect of the Flagellants or *Khlystys*. They claimed to be inspired with the Word and to incarnate Christ. They attained this heavenly communion by the most bestial practices, a monstrous combination of the Christian religion with pagan rites and primitive superstitions. The faithful used to assemble by night in a hut or in a forest clearing, lit by hundreds of tapers. The purpose of these *radenyi*, or ceremonies, was to create a religious ecstasy, an erotic frenzy. After invocations and hymns, the faithful formed a ring and began to sway in rhythm, and then to whirl round and round, spinning faster and faster. As a state of dizziness was essential for the "divine influx," the master of ceremonies flogged any dancer whose vigor abated. The *radenyi* ended in a horrible orgy, everyone rolling on the ground in ecstasy, or in convulsions. They preached that he who is possessed by the "Spirit" belongs not to himself but to the "Spirit" who controls him and is responsible for all his actions and for any sins he may commit.

Rasputin was particularly well suited to receive the "divine influx." In his own courtyard he built a windowless house, which he said was for a *bania* or steam bath, and held mysterious meetings there—doubtless some form of *radenyi*—where he used to give himself up to all sorts of mystico-sadistic practices.

He left his village after having been denounced by a priest; he was then thirty-three. He left on foot as a pilgrim, and in this guise visited the principal Siberian and Russian monasteries. In order to acquire a reputation for saintliness he made use of everything, even his monstrous sexual lapses, which he expiated by spectacular and terrible penances. After the fashion of Hindu fakirs, he underwent privations to develop his strength of will and his hypnotic powers. In monasteries he studied the Bible. His lack of culture was replaced by a prodigious memory, which enabled him to learn by heart long passages that he was incapable of understanding, but with which he managed to bluff, not only simple folk, but also scholars and even the Czarina.

In St. Petersburg he was received at the Monastery of Alexander Nevsky by Father John of Kronstadt, who was at first completely taken in by him. Father John thought that this young Siberian disciple possessed "a spark from God."

The first visit to the capital opened up new perspectives for this crafty, unscrupulous peasant. He went back to his native village with increased ambition and a well-filled purse. His earliest associates had been dissolute priests, more or less enlightened; but little by little he managed to get in with the higher clergy and with the mothers superior of convents who believed that he was "stamped with the seal of God." But this did not change him and he was still up to his old tricks. At Tsaritsyn he raped a nun, under pretense of exorcising her. At Kazan he was seen coming out of a brothel, pushing a naked woman before him and whipping her with a belt. At Tobolsk he seduced the devout wife of an engineer and inspired her with such an extravagant passion that she went about proclaiming her love and glorying in her shame. She considered it an honor that the Saint should have deigned to notice her, and held her relations with him to be one of God's gifts.

His reputation for holiness increased daily. Crowds knelt as he went by: "Our Christ, our Savior, pray for us miserable sinners! God will hear you . . ." He answered: "In the name of the Father, the Son, and the Holy Ghost, I bless you, little brothers. Fear not! Christ will come again soon. Possess your souls in patience in memory of His Agony! For love of Him, mortify your flesh! . . ."

Such was Rasputin in 1905. Then through a devout but childishly simple young missionary he met the Archimandrite Théophane, rector of the Theological Academy of St. Petersburg, and the Czarina's confessor. This honest and pious prelate took him under his protection.

The Siberian prophet soon gathered around him a clique of worldly idlers, given over to occultism and necromancy. The two Montenegrin Grand Duchesses were among the first and most fervent admirers of the "man of God." It was they who, in 1900, had introduced the occultist Philippe to the Court of Russia; now again, it was they who presented Rasputin to the Czar and Czarina, backed by the Archimandrite Théophane who spoke of him in the following terms:

"Gregory Efimovitch is a simple man. Your Majesties will profit by listening to him, for the voice of the Russian land speaks through his lips. I know that he has much to account for. He has sinned and his sins are innumerable and sometimes very black; but each time his repentance is so fervent, and he has such a childlike faith in divine mercy, that I can vouch for his salvation. Each time he repents, he becomes as pure as a newly christened child. God has him in His hands."

Rasputin very shrewdly made no attempts to make himself look other than a peasant. As he himself said: "A *moujik* in clumsy boots entered the Palace and trod its marble floors."

His influence over the Czarina was not due to flattery; far from it. He spoke roughly to her, with bold and even vulgar familiarity, "the voice of the Russian land." M. Paléologue, then French Ambassador in St. Petersburg, relates that, having asked a lady whether she had fallen under the starets' charm, she replied:*

"I? Not in the least! He disgusts me physically, with his dirty hands, coal-black nails, and unkempt beard. Ugh! Yet I admit he amuses me. He has high spirits and a remarkable imagination. He is even very eloquent at times; he has a vivid gift of expression, a deep sense of mystery. He can in turn be familiar, scoffing, violent, joyful, absurd, and poetical. And with all that, no affectations. On the contrary, an incredible lack of manners, a staggering cynicism."

Anna Wirouboff, lady-in-waiting and intimate friend of the Czarina, rapidly became Rasputin's friend and ally. I have already mentioned this unattractive girl who as Anna Taneïev was one of my early playmates. She became lady-in-waiting to the Czarina in 1903, and four years later married a naval officer, Wirouboff. The marriage was celebrated with great pomp in the palace chapel at Tsarskoïe-Selo; the Czarina was the bride's witness. A few days before the ceremony, the Czarina had insisted upon Anna having an interview with

*Quoted from *The Russia of the Czars*, by Maurice Paléologue.

Rasputin. On giving her his blessing, Rasputin said to the fiancée: "Your marriage will not last long, and you won't be happy." This prophecy came true.

The young couple settled at Tsarskoïe-Selo, in a villa near the Alexander Palace. When Wirouboff came home one evening, he found the door of the house closed and was told that the Empress and Rasputin were there with his wife. He waited for them to leave before entering, and then made a violent scene, for he had strictly forbidden his wife to have the starets in the house. It is said that he even struck her. Anna ran away and took refuge with the Czarina, imploring her protection against her husband who, she said, wanted to kill her. She was quickly granted a divorce.

This affair caused a great scandal because of the personages involved, and its consequences were disastrous. The Czarina sided with her protégée, and Rasputin took advantage of this to subjugate Anna once and for all, and she became a docile instrument in his hands.

Anna Wirouboff was not worthy of the friendship shown her by the Czarina. No doubt her attachment to the Czarina was sincere, but it was far from being disinterested. It was that of a servile and intriguing woman for a worried and ailing mistress, whom she did her utmost to isolate from those who could have been her friends by making her distrust them.

Her intimacy with the Czarina gave Anna a privileged position, and Rasputin's appearance on the scene awoke new ambitions in her. She was not intelligent enough to have any political designs, but the idea of playing the important role of a go-between went to her head. Through her, Rasputin was kept informed of the Emperor's and Empress' most intimate secrets, and it was she who facilitated his many intrusions into affairs of state.

The starets' influence soon spread to political circles. Petitioners of all sorts besieged his house: high officials, members of the clergy, fashionable women, and so on. . . .

He found a valuable assistant in the person of a Tibetan therapist called Badmaïev, a most disreputable man who practiced medicine illegally, and claimed to have brought from Tibet all sorts of medicinal plants and magic formulas which he said he had extorted with much trouble from the wise men of his native land. The truth was that he made these nostrums himself, procuring the ingredients with the complicity of a chemist. He dealt in narcotics, anesthetics, and aphrodisiacs, which he christened: "Tibetan Elixir," "Balm of Nyen Tchen," "Essence of Black Lotus," etc. These two charlatans were well fitted to work together.

When disaster threatens, circumstances seem to combine to hasten it on.

The calamitous war with Japan, the disorders of 1905, the Czarevitch's illness—all these were so many misfortunes which in the mind of the unhappy Czarina made it more and more necessary to resort to the help of the Almighty. This was Rasputin's opportunity—this and the Czarina's fatal blindness to the evil in him. The reason for this needs explaining.

Princess Alice of Hesse entered Russia behind a coffin, that of her father-in-law. Her husband was the emperor of a country she knew nothing about, whose language she did not speak, whose people she did not know. She was inevitably the focus of all eyes, the center of all interest, and this increased her natural timidity and nervousness, which were mistaken for coldness and indifference. She was considered haughty and disdainful. A mystical belief in her mission and an intense desire to help her husband—who was deeply affected both by his father's death and by the weight of the Imperial crown—caused her to intervene in affairs of state. This led people to accuse her of a love of power, and to reproach the Czar with not exercising it sufficiently. When she realized that she had failed to gain the affection of the Russian people, and especially that of the court and the aristocracy, the young Czarina retired within herself more than ever.

Her conversion to the Orthodox religion developed her natural tendency to exalted mysticism, which made her an easy prey for a Rasputin, just as she had previously been the prey of occultists such as Papus and Philippe. But the Czarevitch's terrible illness and Rasputin's mysterious power to give him relief did more than anything else to make the unfortunate Czarina a passive tool in the hands of the "man of God." Nothing could shake her faith in the man she considered the savior of her child, the guardian of his health. And the son for whom she had waited so many years, and for whose life she never ceased to tremble, was the heir to the throne! It was by playing on the feelings of a father and a mother who were racked by anxiety for their son and for the future of the dynasty that Rasputin succeeded in reigning supreme over all the Russias.

There is no doubt that the starets possessed hypnotic powers. Stolypin, the Minister of the Interior, who waged a determined war against him, tells how Rasputin, when he had been sent for, attempted to hypnotize him:

"He ran his colorless eyes over me, muttering mysterious and incoherent passages from the Bible, and making strange passes in the air with his hands. I was conscious of a growing feeling of intense antagonism and repulsion for the scoundrel who sat facing me; he was just beginning to gain an ascendancy over me when I managed to regain control over myself and, cutting him short, bluntly told him he was completely in my power."

Stolypin was assassinated a few months after this interview; he had already had a narrow escape when an attempt was made on his life in 1906.

Rasputin's scandalous behavior, his occult influence over the Imperial couple, his obscene morals, stirred the indignation of the more clearsighted people in St. Petersburg. The press itself, braving the censor, denounced the starets' infamous conduct.

Rasputin thought it would be wise to make himself scarce, for a time at least. In March 1911 he seized his pilgrim's staff and left for Jerusalem, and thence for Tsaritsyn where he spent the summer with one of his cronies, a monk by the name of Héliodore. When he came back at the beginning of the following winter, he resumed his dissolute life.

The alleged holiness of the starets could deceive only those who had no direct contact with him. The coachmen who drove him and his women to the public baths, the servants who waited on him during his nocturnal orgies, the secret police who guarded him, all these knew him as he was, and for what he was. It is easy to imagine how this knowledge was exploited by the revolutionary party.

Many of those who had been among Rasputin's partisans saw him at last in his true colors. Archimandrite Théophane deeply regretted his mistake and could not forgive himself for having introduced Rasputin to the court. With great courage he spoke out against him, but merely succeeded in having himself exiled. About the same time the Episcopal See of Tobolsk was given to a venal and ignorant peasant, an old friend of Rasputin; this was done to enable the head of the Holy Synod to recommend the starets for holy orders. This roused the Orthodox Church. Monsignor Hermogène, Bishop of Saratov, was particularly violent. Seconded by a group of priests among whom was the monk Héliodore, the starets' former companion, Bishop Hermogène had a stormy interview with Rasputin in the course of which he told him exactly what he thought of him. "Limb of Satan! Sacrilegious scoundrel! Fornicator! Foul beast!" Rasputin endeavored to give as good as he got, with a torrent of filthy abuse. Monsignor Hermogène, a giant, struck him on the head with his pectoral cross: "Down on your knees, villain! . . . On your knees before the holy icons . . . Ask God's forgiveness for your foul sins! Swear that you will never dare to pollute our beloved Czar's palace with your presence! . . ."

Terror-stricken and covered with blood, Rasputin beat his breast, muttered prayers, and swore to everything they wanted. But no sooner had he made his escape than he ran to Tsarskoïe-Selo to complain. His vengeance was swift: a few days later Monsignor Hermogène lost his bishopric, Héliodore was arrested and confined in a penitentiary. But as a result of this agitation Rasputin was never ordained.

After the Church, it was the Duma's turn to attack him. Representative Pourichkevitch cried: "I would gladly sacrifice myself and kill that scoundrel!" Wladimir Nikolaïevitch Kokovtsow, the Prime Minister, appealed to the Czar and entreated him to send Rasputin back to Siberia. The same day, Rasputin telephoned an intimate friend of Kokovtsow's: "Your friend the Prime Minister tried to

Czar Nicolas II, the Czarina, and their children

frighten *Papa* about me this morning, but with no success. *Papa* and *Mamma* still love me. You can tell this to Wladimir Nikolaïevitch from me." Kokovtsow was dismissed in 1914 under pressure from Rasputin and his gang.

The Czar realized, however, that it was necessary to make some concession to public opinion. For once he stood firm in spite of the Empress' disapproval, and Rasputin was sent back to his village in Siberia.

For two years the starets put it only brief appearances in St. Petersburg, but in spite of his absence he continued to be consulted and obeyed. He had given the following warning as he left: "I know that evil people are lying in wait for me. Don't listen to them! If you forsake me, you'll lose your son and your crown within six months."

A friend of the starets is supposed to have had in his possession a letter from the occultist Papus to the Czarina. It was written toward the end of 1915 and the last sentences were: "From a cabalistic point of view, Rasputin is a vessel similar to Pandora's box; this vessel contains all the vices, all the crimes, all the faults of the Russian people. If it were ever to be broken, its frightful contents would immediately spread all over Russia."

During the autumn of 1912, while the Imperial family was staying at Spala, in Poland, an apparently slight accident caused a terrible attack of hemophilia which endangered the Czarevitch's life. Priests prayed night and day in the church at Spala; a service was held in Moscow before the miraculous icon of the Blessed Virgin of Iverskaïa; in St. Petersburg the people prayed incessantly at the Cathedral of Our Lady of Kazan. Rasputin, who was in constant touch with Spala, telegraphed the Czarina: "God has seen your tears and heard your prayers. Do not grieve: your son will live." The next day the child's temperature went down; two days later he was out of danger, and the poor Czarina's faith in the "holy man" was naturally intensified.

In 1914, Rasputin was stabbed by a peasant woman and his life was in danger for several weeks. Against all expectations his wound healed, and in September he was seen again in St. Petersburg. At first it seemed that he had lost some of his authority. The Czarina was busy with her war work, her ambulance, her hospital train. Those around her said that she had never been in better health. Rasputin never went to the palace without first telephoning: a new development which everyone noticed and many rejoiced over. But around him gravitated a whole party of influential persons who had linked their fortunes with his, and soon he was more powerful than ever.

In July 1915 Sasarine, the new head of the Holy Synod, informed the Czar that it would be impossible for him to continue in office if Rasputin persisted in giving orders to the ecclesiastical administration. He obtained permission from the Sovereign to send Rasputin away, but a month later the starets was back.

The author in the uniform of the Corps des Pages

chapter XXII

Being convinced of the necessity for action, I discussed the matter with Irina and found she agreed with me completely. I imagined that it would be easy to find a few determined men ready to help me to find a way of eliminating Rasputin. The conversation I had on the subject with different influential persons left me with few illusions. The very men who were the most violent whenever the starets' name was mentioned became reticent at once when I told them the time had come to act. Fear of compromising themselves, and of disturbing the quiet tenor of their lives, turned them suddenly into optimists about Rasputin.

But the President of the Duma, Rodzianko, was of a very different opinion: "What can one do when all the ministers and most of the people in close contact with His Majesty are the tools of Rasputin? The only solution is to kill the scoundrel, but there's not a man in Russia who has the guts to do it. If I weren't so old, I would do it myself."

These words decided me; but how can one deliberately prepare to murder a man in cold blood?

I have repeatedly stated that I am by nature a peaceful man. The very idea of spilling blood fills me with horror. Yet the more I thought about it the more convinced I was that I would have to conquer my personal feelings in this matter.

During Dimitri's absence at Headquarters I saw a good deal of a certain Captain Soukhotin who had been wounded and was undergoing treatment in St. Petersburg. I confided in this trusted friend and asked if he would help me in my plan. He consented without a moment's hesitation.

Our conversation took place on the day of Dimitri's return, and I saw him the day after: Dimitri made no secret of the fact that the idea of killing Rasputin had haunted him for months, but he had not yet found a way of doing it. He told me what a depressing impression he had got at General Headquarters. He was convinced that the drugs administered to the Czar were paralyzing his will power, and were given with this intention. Dimitri was obliged to return to Headquarters shortly, but was certain he would not remain there long, as General Woeïkoff, the Palace Commandant, seemed determined to keep him as far away from the Emperor as he could.

Captain Soukhotin came to see me that evening. I told him of my conversation with the Grand Duke, and we immediately set about making a plan of action. It was agreed that the first thing for me to do was to get into closer contact with the starets and win his confidence, so that he himself should keep us informed of his intentions.

We had not lost all hope of removing him by peaceful means, such as the offer of a huge bribe; but we had to decide on the method to use in case this failed and we were obliged to resort to violence. I proposed that we cast lots to decide which of us would shoot the starets.

A few days later, Mlle G., the friend who had first introduced me to Rasputin in 1909, invited me to her mother's house to meet Gregory Efimovitch, who wanted very much to see me again.

Luck seemed to be on my side. I felt, however, a certain repugnance to deceiving Mlle G., for she could have no suspicion of my real motives in accepting her invitation.

So the following day I went to the G.s' and arrived a few minutes before the starets. I found him much changed. He had become very fat and his face was puffy. He no longer wore a humble caftan but an embroidered blue silk blouse and full velvet breeches. His offensive familiarity and insolent assurance made him seem still more obnoxious than at our first meeting.

On seeing me, he winked and smiled; then he came up to me and embraced me. I had difficulty in concealing my repugnance when he touched me. He seemed anxious about something, and walked nervously up and down the room. He asked several times whether anyone had telephoned for him; finally he sat down beside me and inquired about what I had been doing. He also asked when I was going to the front. I tried to reply politely, but his patronizing tone irritated me beyond words.

Having found out all he wanted to know about me, Rasputin launched out into an incoherent speech about God and brotherly love. I attempted in vain to make some sense of it and wondered if there was anything personal in his sermon; but the more I listened the more obvious it became that he himself did not understand what he was saying. While he held forth, I watched Mme and Mlle G.'s attitude of pious veneration. They drank in every word he said, and for them it seemed to hold some profound mystical meaning.

As Rasputin was fond of saying that he had the gift of curing all diseases, I thought it would serve my purpose to ask him to try his talents on me. So I talked about my health, complaining of an intense fatigue which the doctors seemed powerless to relieve.

"I'll cure you," he said. "Doctors don't know anything.... My dear fellow, I can cure anyone, for I work in God's own way, with divine remedies and not with ordinary drugs. You'll see for yourself." At that moment, the telephone rang: "It's for me," he said; "go and see what it's about." The order was given to Mlle G., who rose obediently without showing the least surprise at his imperious tone.

He was right, the telephone message was for him. He hung up and, looking much perturbed, left in a hurry.

I decided not to attempt to see him again until he himself invited me.

I did not have long to wait. That same evening, Mlle G. sent me a note conveying Rasputin's apologies for leaving so abruptly. She asked me to come back the next day and to bring my guitar, at the starets' request, for he had been told that I sang and he wanted to hear me.

Once again I was the first to arrive. I took the opportunity to ask Mlle G. why he had left so hurriedly the day before. "Because he was told that an important affair was shaping badly. But," she added quickly, "everything has been put right. Gregory Efimovitch flew into a rage, he had to do a great deal of shouting; then they were scared over there and gave in."

"Where is 'over there'?" I asked.

Mlle G. hesitated but ended by unwillingly replying: "At Tsarskoïe-Selo."

I learned finally that the business which had upset the starets so much was the nomination of Protopopoff as Minister of the Interior. Rasputin's faction wanted Protopopoff to have this post at all costs, while others advised the Czar against it. It sufficed for the starets to go himself to Tsarskoïe-Selo to achieve success.

Rasputin arrived in excellent spirits, and very communicative: "Please forgive me for my behavior yesterday, dear boy," he said to me. "What could I do? The wicked must be punished, and they have become very numerous of late." He then addressed Mlle G.: "I have settled everything, I had to go myself to the palace. When I reached it, I found myself face to face with Anouchka.* She did nothing but whimper and repeat over and over again 'We have failed, Gregory Efimovitch, you are our only hope. Thank Heaven you've come!' I was received at once. *She* was in a bad temper, *he* strode up and down the room. I raised my voice and they calmed down at once, particularly when I threatened to go away and leave them to their fate; they then agreed to everything."

We went to the dining room. Mlle G. poured out tea and offered Rasputin an assortment of cakes and dainties.

"See how good and kind she is," he said, "she always thinks of me. And have you brought your guitar?"

"Yes, I have it here."

"Very well then, sing, and we'll listen to you."

Making a great effort to control myself, I took up my guitar and sang a gypsy ballad.

"You sing very well," he said; "you sing with a great deal of feeling. Sing something else."

I sang some more songs, some gay, some sad. Rasputin begged me to continue.

*Anna Wirouboff.

"I see you like my singing," I said, "but you have no idea how ill I feel. It's not that I am lacking in energy, I am not afraid of work, but my health does not improve, in spite of the doctors."

"I will put you right in no time. We will go and hear the gypsies together, and your complaint will vanish as if by magic."

I laughed and answered: "I've been there many times and never felt any the better for it."

Rasputin also laughed. "It's quite another matter, my dear boy, if you go there with *me*. You'll have a much better time when I am with you. Come along, you'll see that everything will be splendid."

He then told me, in much detail, how he spent his time when he went to see the gypsies, how he sang and danced with them.

Mlle G. and her mother looked very uneasy. The starets' uncalled-for frankness embarrassed them. "Don't believe a word of it," they said; "Gregory Efimovitch is joking, and inventing tales about himself."

This attempt to defend his reputation put Rasputin in such a rage that he banged on the table and started to scold the two ladies violently. They said no more. Then, turning to me, Rasputin said: "Well, are you coming with me? I tell you that I can cure you . . . you'll see; you'll be grateful to me later on; we'll take her with us."

Mlle G. blushed; her mother protested. "What's the matter with you, Gregory Efimovitch?" she asked nervously. "Why do you say such dreadful things about yourself, and why bring my daughter into it? She wants to pray with you, and you want to take her to the gypsies. It's wrong to talk in such a way . . ."

"What on earth is the matter with you?" asked Rasputin, giving her an ugly look. "Don't you know one can go anywhere with me without sinning?" He turned to me again: "As for you, dear boy, don't listen to her, do as I say and everything will be all right."

The idea of paying the gypsies a visit did not suit me at all, but, not wishing to refuse outright, I replied that I was one of the Corps des Pages and that such places of amusement were out of bounds.

Rasputin insisted; he said that I could disguise myself, and assured me that no one would hear of the outing. But I replied evasively and promised to telephone him later.

On bidding me good-by he said, "I want to see you often. Come to tea with me. But let me know beforehand." And he slapped me on the shoulder several times with great familiarity.

My intimacy with Rasputin—so indispensable to our plan—increased each day. But what an effort it was! I felt polluted every time I met him. I telephoned that same evening to tell him that it was impossible for me to visit the gypsies as I had to pass an examination the next day, and had to prepare for it. This was perfectly true and I had to cancel all my social engagements for the time being.

Some days later, I met Mlle G. "Aren't you ashamed of yourself?" she asked. "Gregory Efimovitch is still expecting a visit from you." I accepted her invitation to go to see the starets with her on the following day.

When we reached the Fontanka Canal, we left the car at the corner of Gorokhovaïa Street and walked to number 64 where Rasputin lived. This was a necessary precaution for anyone who wished to avoid attracting the attention of the police who watched his house. Mlle G. told me that the policemen who guarded the starets were posted on the main stairs, so we took the back stairs to reach his flat. Rasputin himself opened the door: "Ah, here you are at last!" he exclaimed on seeing me. "I was beginning to feel really annoyed with you: I've been expecting you for several days."

He led us through the kitchen to the bedroom; it was small and very simply furnished. In a corner, close to the wall, was a narrow bed with a red fox bedspread, a present from Anna Wirouboff. Near the bed was a big chest of painted wood; in the opposite corner were icons before which burned a small lamp. Portraits of the Czar and Czarina hung on the walls along with crude engravings representing Biblical scenes. We went from there to the dining room where tea was waiting for us.

Water was boiling in the samovar; on the tables were a number of plates filled with biscuits, cakes, and nuts; glass bowls contained jam and fruit and other delicacies; in the center stood a great basket of flowers.

The furniture was of massive oak, the chairs had very high backs, a bulky dresser full of crockery took up most of one wall. There were a few badly painted pictures, and a bronze chandelier with glass shades lighted the table.

The flat had an air of middle-class solidity. Rasputin served tea; conversation flagged at first—we were constantly interrupted by telephone calls and by the arrival of visitors who were received in the next room. This incessant coming and going seemed to annoy him. During one of his absences a great basket of flowers was brought into the dining room; a note was pinned to it.

"Is that for Gregory Efimovitch?" I asked Mlle G.

She nodded. Rasputin came back shortly and, without a glance at the flowers, sat down by me and poured himself some tea.

"Gregory Efimovitch," I remarked, "you are given flowers, like a prima donna."

He laughed: "Silly creatures these women, silly creatures who spoil me. They send me flowers every day, they know I like them." He then said to Mlle G.: "Go into the next room for a while, I want to talk to him."

She rose obediently and left the room.

When we were alone, Rasputin drew his chair closer to mine and took my hand in his: "Well, my dear boy, how do you like my flat? Come to see me oftener, it will do you a world of good." He stared intently at me: "Don't be frightened of me," he continued in a caressing voice, "you'll see what kind of a man I am when you know me better. I am all-powerful. *Papa* and *Mamma* listen to me, so you should listen to me too. I'm going to see them this afternoon, and I'll tell them you had tea with me. They'll be so pleased."

I much disliked the idea of the Czarina being told of my visit to Rasputin. I knew that she would immediately tell Anna Wirouboff of my newly made friendship with Rasputin, and that this would seem suspicious to her. Anna knew my opinion of the starets only too well, for I had discussed him with her. "Listen, Gregory Efimovitch," I said, "it might be better if you didn't mention it. If my parents knew that I came here they would be annoyed, and I want to avoid that at all costs."

Rasputin agreed with me and promised not to say anything. He began to talk politics, and criticized the Duma: "They spend their time slandering me, and that distresses the Czar. But they won't do it much longer. I'll soon have the Duma dissolved and send its representatives to the front. Then they'll see where their gossiping led them, and they'll remember me."

"Tell me, Gregory Efimovitch, are you really powerful enough to dissolve the Duma? How would you go about it?"

"Why, my dear fellow, it's perfectly easy; when you become my friend and ally, you'll be told everything. For the time being, I'll tell you this much: the Czarina has a wise, strong mind and I can get anything and everything from her. As for *him*, he's a simple soul. He was not cut out to be a sovereign; he is made for family life, to admire nature and flowers, but not to reign. That's beyond his strength. So, with God's blessing, we come to his rescue."

Controlling my irritation, I asked him in the most natural way whether he was sure of his associates: "How can you tell, Gregory Efimovitch, what those people want of you, and what their aims are? Supposing they had criminal intentions?"

Rasputin smiled indulgently: "So you want to teach the good Lord what he should do? He hasn't sent me to help the Lord's Anointed in vain. I can't say it often enough: they would all have died if I hadn't been there. I stand on no ceremony with them; if they don't obey implicitly, I bang on the table with my fist, get up, and go. Then they run after me, imploring: 'Don't go, Gregory Efimovitch, we'll do anything you wish, so long as you don't forsake us.' And that's why, my dear fellow, they love and respect me. The other day, I talked to *him* about someone who should be given a post, but *he* keeps on postponing the nomination. So I threatened to leave them: 'I'll go to Siberia,' I announced, 'and you'll stay here and rot all by yourselves. You'll lose your son through your own fault if you turn away from God, and then you'll fall into the clutches of the devil.' That's the way I speak to them; but I haven't finished my work. There are still a lot of bad people about them who spend their time whispering in their ears that Gregory Efimovitch is a wicked man who works for their downfall. . . . It's ridiculous. Why should I want to ruin them? They are good and pious."

"Gregory Efimovitch," I answered, "the fact that the Emperor and Empress trust you isn't enough. Surely you know what's said about you? You are most severely criticized in Russia, and even abroad the newspapers write about you disparagingly. That's why I believe if you really loved the Imperial family you'd go away forever. Otherwise, who knows? Someone might do you grievous harm."

"No, no, my dear boy, you talk like this because you know nothing about it. God would not allow such a thing to happen, for it has pleased Him to send me to help them in their difficulties. I don't care what a lot of nincompoops write and say, I scorn them, they're only harming themselves."

Rasputin rose and walked about nervously. I watched him intently; he had become gloomy and anxious. Suddenly he leaned toward me, and gave me a long searching look.

I turned as cold as ice, for I felt the tremendous power of his gaze. Without taking his eyes off me, he lightly ran his hand over the nape of my neck and, in a soft insinuating voice, asked me if I would have a glass of wine. I accepted and he fetched a bottle of Madeira, filled a glass for himself, another for me, and drank to my health:

"When will you come to see me again?" he asked.

At that moment, Mlle G. came in and reminded him that it was time he went to Tsarskoïe-Selo.

"And here I've been gossiping! I'd completely forgotten that they're waiting for me there. Anyway, there's no great harm done ... it's not the first time it's happened. Sometimes they ring me up on the telephone, I'm sent for, and I don't go. Later on, I turn up unexpectedly. Then they're overjoyed! My visits are all the more appreciated." He added: "Well, good-by, my dear boy." Then, turning to Mlle G., he said, pointing at me: "He's intelligent, most intelligent, provided his mind doesn't get warped. If he continues to obey me, everything will be all right. Isn't it so, my child? Make it clear to him, so he'll understand ... Well, good-by, come and see me again." He embraced me.

As soon as he had left, Mlle G. and I made our way out down the back stairs. "There's such a comfortable, easy atmosphere at Gregory Efimovitch's," she remarked. "In his presence all the worries and troubles of this world are forgotten. Don't you think so? He has the gift of making one feel serene and peaceful."

I did not want to contradict her. But I gave her a hint: "Gregory Efimovitch would do well to leave St. Petersburg as quickly as possible."

"Why?"

"Because someone will end by murdering him. I'm quite sure of this, and I advise you to exert your utmost influence to make him realize that he's in danger. He must go away."

"Oh no!" She looked terrified. "Such a thing will never happen. God would not allow it. Do you realize that he's our only consolation, our only help? How right the Empress is to believe that as long as he stays here nothing can happen to her son. Gregory Efimovitch says so himself: 'If I am killed, the Czarevitch will die.' Several attempts have been made on his life, but God has kept him safe. He has become very wary now, and he is so carefully guarded that there's no reason to fear for him."

We had reached the G.s' house. "When shall I see you again?" asked Mlle G.

"Telephone me after you have seen him again."

I was anxious to hear what impression our conversation had made on Rasputin. All hope of his leaving without our having to resort to violence now seemed vain. He knew his power and believed himself absolutely safe. The idea of a bribe had to be abandoned, for he obviously had ample means, and if it was true that he was working for the Germans (even though he was perhaps only half aware of the fact), he could get infinitely larger sums from them than any we could offer him.

My military training at the Corps des Pages left me very little free time. I went home tired but could not rest; I was possessed by the haunting memory of Rasputin. I tried to weigh up his responsibility; in my mind's eye I pictured the monstrous plot against Russia of which he was the moving spirit. Did he realize what he was doing? The idea harassed me; for hours on end, I went over everything I knew about him, trying to understand the contradictions in his character and to find excuses for his infamous behavior. Then once again a flood of indignation swept over me as I remembered his licentiousness, his incredible unscrupulousness and, above all, his abominable hypocrisy toward the Imperial family.

Gradually, however, a clearer, simpler picture of Rasputin took shape in my mind.

He was just an uncultured, cynical, avid, and unscrupulous peasant who had reached the pinnacle of power owing to a chain of circumstances. His boundless influence over the Czar and Czarina, the adoration of his female admirers, his continual orgies, and the idleness in which he lived and to which he was not accustomed, had completely destroyed what good remained in him. But who were the people who so skillfully exploited and directed him from a distance, without his being aware of it? It is most improbable that Rasputin knew the real intentions of his masters, or even their true identity; he rarely remembered the names of the people he saw, and was in the habit of giving each one a fancy nickname. In one of our later conversations, alluding to his mysterious friends, he called them "the greens." It is likely that he had never even seen them and only communicated with them through a third person. " 'The greens' live in Sweden; you shall go there to meet them," he said.

"But aren't there 'greens' in Russia too?" I asked.

"No, just the 'greenish,' who are friends of theirs and of ours. They are intelligent people."

A few days later, Mlle G. telephoned that the starets had invited me once more to visit the gypsies with him. I again gave my examinations at the Corps des Pages as an excuse for declining the invitation, but added that if Gregory Efimovitch wished to see me I would go to his house for tea.

I went there the next day. He was in a particularly jovial mood and I reminded him of his promise to cure me.

"Oh, you'll see, it will only take a few days," he said. "But let's have a cup of tea first, then we'll go to my study where no one will disturb us. I shall pray to the Lord and then rid your body of disease. Just obey me, my dear boy, and you'll see, all will be well."

After tea, Rasputin took me into his study for the first time; it was a small room furnished with a sofa, a few leather armchairs and a large table littered with papers.

The starets made me lie down on the sofa. Then, staring intently at me, he gently ran his hand over my chest, neck, and head, after which he knelt down, laid both hands on my forehead and murmured a prayer. His face was so close to mine that I could see only his eyes. He remained in this position for some time, then rising brusquely he made mesmeric passes over my body.

Rasputin had tremendous hypnotic power. I felt as if some active energy were pouring heat, like a warm current, into my whole being. I fell into a torpor, and my body grew numb; I tried to speak, but my tongue no longer obeyed me and I gradually slipped into a drowsy state, as though a powerful narcotic had been administered to me. All I could see was Rasputin's glittering eyes: two phosphorescent beams of light melting into a great luminous ring which at times drew nearer and then moved farther away.

I heard the voice of the starets but could not understand what he said.

I remained in this state, without being able to cry out or to move. My mind alone was free, and I fully realized that I was gradually falling into the power of this evil man. Then I felt stirring in me the will to fight his hypnosis. Little by little the desire to resist grew stronger and stronger, forming a protective armor around me. I had the feeling that a merciless struggle was being fought out between Rasputin and me, between his personality and mine. I knew that I was preventing him from getting complete mastery over me, but still I could not move: I had to wait until he ordered me to get up.

Soon I was able to distinguish his silhouette, his face and eyes; the dreadful ring of light had entirely disappeared. "That's enough for the present, my dear boy," said Rasputin.

Although he watched me closely, he did not realize that he could not read all my thoughts; my resistance to his hypnotic power had escaped him. A satisfied smile lit up his face, and the assurance in his voice betrayed his conviction that he had got me in his power.

He pulled me roughly by the arm; I sat up, but my head swam

and my whole body felt weak. I managed to get to my feet and take a few steps, but my legs felt paralyzed and refused to obey me.

Rasputin continued to watch all my movements. "It's God's grace," he said finally, "you'll soon notice how much better you are."

As I said good-by he made me promise to come back soon.

After this experiment in hypnotism, I went to see Rasputin very often. The "cure" was continued, the starets' confidence in his patient increased. "Really, you have a great deal of common sense, my dear boy," he declared one day. "You understand everything right away. I'll have you appointed minister, if you like."

The offer took me aback; I knew how easy it was for him to carry out his promise, and I was horrified at the thought of being known as the protégé of such a man. I laughed and answered: "I'll give you my help willingly, but please, never dream of making a minister of me."

"Why do you laugh? Perhaps you think I can't do what I say? I can do anything and everything I like, and everyone obeys me. You'll see. You'll be made a minister."

He spoke with such assurance that I felt extremely uneasy. I could already imagine the general astonishment when the appointment was announced in the newspapers.

"I beg of you, Gregory Efimovitch, do nothing of the sort. What kind of a minister would I make, anyway? And what's the use? It would be far better for me to help you secretly."

"Perhaps you're right," replied Rasputin, "have it your own way." He continued: "It isn't everybody who thinks as you do; most people who come to me say, 'Do this for me, do that for me.' Everybody wants something."

"And how do you fulfill these requests?"

"I send them to a minister or some other influential person with a personal note. Sometimes I send them directly to Tsarskoïe-Selo. That's how I hand out appointments."

"And the ministers obey you?"

"Every one of them!" cried Rasputin. "They all owe their positions to me. How could they disobey me? They know very well that if they don't obey me, they'll come to a bad end . . ." After a moment's silence he continued: "Every one of them without exception is afraid of me. All I have to do to enforce my will is to bang my hand on the table. That's the way you aristocrats should be treated. You're filled with envy because I walk about the palace in great clumsy boots. Every one of you is a mountain of pride, and it's pride, my dear boy, that breeds sin. If you wish to please God, you must, above all, stifle any feelings of pride."

Rasputin burst into cynical laughter; he was tipsy and in a confidential mood. He went on to disclose his method for fighting pride. "And that's that, my dear fellow," he continued, smiling strangely. "Women are worse than men and have to be dealt with first. Yes, this is how I proceed: I take all the ladies to the public baths. I just say: 'And now undress and wash the *moujik.*' If they put on airs, I have a good way of convincing them and . . . they soon swallow their pride."

I listened in horrified silence to the abominable account which followed, the details of which are impossible to repeat. I was afraid to interrupt him, and, as he talked, he emptied glass after glass. "But why aren't you drinking?" he asked. "Are you afraid of wine? Yet it's the best of medicines; it cures every ill and isn't made up in a drugstore. It's a God-given remedy to strengthen body and soul. Wine makes me conscious of the tremendous power the Lord has bestowed on me. And, by the bye, do you know Badmaïev? There's a real doctor for you, who knows how to make up his own remedies. As for fellows like Botkine and Derevenko,* they know nothing. Badmaïev uses herbs provided by nature herself; they can be found in forests, in fields, on mountains . . . God makes them grow, that's why they have divine properties."

"Tell me, Gregory Efimovitch," I asked with some trepidation, "aren't the Czar and the Czarevitch treated with these herbs?"

"Most certainly they are. *She herself* and Anouchka see to it, but they are afraid that Botkine will hear of it. I tell them constantly: 'If one of your doctors ever hears about my remedies, it will go very badly for the patient.' So they take great precautions."

*Physicians of the Imperial family.

"What kind of medicine do you give to the Emperor and the Czarevitch?"

"All kinds, my dear fellow. The Emperor is given a tea which causes divine grace to descend on him. His heart is filled with peace, everything looks good and cheerful to him. And anyway," continued Rasputin, "what kind of a Czar is he? He's just a child of God. But you'll see how we'll settle things later on. Everything will be for the best then."

"What do you mean, Gregory Efimovitch? What will be for the best?"

"You are too inquisitive, you want to know everything . . . when the time comes, you shall know it all."

I had never seen Rasputin so communicative. Obviously, so much wine had loosened his tongue. I wanted to seize this opportunity to learn as much as possible about the plots that were being hatched. I then suggested that we should go on drinking. For a long time we silently filled our glasses. Rasputin drained his at a gulp, while I only pretended to drink. After finishing a bottle of very heavy Madeira, he staggered to the sideboard to fetch another one. I filled his glass and feigning to replenish mine took up the conversation where we had left it: "Gregory Efimovitch, do you remember having said some time ago that you wanted me for an ally? I'll help you with pleasure, but you must tell me more about your plans. You've just said that there will soon be more changes; but when will that be? And why don't you tell me about them?"

Rasputin stared at me intently; half closing his eyes, he said after a few moments of thought: "This is what is going to happen my dear fellow: enough of this war, enough bloodshed. It's time to end this slaughter. Isn't Germany our brother too? The Lord said: 'Thou shalt love thine enemy as thine own brother.' That's why the war must cease. *He* constantly opposes this; *she* won't hear of it either. Someone is certainly giving them bad advice. But what does it matter? If I give an order, they'll have to do as I say. But it's still early in the day, everything isn't quite ready.

"When we've settled this matter, we'll make Alexandra regent during her son's minority. As for *him*, we'll send him to Livadia for a rest. He'll be glad to go, he's worn out and needs a rest. Down there, at Livadia, with his flowers, he'll be closer to God. He has enough sins on his conscience to atone for. A whole life of prayer wouldn't be enough to atone for this war. The Czarina is a very wise woman, a second Catherine the Great. Anyway, she's been running everything lately, and, you'll see, the more she does, the better things will be. She's promised to begin by sending away all those chatterboxes at the Duma. May they go to the devil! Look at them, they have decided to rebel against the Lord's Anointed. Well, we'll give them a sound drubbing. They should have been sent packing long ago. All those who have found fault with me and complained will come to a bad end."

Rasputin grew more and more excited. Under the influence of the wine, he forgot to keep a watch over his tongue. "I'm like a hunted animal," he said. "All the aristocrats want to destroy me because I stand in their way. On the other hand, the masses respect me because in spite of my caftan and heavy boots I've managed to become the Sovereign's adviser. It's God's will. God has given me this power. I can read men's most intimate thoughts. You have common sense, you will help me. I can arrange for you to meet certain people . . . it will bring you a lot of money. But perhaps you don't need it, perhaps you're richer than the Czar himself. Well, you can give the money to the poor! Everyone is the happier for a few extra pennies."

The bell pealed violently; Rasputin jumped. Obviously he expected someone, but being engrossed in our conversation he had completely forgotten the appointment. Now that he was brought back to earth, he seemed afraid that the newcomers might see me in his house.

He jumped up, took me to his study, and hastily went out leaving me there alone. I heard him staggering to the front door. On his way, he bumped into some object which fell to the ground, at which he let out an oath. His legs may have been shaky but his head was perfectly clear.

I heard the newcomers' voices in the dining room. I strained my ears, but the conversation went on in such a low tone that it was impossible for me to catch what was said. The dining room was separated from the study by a narrow passage. I softly half-opened the door; that of the dining room was ajar so I could see the starets in the seat which he had occupied during our conversation a few moments before, surrounded by seven shady-looking men. Four of them were of a distinctly Jewish type, the other three were fair and curiously alike in appearance. Rasputin talked briskly, his visitors took notes, held whispered consultations, and occasionally laughed. They looked like a group of conspirators.

An idea crossed my mind: could these be the "greenish" mentioned by Rasputin? The more I examined them, the more certain I became that I was looking at a gang of spies.

I drew away from the door in disgust; I longed to flee from that cursèd place, but it was impossible to leave the room unnoticed, as it had only one exit.

After what seemed an eternity, Rasputin reappeared; he was very cheerful, and seemed very pleased with himself. Feeling that I could no longer control my repulsion for him, I quickly said good-by and fled from the house.

Each of my visits to Rasputin convinced me more and more that he was the cause of Russia's disasters, and that if he disappeared the diabolical spell cast over our Czar and Czarina would vanish with him.

It seemed as though fate had led me to him so that I could see for myself his evil, destructive role. So, why wait? To spare his life only meant increasing the number of war victims and prolonging the country's misery. Was there a single honest man in Russia who did not sincerely wish for his death?

It was no longer a matter of knowing whether Rasputin ought to disappear, but only whether I was the right person to kill him. Our first plans to kill him in his flat had to be abandoned. In the middle of a war, at a time when a great offensive was being prepared, when people's nerves were strung to the breaking point, to assassinate Rasputin openly might have been interpreted as a demonstration of hostility against the Imperial family. Rasputin had to be made away with secretly, without anyone knowing the circumstances of his death or the names of those who brought it about.

I imagined that Maklakoff and Pourichkevitch, who had violently attacked the starets in the Duma (I had heard them myself) would be disposed to advise and perhaps help me. I resolved to call on them, for it seemed important that members of all classes should participate in this momentous affair. Dimitri belonged to the Imperial family, I was a member of the nobility, Soukhotin was an officer; I would have liked a politician, someone from the Duma, to join us.

I first went to see Maklakoff. Our conversation was brief. I disclosed my scheme in a few words and asked for his opinion. Maklakoff avoided giving me a direct answer. His indecision and distrust were shown clearly enough by the following question: "Why did you come to see me, particularly?"

"I have attended sessions in the Duma, and I heard your speech."

I was convinced that in his heart of hearts he approved of my intentions, but his attitude disappointed me. Did he lack confidence in me, or was he afraid of being embroiled in a dangerous adventure? No matter what the reason, I quickly realized he was not to be counted on.

Pourichkevitch gave me a very different reception. I had barely time to tell him of my intentions concerning Rasputin when he assured me of his co-operation with his usual ardor and warmth. But he thought it his duty to warn me that Rasputin was well guarded, and that it would be difficult to get into contact with him.

"That's already done," I remarked. I then described my visits to the starets, and our conversations. I also spoke to him about the Grand Duke Dimitri, Captain Soukhotin, and my visit to Maklakoff. The latter's reticence did not surprise him, but he promised to speak to Maklakoff and try to induce him to join us.

Pourichkevitch was also of the opinion that Rasputin should be done away with secretly. At a meeting with Dimitri and Soukhotin, we decided that poison was the surest means of killing him without leaving any trace of murder.

Our house on the Moïka was chosen as the place of execution; I was fitting up an apartment in the basement which lent itself admirably to the accomplishment of our scheme.

This decision at first gave me a feeling of disgust: the prospect of luring a man to my house to kill him horrified me. No matter what the man was, I could not bring myself to plan the murder of a guest.

My friends shared my scruples but, after lengthy discussions, we decided to abide by our plan: our country had to be saved at all costs, even by doing violence to our most sacred feelings.

We accepted a fifth accomplice, proposed by Pourichkevitch, namely the doctor of his military detachment, Dr. Lazovert. We agreed to give Rasputin a sufficient dose of cyanide of potassium to kill him instantly. I was to remain alone with him while he was in my house. The others would stand by, to come to my help in case of need.

But no matter what were the consequences of our act, we resolved never to disclose our participation in Rasputin's murder.

A few days after this meeting, Dimitri and Pourichkevitch both left for the front.

While awaiting their return, I went back to see Maklakoff on Pourichkevitch's advice. I was agreeably surprised by the change in his attitude. He approved of our plan, but when I proposed that he should join us, he replied that he would probably have to go to Moscow on important business about the middle of December. In spite of this, I unfolded our plan in detail. He listened with the greatest attention . . . but gave no signs of wishing to take an active part in our conspiracy.

As I left, he wished me good luck and presented me with a rubber club: "Take it, one never knows," he said with a smile.

Each time I went to see Rasputin, I loathed myself; these visits had become an almost unbearable torture.

Shortly before Dimitri and Pourichkevitch returned, I went to see him again.

He was in a very good temper. "Why are you in such good spirits?" I asked.

"Because I've just made a really good deal. Matters will soon come to a head, and it'll be our turn to rejoice."

"What is it all about?" I inquired.

"What's it all about? What's it all about?" repeated Rasputin, mimicking me. "You're afraid of me," he continued, "and that's why you've stopped coming to see me. And yet, I have lots of interesting things to tell you . . . well, I won't, because you're frightened of me and frightened of everything. If you had more courage, I'd have told you everything."

I tried to explain that I was cramming for an examination at the Corps des Pages and that this took up all my time; that was the reason for my apparent neglect. But I could not convince him. "I know, I know . . . you're afraid, and your parents won't allow you to come here. Your mamma is hand in glove with Elisabeth, isn't she? And they both have but one thought: to send me away from here. They won't succeed, indeed they won't, no one will listen to them; they're much too fond of me at Tsarskoïe-Selo."

"Gregory Efimovitch, your behavior at Tsarkoïe-Selo is quite different from what it is elsewhere. You only talk of God there, and that's why you're believed in and loved."

"And why shouldn't I talk to them about God, my dear fellow? They are very pious and such talk pleases them. . . . They understand everything, forgive everything, and appreciate me. It's not the least use running me down to them, for no matter what is told them they don't believe a word of it. I have often said to them: 'You'll see that I'll be slandered. Remember then how Christ was persecuted. He too suffered for the sake of truth.' They listen to everyone, but they act only according to the dictates of conscience. As for *him*," continued Rasputin, "whenever he leaves Tsarskoïe-Selo, he listens to everything that wicked people tell him; I've had a lot of trouble with him lately. I try to make him understand that he must put an end to this butchery. 'All men are brothers,' I tell him, 'Does it matter whether they are French or German?' But I can do nothing with him. He doggedly repeats that he'd be 'ashamed' to sign a peace. And what is there to be ashamed of, when it means the salvation of his brothers? He is about to send more men to their death, thousands of them. That is what he should be ashamed of. *She* is a good and wise woman. But what does he understand? He hasn't the makings of an emperor. He's just one of God's children. What I fear is that the Grand Duke Nicolas Nikolaïevitch will make difficulties for us if he hears anything. But thank God, he's far away and he isn't powerful enough to get at us. The Czarina saw the danger and he was sent as far away as possible to prevent his meddling."

"In my opinion," I replied, "it was a great blunder to relieve the Grand Duke of his command. The whole of Russia worships him. The Army should not have been deprived of its beloved chief at a time like this."

"Don't give yourself airs, my dear boy. The decision was made because it was necessary, and a very good thing too." Rasputin rose and began striding up and down, muttering. He stopped suddenly, rushed up to me, and seized my hand. His expression became very strange: "Come with me to the gypsies," he said. "If you'll come, I'll tell you everything, down to the smallest detail."

I consented, but at that moment the telephone rang: Rasputin was summoned to Tsarskoïe-Selo. Taking advantage of his disappointment at not going to see the gypsies with me, I invited him to spend an evening with me soon, at the Moïka.

He had long wished to meet my wife. Believing her to be in St. Petersburg, and knowing that my parents were in the Crimea, he accepted my invitation. The truth was that Irina was also in the Crimea, but I thought Rasputin would be more likely to accept my invitation if he thought he had a chance of meeting her.

Dimitri and Pourichkevitch returned from the front some days later, and it was agreed that I should invite Rasputin to the Moïka on the evening of December 29.

He accepted on the understanding that I would come for him myself and take him home afterward. He told me to come up the back stairs and said he would notify the janitor that someone would come for him at midnight.

The simple way in which he consented to everything, and even went out of his way to make things easier for me, horrified and surprised me.

The Youssoupoff palace, on the Moïka Canal in Saint Petersburg

chapter XXIII

As I was alone in St. Petersburg, I was staying with my brothers-in-law at the Grand Duke Alexander's palace. On December 29, I spent most of the day preparing for my examinations which were to be held next day. As soon as I had a free moment I went home to make the final arrangements.

I intended to receive Rasputin in the flat which I was fitting up in the Moïka basement: arches divided it in two; the larger half was to be used as a dining room. From the other half, the staircase which I have already mentioned led to my rooms on the floor above. Halfway up was a door opening onto the courtyard. The larger room had a low, vaulted ceiling and was lighted by two small windows which were on a level with the ground and looked out on the Moïka. The walls were of gray stone, the flooring of granite. To avoid arousing Rasputin's suspicions—for he might have been surprised at being received in a bare cellar—it was indispensable that the room should be furnished and appear to be lived in.

When I arrived, I found workmen busy laying down carpets and putting up curtains. Three large red Chinese porcelain vases had already been placed in niches hollowed out of the walls. Various objects which I had selected were being carried in: carved wooden chairs of oak, small tables covered with ancient embroideries, ivory bowls, and a quantity of other curios. I can picture the room to this day in all its details, and I have good reason to remember a certain cabinet of inlaid ebony which was a mass of little mirrors, tiny bronze columns, and secret drawers. On it stood a crucifix of rock crystal and silver, a beautiful specimen of sixteenth-century Italian workmanship. On the great red granite mantelpiece were placed golden bowls, antique majolica plates, and a sculptured ivory group. A large Persian carpet covered the floor and, in a corner, in front of the ebony cabinet, lay a white bearskin rug.

In the middle of the room stood the table at which Rasputin was to drink his last cup of tea.

My two servants, Gregory and Ivan, helped me to arrange the furniture. I asked them to prepare tea for six, to buy biscuits and cakes, and to bring wine from the cellar. I told them that I was expecting some friends at eleven that evening, and that they could wait in the servants' hall until I rang for them.

When everything was settled, I went up to my room where Colonel Vogel, my crammer, was waiting to coach me for the last time before my exams. The lesson was over by six o'clock; before going back to dine with my brothers-in-law, I went into the church of Our Lady of Kazan. Deep in prayer, I lost all sense of time. When I left the cathedral after what seemed to me but a few moments, I was astonished to find I had been there almost two hours. I had a strange feeling of lightness, of well-being, almost of happiness. . . . I hurried to my father-in-law's palace where I had a light dinner before returning to the Moïka.

By eleven o'clock everything was ready in the basement. Comfortably furnished and well-lighted, this underground room had lost its grim look. On the table the samovar smoked, surrounded by plates filled with the cakes and dainties that Rasputin liked so much. An array of bottles and glasses stood on a sideboard. Ancient lanterns of colored glass lighted the room from the ceiling; the heavy red damask portières were lowered. On the granite hearth, a log fire crackled and scattered sparks on the flagstones. One felt isolated from the rest of the world and it seemed as though, no matter what happened, the events of that night would remain forever buried in the silence of those thick walls.

The bell rang, announcing the arrival of Dimitri and my other friends. I showed them into the dining room and they stood for a little while, silently examining the spot where Rasputin was to meet his end.

I took from the ebony cabinet a box containing the poison and laid it on the table. Dr. Lazovert put on rubber gloves and ground the cyanide of potassium crystals to powder. Then, lifting the top of each cake, he sprinkled the inside with a dose of poison which, according to him, was sufficient to kill several men instantly. There was an impressive silence. We all followed the doctor's movements with emotion. There remained the glasses into which cyanide was to be poured. It was decided to do this at the last moment so that the poison should not evaporate and lose its potency. We had to give the impression of having just finished supper—for I had warned Rasputin that when we had guests we took our meals in the basement and that I sometimes stayed there alone to read or work while my friends went upstairs to smoke in my study. So we disarranged the table, pushed the chairs back, and poured tea into the cups. It was agreed that when I went to fetch the starets, Dimitri, Pourichkevitch, and Soukhotin would go upstairs and play the gramophone, choosing lively tunes. I wanted to keep Rasputin in a good humor and remove any distrust that might be lurking in his mind.

When everything was ready, I put on an overcoat and drew a fur cap over my ears, completely concealing my face. Doctor Lazovert, in a chauffeur's uniform, started up the engine and we got into the car which was waiting in the courtyard by the side entrance. On reaching Rasputin's house, I had to parley with the janitor before he agreed to let me in. In accordance with Rasputin's instructions, I went up the back staircase; I had to grope my way up in the dark, and only with the greatest difficulty found the starets' door. I rang the bell.

"Who's that?" called a voice from inside.

I began to tremble, "It's I, Gregory Efimovitch. I've come for you."

I could hear Rasputin moving about the hall. The chain was unfastened, the heavy lock grated. I felt very ill at ease.

He opened the door and I went into the kitchen. It was dark. I imagined that someone was spying on me from the next room. Instinctively, I turned up my collar and pulled my cap down over my eyes.

"Why are you trying to hide?" asked Rasputin.

"Didn't we agree that no one was to know you were going out with me tonight?"

"True, true; I haven't said a word about it to anyone in the house, I've even sent away all the *tainiks*.* I'll go and dress."

I accompanied him to his bedroom; it was lighted only by the little lamp burning before the icons. Rasputin lit a candle; I noticed that his bed was crumpled. He had probably been resting. Near the bed were his overcoat and beaver cap, and his high felt-lined galoshes.

Rasputin wore a silk blouse embroidered in cornflowers, with a thick raspberry-colored cord as a belt. His velvet breeches and highly polished boots seemed brand-new; he had brushed his hair and carefully combed his beard. As he came close to me, I smelled a strong odor of cheap soap which indicated that he had taken pains with his appearance. I had never seen him look so clean and tidy.

"Well, Gregory Efimovitch, it's time to go; it's past midnight."

"What about the gypsies? Shall we pay them a visit?"

"I don't know; perhaps," I answered.

"There will be no one at your house but us tonight?" he asked, with a note of anxiety in his voice.

I reassured him by saying that he would meet no one that he might not care to see, and that my mother was in the Crimea.

"I don't like your mother. I know she hates me; she's a friend of Elisabeth's. Both of them plot against me and spread slander about me too. The Czarina herself has often told me that they were my worst enemies. Why, no earlier than this evening, Protopopoff came to see me and made me swear not to go out for a few days. 'They'll kill you,' he declared. 'Your enemies are bent on mischief!' But they'd just be wasting time and trouble; they won't succeed, they are not powerful enough . . . But that's enough, come on, let's go."

I picked up the overcoat and helped him on with it.

Suddenly, a feeling of great pity for the man swept over me. I was ashamed of the despicable deceit, the horrible trickery to which I was obliged to resort. At that moment I was filled with self-contempt, and wondered how I could even have thought of such a cowardly

*Members of the secret police.

crime. I could not understand how I had brought myself to decide on it.

I looked at my victim with dread, as he stood before me, quiet and trusting. What had become of his second sight? What good did his gift of foretelling the future do him? Of what use was his faculty for reading the thoughts of others, if he was blind to the dreadful trap that was laid for him? It seemed as though fate had clouded his mind . . . to allow justice to deal with him according to his deserts. . . .

But suddenly, in a lightning flash of memory, I seemed to recall every stage of Rasputin's infamous life. My qualms of conscience disappeared, making room for a firm determination to complete my task.

We walked to the dark landing, and Rasputin closed the door behind him.

Once more I heard the grating of the lock echoing down the staircase; we were in pitch-black darkness. I felt fingers roughly clutching at my hand. "I will show you the way," said the starets, dragging me down the stairs.

His grip hurt me, I felt like crying out and breaking away, but a sort of numbness came over me. I don't remember what he said to me, or whether I answered him; my one thought was to be out of the dark house as quickly as possible, to get back to the light, and to free myself from that hateful clutch. As soon as we were outside, my fears vanished and I recovered my self-control.

We entered the car and drove off. I looked behind us to see whether the police were following; but there was no one, the streets were deserted.

We drove a roundabout way to Moïka, entered the courtyard and, once more, the car drew up at the side entrance.

As we entered the house, I could hear my friends talking while the gramophone played "Yankee Doodle went to town."

"What's all this?" asked Rasputin. "Is someone giving a party here?"

"No, just my wife entertaining a few friends; they'll be going soon. Meanwhile, let's have a cup of tea in the dining room."

We went down to the basement. As soon as Rasputin entered the room, he took off his overcoat and began inspecting the furniture with great interest. He was particularly fascinated by the little ebony cabinet, and took a childlike pleasure in opening and shutting the drawers, exploring it inside and out.

Then, at the fateful moment, I made a last attempt to persuade him to leave St. Petersburg. His refusal sealed his fate. I offered him wine and tea; to my great disappointment, he refused both. Had something made him suspicious? I was determined, come what may, that he should not leave the house alive.

We sat down at the table and began to talk. We reviewed our mutual acquaintances, not forgetting Anna Wirouboff and, naturally, touched on Tsarskoïe-Selo. "Gregory Efimovitch," I asked, "why did Protopopoff come to see you? Is he still afraid of a conspiracy?"

"Why yes, my dear boy, he is; it seems that my plain speaking annoys a lot of people. The aristocrats can't get used to the idea that a humble peasant should be welcome at the Imperial Palace.... They are consumed with envy and fury ... but I'm not afraid of them. They can't do anything to me. I'm protected against ill fortune. There have been several attempts on my life but the Lord has always frustrated these plots. Disaster will come to anyone who lifts a finger against me."

Rasputin's words echoed ominously through the very room in which he was to die, but nothing could deter me now. While he talked, my one idea was to make him drink some wine and eat the cakes.

After exhausting his customary topics of conversation, Rasputin asked for some tea. I immediately poured out a cup and handed him a plate of biscuits. Why was it that I offered him the only biscuits that were not poisoned? I even hesitated before handing him the cakes sprinkled with cyanide.

He refused them at first: "I don't want any, they're too sweet." At last, however, he took one, then another.... I watched him, horror-stricken. The poison should have acted immediately but, to my amazement, Rasputin went on talking quite calmly.

I then suggested that he should sample our Crimean wines. He once more refused. Time was passing, I was becoming nervous; in spite of his refusal, I filled two glasses. But, as in the case of the biscuits—and just as inexplicably—I again avoided using a glass containing cyanide. Rasputin changed his mind and accepted the wine I handed him. He drank it with enjoyment, found it to his taste, and asked whether we made a great deal of wine in the Crimea. He seemed surprised to hear that we had cellars full of it.

"Pour me out some Madeira," he said. This time I wanted to give it to him in a glass containing cyanide, but he protested: "I'll have it in the same glass."

"You can't, Gregory Efimovitch," I replied. "You can't mix two kinds of wines."

"It doesn't matter, I'll use the same glass, I tell you . . ."

I had to give in without pressing the point, but I managed, as if by mistake, to drop the glass from which he had drunk, and immediately poured the Madeira into a glass containing cyanide. Rasputin did not say anything.

I stood watching him drink, expecting any moment to see him collapse.

But he continued slowly to sip his wine like a connoisseur. His face did not change, only from time to time he put his hand to his throat as though he had some difficulty in swallowing. He rose and took a few steps. When I asked him what was the matter, he answered: "Why, nothing, just a tickling in my throat."

"The Madeira's good," he remarked; "give me some more."

Meanwhile, the poison continued to have no effect, and the starets went on walking calmly about the room.

I picked up another glass containing cyanide, filled it with wine, and handed it to Rasputin.

He drank it as he had the others, and still with no result.

There remained only one poisoned glass on the tray. Then, as I was feeling desperate, and must try to make him do as I did, I began drinking myself.

A silence fell upon us as we sat facing each other.

He looked at me; there was a malicious expression in his eyes, as if to say: "Now, see, you're wasting your time, you can't do anything to me."

Suddenly his expression changed to one of fierce anger; I had never seen him look so terrifying. He fixed his fiendish eyes on me, and at that moment I was filled with such hatred that I wanted to leap at him and strangle him with my bare hands.

The silence became ominous. I had the feeling that he knew why I had brought him to my house, and what I had set out to do. We seemed to be engaged in a strange and terrible struggle. Another moment and I would have been beaten, annihilated. Under Rasputin's heavy gaze, I felt all my self-possession leaving me; an indescribable numbness came over me, my head swam. . . .

When I came to myself, he was still seated in the same place, his head in his hands. I could not see his eyes. I had got back my self-control, and offered him another cup of tea.

"Pour me a cup," he said in a muffled voice, "I'm very thirsty." He raised his head, his eyes were dull, and I thought he avoided looking at me.

While I poured the tea, he rose and began walking up and down. Catching sight of my guitar which I had left on a chair, he said: "Play something cheerful, I like listening to your singing."

I found it difficult to sing anything at such a moment, especially anything cheerful. "I really don't feel up to it," I said. However, I took the guitar and sang a sad Russian ditty.

He sat down and at first listened attentively; then his head drooped and his eyes closed. I thought he was dozing. When I finished the song, he opened his eyes and looked gloomily at me: "Sing another. I'm very fond of this kind of music and you put so much soul into it."

I sang once more but I did not recognize my own voice.

Time went by; the clock said two-thirty . . . the nightmare had lasted two interminable hours. What would happen, I thought, if I had lost my nerve?

Upstairs my friends were evidently growing impatient, to judge by the racket they made. I was afraid that they might be unable to bear the suspense any longer and just come bursting in.

Rasputin raised his head: "What's all that noise?"

"Probably the guests leaving," I answered. "I'll go and see what's up."

In my study, Dimitri, Pourichkevitch, and Soukhotin rushed at me, and plied me with questions.

"Well, have you done it? Is it over?"

"The poison hasn't acted," I replied.

They stared at me in amazement.

"It's impossible!" cried the Grand Duke.

"But the dose was enormous! Did he take the whole lot?" asked the others.

"Every bit," I answered.

After a short discussion, we agreed to go down in a body, throw ourselves on Rasputin, and strangle him. We were already on the way down, when I was brought to a halt by the fear that we would ruin the whole scheme by our precipitation: the sudden appearance of a lot of strangers would certainly arouse Rasputin's suspicions. And who could tell what such a diabolical person was capable of doing?

I convinced my friends with great difficulty that it would be best for me to act alone. I took Dimitri's revolver and went back to the basement.

Rasputin sat where I had left him; his head drooping and his breathing labored. I went up quietly and sat down by him, but he paid no attention to me. After a few minutes of horrible silence, he slowly lifted his head and turned vacant eyes in my direction.

"Are you feeling ill?" I asked.

"Yes, my head is heavy and I've a burning sensation in my stomach. Give me another little glass of wine. It'll do me good."

I handed him some Madeira; he drank it at a gulp; it revived him and he recovered his spirits. I saw that he was himself again and that his brain was functioning quite normally. Suddenly he suggested that we should go to the gypsies together. I refused, giving the lateness of the hour as an excuse.

"That doesn't matter," he said. "They're quite used to that; sometimes they wait up for me all night. I'm often detained at Tsarskoïe-Selo by important business, or simply to talk about God. . . . When this happens I drive straight to the gypsies in a car. The body, too, needs a rest . . . isn't it so? All our thoughts belong to God, they are His, but our bodies belong to ourselves: That's the way it is!" added Rasputin with a wink.

I certainly did not expect to hear such talk from a man who had just swallowed an enormous dose of poison. I was particularly struck by the fact that Rasputin, who had a quite remarkable gift of intuition, should be so far from realizing that he was near death. How was it that his piercing eyes had not noticed that I was holding a revolver behind my back, ready to point it at him?

I turned my head and saw the crystal crucifix. I rose to look at it more closely.

"What are you staring at that crucifix for?" asked Rasputin.

"I like it," I replied, "it's so beautiful."

"It is indeed beautiful," he said. "It must have cost a lot. How much did you pay for it?" As he spoke, he took a few steps toward me and, without waiting for an answer, added: "For my part, I like the cabinet better." He went up to it, opened it, and started to examine it again.

"Gregory Efimovitch," I said, "you'd far better look at the crucifix and say a prayer."

Rasputin cast a surprised, almost frightened glance at me. I read in it an expression which I had never known him to have: it was at once gentle and submissive. He came quite close to me and looked me full in the face. It was as though he had at last read something in my eyes, something he had not expected to find. I realized that the hour had come. "O Lord," I prayed, "give me the strength to finish it."

Rasputin stood before me motionless, his head bent and his eyes on the crucifix. I slowly raised the revolver. Where should I aim, at the temple or at the heart?

A shudder swept over me; my arm grew rigid, I aimed at his heart and pulled the trigger. Rasputin gave a wild scream and crumpled up on the bearskin.

For a moment I was appalled to discover how easy it was to kill a man. A flick of the finger and what had been a living, breathing man only a second before, now lay on the floor like a broken doll.

On hearing the shot my friends rushed in, but in their frantic haste they brushed against the switch and turned out the light. Someone bumped into me and cried out; I stood motionless for fear of treading on the body. At last, someone turned the light on.

Rasputin lay on his back. His features twitched in nervous spasms; his hands were clenched, his eyes closed. A bloodstain was spreading on his silk blouse. A few moments later all movement ceased. We bent over his body to examine it.

The doctor declared that the bullet had struck him in the region of the heart. There was no possibility of doubt: Rasputin was dead. Dimitri and Pourichkevitch lifted him from the bearskin and laid him on the flagstones. We turned off the light and went up to my room, after locking the basement door.

Our hearts were full of hope, for we were convinced that what had just taken place would save Russia and the dynasty from ruin and dishonor.

In accordance with our plan, Dimitri, Soukhotin, and the Doctor were to pretend to take Rasputin back to his house, in case the secret police had followed us without our knowing it. Soukhotin was to pass himself off as the starets and, wearing Rasputin's overcoat and cap, would drive off in Pourichkevitch's open car along with Dimitri and the Doctor. They were to return to the Moïka in the Grand Duke's closed car, after which they would take the body to Petrovski Island.

Pourichkevitch and I remained at the Moïka. While we waited for our friends, we talked of the future of our country, now that it was freed once and for all from its evil genius. How could we foresee that those who ought to have seized this unique opportunity would not have the will, or the skill, to do so?

As we talked I was suddenly filled with a vague misgiving; an irresistible impulse forced me to go down to the basement.

Rasputin lay exactly where we had left him. I felt his pulse: not a beat, he was dead.

Scarcely knowing what I was doing I seized the corpse by the arms and shook it violently. It leaned to one side and fell back. I was just about to go, when I suddenly noticed an almost imperceptible quivering of his left eyelid. I bent over and watched him closely; slight tremors contracted his face.

All of a sudden, I saw the left eye open. . . . A few seconds later his right eyelid began to quiver, then opened. I then saw both eyes—the green eyes of a viper—staring at me with an expression of diabolical hatred. The blood ran cold in my veins. My muscles turned to stone. I wanted to run away, to call for help, but my legs refused to obey me and not a sound came from my throat.

I stood rooted to the flagstones as if caught in the toils of a nightmare.

Then a terrible thing happened: with a sudden violent effort Rasputin leapt to his feet, foaming at the mouth. A wild roar echoed through the vaulted rooms, and his hands convulsively thrashed the air. He rushed at me, trying to get at my throat, and sank his fingers into my shoulder like steel claws. His eyes were bursting from their sockets, blood oozed from his lips. And all the time he called me by name, in a low raucous voice.

No words can express the horror I felt. I tried to free myself but was powerless in his vicelike grip. A ferocious struggle began. . . .

This devil who was dying of poison, who had a bullet in his heart, must have been raised from the dead by the powers of evil. There was something appalling and monstrous in his diabolical refusal to die.

I realized now who Rasputin really was. It was the reincarnation of Satan himself who held me in his clutches and would never let me go till my dying day.

By a superhuman effort I succeeded in freeing myself from his grasp.

He fell on his back, gasping horribly and still holding in his hand the epaulette he had torn from my tunic during our struggle. For a while he lay motionless on the floor. Then after a few seconds, he moved. I rushed upstairs and called Pourichkevitch, who was in my study.

"Quick, quick, come down!" I cried. "He's still alive!"

At that moment, I heard a noise behind me; I seized the rubber club Maklakoff had given me (he had said: "one never knows") and rushed downstairs, followed by Pourichkevitch, revolver in hand. We found Rasputin climbing the stairs.

He was crawling on hands and knees, gasping and roaring like a wounded animal. He gave a desperate leap and managed to reach the secret door which led into the courtyard. Knowing that the door was locked, I waited on the landing above, grasping my rubber club.

To my horror and amazement, I saw the door open and Rasputin disappear. Pourichkevitch sprang after him. Two shots echoed through the night. The idea that he might escape was intolerable! Rushing out of the house by the main entrance, I ran along the Moïka to cut him off in case Pourichkevitch had missed him.

The courtyard had three entrances, but only the middle one was unlocked. Through the iron railings, I could see Rasputin making straight for it.

I heard a third shot, then a fourth.... I saw Rasputin totter and fall beside a heap of snow. Pourichkevitch ran up to him, stood for a few seconds looking at the body, then, having made sure that this time all was over, went swiftly into the house. I called, but he did not hear me.

The quay and the adjacent streets were deserted; apparently the shots had not been heard. When I had reassured myself on this point, I entered the courtyard and went up to the snow-heap behind which lay Rasputin. He gave no sign of life.

But, at that moment, I saw two of my servants running up from one side and a policeman from the other.

I went up to the policeman and spoke to him; I stood so as to make him turn his back to the spot where Rasputin lay.

"Your Highness," he said on recognizing me, "I heard revolver shots. What has happened?"

"Nothing of any consequence," I replied, "just a little horseplay. I gave a small party this evening and one of my friends who had drunk a little too much amused himself by firing his revolver into the air. If anyone questions you, just say that everything's all right, and that there is no harm done!"

As I spoke, I led him to the gate. I then returned to the corpse by which the two servants were standing. Rasputin's body still lay in a crumpled heap on the same spot, but his position had changed.

My God, I thought, can he still be alive?

I was terror-stricken at the bare thought that he might suddenly get up again. I ran toward the house, calling Pourichkevitch, who had disappeared indoors. I felt sick, and Rasputin's hollow voice calling my name still rang in my ears. Staggering up to my dressing room, I drank a glass of water. At that moment Pourichkevitch entered the room: "Ah! there you are! I've been looking for you everywhere!" he cried.

My sight was blurred, I thought I was going to faint. Pourichkevitch helped me to my study. We had scarcely reached it when my manservant came to say that the policeman I had talked to a few moments before wished to see me again. The shots, it seems, had been heard from the police station, and my constable, whose beat it was, had been sent for to make a report on what had happened. As his version of the affair was considered unsatisfactory, the police insisted on fuller details.

When the constable entered the room, Pourichkevitch addressed him in a loud voice: "Have you ever heard of Rasputin? The man who plotted to ruin our country, the Czar, and your brother-soldiers? The man who betrayed us to Germany, do you hear?"

Not understanding what was expected of him, the policeman remained silent.

"Do you know who I am?" continued Pourichkevitch. "I am Wladimir Mitrophanovitch Pourichkevitch, member of the Duma. The shots you heard killed Rasputin. If you love your country and your Czar, you'll keep your mouth shut."

I listened with horror to this amazing statement, which came so unexpectedly that I had no chance to interrupt. Pourichkevitch was in such a state of excitement that he did not realize what he was saying.

Finally, the policeman spoke: "You did right and I won't say a word unless I'm put on oath. I would then have to tell the truth as it would be a sin to lie."

Pourichkevitch followed him out.

My manservant then informed me that Rasputin's body had been placed on the lower landing of the staircase. I felt very ill, my head swam, and I could scarcely walk. I rose with difficulty, automatically picked up my rubber club, and left the study.

As I reached the top of the stairs, I saw Rasputin stretched out on the landing, blood flowing from his many wounds. It was a loathsome sight. Suddenly, everything went black, I felt the ground slipping from under my feet, and I fell headlong down the stairs.

Pourichkevitch and Ivan found me, a few minutes later, lying side by side with Rasputin; the murderer and his victim. I was unconscious and he and Ivan had to carry me to my bedroom.

Meanwhile Dimitri, Soukhotin, and Doctor Lazovert came back in a closed car to fetch Rasputin's body. When Pourichkevitch told them what had happened, they decided to let me rest and go off without me. They wrapped the corpse in a piece of heavy linen, shoved it into the car, and drove to Petrovski Island. There, from the top of the bridge, they hurled it into the river.

On regaining consciousness I felt as though I had just recovered from a serious illness. The air I breathed in so deeply seemed fresh, clean, and pure, as after a storm. I seemed to come to life again.

With the help of my servant I washed up all traces of blood which might give us away. When everything was in order I walked out into the courtyard. I had to think of some story to explain the revolver shots. This is what I decided to say: one of my guests while considerably the worse for liquor had tried to shoot one of our watchdogs in the courtyard when he was leaving.

I then sent for the two servants who had seen the end of the tragedy and explained what had really happened. They listened in silence and promised to keep my secret.

It was almost five in the morning when I left the Moïka to return to the Grand Duke Alexander's palace. I felt full of courage and confidence at the thought that the first steps to save Russia had been taken.

I found my brother-in-law Theodore in my room. He had spent a sleepless night, anxiously waiting for me to come back. "Thank God you are here at last," he said. "Well?"

"Rasputin is dead," I replied, "but I'm not in a fit state to talk about it; I am dropping with fatigue."

Realizing that I would need all my strength on the morrow to face the cross-examinations, the investigations, and perhaps even worse, I went to bed and at once fell into a deep sleep.

chapter XXIV

I slept until ten o'clock. I had barely opened my eyes when I was told that General Grigorieff, the police superintendent of our district, wanted to see me on very important business. I dressed quickly and went into the next room where the general was waiting for me.

"Your visit is probably connected with the shots fired in the courtyard of our house last night," I said.

"Exactly. My object is to ask you for a detailed account of what happened. Wasn't Rasputin among your guests?"

"Rasputin never comes to my house," I replied.

"The reason I ask is that the revolver shots that were heard coincided with his disappearance; the Chief Commissioner of Police has ordered me to send him a report as quickly as possible."

The fact that the shots fired at the Moïka were at once connected with Rasputin's disappearance was extremely alarming. I hesitated before answering and chose my words with care: "Who told you that Rasputin had disappeared?"

From what General Grigorieff said, it appeared that the policeman last night had taken fright and had repeated Pourichkevitch's imprudent words to his chiefs.

I tried to look unconcerned. I was bound by the oath we had taken not to divulge our secret. We still hoped to be able to conceal the true facts.

"General, I'm very glad that you came to see me yourself. It would be most unfortunate if a report made by a policeman under a misapprehension were to have any disagreeable consequences."

I then recited my story about the dog shot at by a drunken guest.

I added that when the policeman, on hearing the shots, had rushed in, Pourichkevitch, the last of my guests to leave, had gone up to the man and said a few hurried words in his ear. "I have no idea what they were," I continued, "but from what you say yourself, I presume that Pourichkevitch, who was drunk, must have spoken of the dog, comparing him perhaps to Rasputin and expressing his regret that it was the dog, and not the starets, who had been shot at. Apparently the policeman didn't understand a word of what was told him."

My explanation seemed to satisfy the General, but he wished to know who my other guests had been besides Pourichkevitch.

"I'd rather not give their names," I replied, "as I don't want them to be worried by a lot of unnecessary inquiries about something of so little importance."

"Thank you very much for the information you've given me," said the General, "I'll tell the Chief Commissioner exactly what you said."

I asked him to inform the Commissioner that I would like to see him and would be obliged if he would give me an appointment.

When the police superintendent had left, I was told that Mlle G. was on the telephone.

"What have you done with Gregory Efimovitch?" she cried.

"Gregory Efimovitch? What a strange question!"

"Why strange? Didn't he spend the evening with you yesterday?" Her voice betrayed her agitation. "Where is he? For Heaven's sake, come and see me immediately, I'm in a frightful state."

The prospect of a conversation with her was extremely painful but, alas, unavoidable, and half an hour later I was in her drawing room. She rushed up to me and said in a stifled voice: "What have you done with him? They say he was murdered at your house and that it was you who killed him."

I tried to reassure her and repeated the story I had invented.

"It's all too horrible," she said. "The Empress and Anna are convinced that you murdered him last night at your house."

"Will you telephone to Tsarskoïe-Selo and ask if the Empress will receive me? I'll explain the whole thing to her, but be quick."

Mlle G. telephoned to Tsarskoïe-Selo and was told that Her Majesty was expecting me.

As I was leaving, she took me by the arm: "Don't go to Tsarskoïe-Selo, I beseech you," she said. "Something dreadful will happen to you if you do; they'll never believe you are innocent of the crime. They've completely lost their heads. They are furious with me, and accuse me of having betrayed them. Ah! why did I listen to you? I should never have telephoned to Tsarskoïe-Selo. You mustn't go there!"

Her distress touched me, for it was evident that it was not entirely due to Rasputin's disappearance; she was also genuinely worried about me. "May God protect you," she said in a low voice. "I'll pray for you."

I was just leaving the drawing room when the telephone rang. It was Anna Wirouboff who was calling from Tsarskoïe-Selo to say that the Empress had had a fainting fit; she could not receive me and requested me to send her a written report on all I knew about Rasputin's disappearance.

A short way down the street, I met a friend from the Corps des Pages; he ran up to me, all excited: "Felix, have you heard the news? Rasputin has been killed."

"No, really? Who killed him?"

"It's said he was killed at the gypsies', but no one seems to know who murdered him."

"Thank God!" I cried. "I hope it's true."

On returning to the Grand Duke Alexander's palace, I found a note from the Chief Commissioner of Police, General Balk, requesting me to call on him.

The police headquarters were in a state of ferment; I found the General seated at his desk, looking extremely preoccupied. I told him that I wished to explain the misunderstanding caused by Pourichkevitch's words. I would like to have the matter cleared up as quickly as possible, as I had a few days' leave and was going that same evening to the Crimea, where my family were expecting me.

The Commissioner replied that the explanation I had given General Grigorieff was considered satisfactory and that consequently he saw nothing to prevent my departure, but he warned me that the Empress had given orders to search our house on the Moïka. The

ABOVE: *A photograph found in the author's desk after Rasputin's death*
(I do not remember this photograph having been taken.—F.Y.)
FACING PAGE: *The back of the photograph, inscribed in Rasputin's handwriting, "Bless you, my boy. Live not in darkness, but seek the light.—Gregory."*

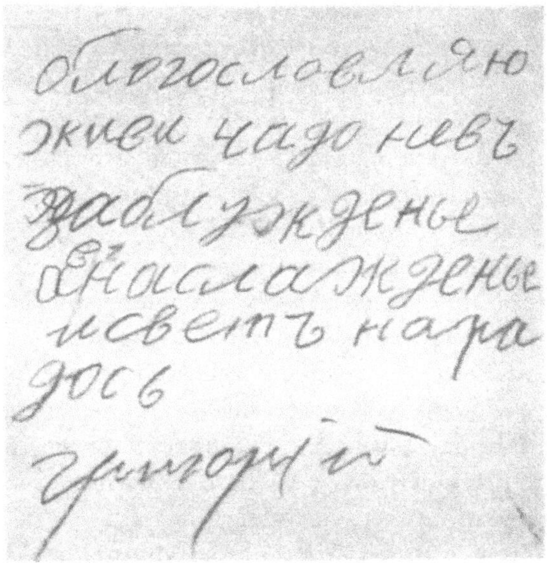
благословляю
экиен чадо невъ
заблужденье
в наслажденье
и светъ нара
досб
Григорій

fact that the shots fired there coincided with Rasputin's disappearance seemed, to say the least of it, suspicious.

I answered: "Our house is occupied by my wife. She is the Emperor's niece, and residences of members of the Imperial family may not be searched without an order from the Emperor himself."

The Commissioner was obliged to agree, and canceled the search warrant on the spot.

I was immensely relieved, as I feared that although we had cleaned the rooms last night something might have escaped us, and a visit from the police was to be avoided at all costs until we were sure that no trace of the murder was left. My mind at rest on that score, I took my leave of General Balk and went back to the Moïka.

On inspecting the scene of the tragedy, I found that my fears were all too well founded. By daylight, dark stains could be clearly seen on the steps. Ivan and I cleaned the whole place thoroughly once again, and when we had finished I went to lunch with Dimitri. Soukhotin came in after lunch. We asked him to go and fetch Pourichkevitch. In view of the fact that we were all leaving town—the Grand Duke for General Headquarters, Pourichkevitch for the front, and myself for the Crimea—it was imperative that we should meet and decide on the line we would take if any one of us were detained in St. Petersburg, or arrested. As soon as Pourichkevitch arrived we agreed, no matter what new evidence was brought up against us, that we would stick to the story I had told General Grigorieff.

And so the first step had been taken; the way lay open to those who had the means of continuing the struggle against Rasputinism. As far as we were concerned, our role was over, for the time being.

I said good-by to my friends and returned to the Moïka. When I got there I was told that all our servants had been questioned during the course of the day. I did not know the result of the examination, and although I considered the procedure somewhat arbitrary, what I heard from my servants left me feeling hopeful.

I decided to go and see Makaroff, the Minister of Justice, to try and discover how the land lay. I found the same confusion at the Ministry of Justice as at police headquarters. I had never seen Makaroff, and took an immediate liking to him. He was an elderly man with gray hair and a beard, a thin face, pleasant features, and a very gentle voice.

I explained to him the reason for my visit and at his request repeated my story about the dog which, by this time, I knew by heart.

When I got to Pourichkevitch's conversation with the policeman, the minister interrupted me: "I know Pourichkevitch very well and I know that he never drinks; what's more, if I am not mistaken, he belongs to a temperance society."

"I assure you that, on this occasion, he belied his reputation for temperance and broke his pledge. It was difficult for him to refuse to drink last night, as I was having a housewarming. If Pourichkevitch is usually as abstemious as you say, a few glasses of wine were probably enough to intoxicate him."

Then I asked the Minister if my servants would be questioned again and whether they were likely to have any further trouble. They were all very worried, as I was leaving for the Crimea that night.

The Minister set my mind at rest: he said that the police would most probably be satisfied with the evidence they had already got. He promised not to allow our house to be searched, and that he would pay no attention to the rumors that were rife. I asked whether I might leave St. Petersburg; he answered in the affirmative and once more expressed his regret for the annoyance I had been caused. I had a strong feeling that neither General Grigorieff, nor the Chief Commissioner, nor the Minister of Justice was taken in by what I had told them.

On leaving the Ministry of Justice, I went to see the President of the Duma, Rodzianko—a distant connection of mine whom I liked very much. Both he and his wife had known of my intention to kill Rasputin, and anxiously awaited news of me. I found them in a highly nervous state. Aunt Rodzianko kissed me tearfully and blessed me. Uncle Rodzianko applauded my conduct in a voice of thunder. Their kindly attitude encouraged and soothed me; I very much appreciated their sincere and warm sympathy; and at this juncture, when I was going through such an ordeal entirely by myself, it was doubly precious. But I could not stay long with them as my train was due to leave at nine, and I still had to pack.

Before I went, I gave them a brief account of the whole affair. "From now on," I told them, "we will do nothing more and will leave to others the task of carrying on our work. Pray God that concerted action will be taken, and that the Emperor's eyes will be opened before it is too late. Such an opportunity will never occur again."

"I am sure that everyone will consider Rasputin's assassination an act of patriotism," replied Rodzianko, "and that all true Russians will unite to save their country."

On reaching the Grand Duke Alexander's palace, the porter told me that the lady with whom I had an appointment at seven o'clock was waiting for me in the small sitting room next to my bedroom.

As I had made no appointment with any lady, I asked the porter to describe the visitor: she was dressed in black, but he could not make out her features as she was wearing a thick veil. This all seemed very mysterious, so I went straight to my room and half-opened the door which communicated with the sitting room. I recognized my visitor as one of Rasputin's most fervent admirers. I called the porter, and told him to tell the lady that I would not be in until very late; after which, I started hurriedly to pack.

As I went down to dinner, I met my friend Oswald Rayner, a British officer whom I had known at Oxford. He knew of our conspiracy and had come in search of news. I hastened to set his mind at ease.

In the dining room I found my wife's three brothers who were also going to the Crimea, their English tutor Mr. Stuart, the Grand Duchess Xenia Alexandrovna's lady-in-waiting Mlle Evreinoff, and several others.

Everyone discussed Rasputin's mysterious disappearance. Some did not believe him to be dead, and said that all the rumors afloat were pure inventions; some, claiming to have it on the best authority, from eye-witnesses even, declared that the starets had been assassinated during an orgy at the gypsies'; others stated that Rasputin's murder had taken place at the Moïka. Although no one thought I had taken an active part in the assassination, they were all convinced that I knew the particulars and hoped that, if enough questions were fired at me, I would give myself away. But I managed to look unconcerned, and took part sincerely in the general rejoicing.

The telephone never stopped ringing. The whole town believed that I was responsible for Rasputin's disappearance. Directors of factories and representatives of various businesses rang up to tell me that their workmen had decided to form a bodyguard to protect me if the need arose.

I told them all that the stories going about were untrue and that I had nothing to do with the matter.

Half an hour before the train left, I said good-by to everybody and drove away with my wife's three brothers, Princes Andrew, Theodore, and Nikita, the latter's tutor, and my friend Captain Rayner. When we got to the station, I noticed a considerable force of police.

Had there been an order for my arrest? I wondered. As I was about to pass the colonel of the military police, he came up to me and mumbled something incomprehensible in a voice shaking with emotion.

"Speak up, Colonel, I can't hear you," I said.

Regaining a little self-assurance, he raised his voice: "By order of Her Majesty the Empress, you are forbidden to leave St. Petersburg. You are to return to the Grand Duke Alexander's palace and stay there until further notice."

"I am sorry," I replied, "that doesn't suit me at all." Then turning to my friends, I repeated the order I had just received. They were extremely surprised at the news of my arrest. "What's the matter? What's happened?" asked poor Mr. Stuart, the English tutor, who had no idea of what was going on.

Andrew and Theodore decided to postpone their journey in order to stay with me. We thought it better, however, for little Nikita to leave for the Crimea with his tutor.

We took them to the train, followed by the police who were probably afraid that I might give them the slip. A large crowd gathered, staring inquisitively at our little group as it moved down the platform, surrounded by the police.

I went into the compartment to say good-by to Nikita; the police looked more and more nervous. I set their minds at rest by declaring that I had no intention of taking French leave.

When the train started, we drove back to the palace. I felt very tired after such an eventful day. I went to my room, asking Theodore and my friend Rayner to stay with me.

A little later, the Grand Duke Nicolas Mikhaïlovitch was announced. His visit at such a late hour boded no good. He had obviously come to find out what had happened; I was tired and did not feel like going over the whole thing again.

Theodore and Rayner left me when the Grand Duke came in: "Well," he said, "what have you been up to?"

"Is it possible that you too believe all that nonsense? The whole business is nothing but a series of misunderstandings. I had nothing to do with it."

"Tell it to the marines! I know all about it. I know every detail, even to the names of the ladies who were at your party."

His last words proved that he knew absolutely nothing, and was only trying to bluff me into talking. I don't know whether or not he believed the story I reeled off once more for his benefit, but he did not want to seem convinced by it, and left looking slightly incredulous and a trifle vexed at not having discovered anything new.

When he had gone, I told my brothers-in-law and Rayner that I had decided to stay with the Grand Duke Dimitri and would move over to his palace the next day. I gave them instructions as to what they were to say if they were questioned. All three promised to carry out my wishes implicitly.

The events of the night before came back to me with horrible intensity; then my mind grew hazy, my head heavy, and I fell asleep.

Early next morning, I went to Dimitri's palace; the Grand Duke was astonished to see me, as he thought I had left for the Crimea. I told him all that had happened since we parted, and asked him if he could put me up, so that we could be together during the anxious days that lay before us.

He then told me that he had been obliged, the evening before, to leave the Michael Theater before the end of the performance so as to escape an ovation from the audience. On returning home, he was told that the Empress believed him to be one of the prime movers in the murder of Rasputin. He had immediately telephoned to Tsarskoïe-Selo to ask for an audience. This had been flatly refused.

A few minutes later I went to the room he had prepared for me, and skimmed through the newspapers. They contained a brief announcement to the effect that the starets Gregory Rasputin had been murdered during the night of December 29.

The morning passed quietly. About one o'clock, while we were still at lunch, General Maximovitch, the Emperor's aide-de-camp, asked to speak to the Grand Duke on the telephone.

Dimitri left the room to answer the call, and returned looking upset: "I'm under arrest by order of the Empress," he said. "She has no right to issue such an order. Only the Emperor can have me arrested."

While we were discussing this unpleasant news, General Maximovitch himself was announced. As soon as he was shown in, he said to the Grand Duke: "Her Majesty the Empress requests his Imperial Highness not to leave his palace."

"Does this mean that I am under arrest?"

"No, you are not under arrest, but Her Majesty insists that you do not leave your palace."

The Grand Duke replied, raising his voice: "I consider that this is equivalent to an arrest. Tell Her Majesty the Empress that I will obey her wish." Coldly saluting General Maximovitch, the Grand Duke left the room.

All the members of the Imperial family who were in St. Petersburg came to call on Dimitri. The Grand Duke Nicolas Mikhaïlovitch came several times a day, or telephoned the wildest, most improbable news, couched in such mysterious terms that we never really knew what it was all about. He always tried to bluff us that he knew all about the conspiracy, hoping by this means to worm our secret out of us.

He took an active part in the search for Rasputin's body. He warned us that the Czarina, convinced of our complicity in Rasputin's assassination, demanded that we be shot at once. He added that this had raised a storm of protest; even Protopopoff had advised her to wait until the Czar returned. The latter was kept in touch with events by telegram, and was expected back shortly.

I heard at the same time from Mlle G. that about twenty of Rasputin's most fervent followers had met in her flat and sworn to avenge him. She had been present, and strongly urged us to take every precaution to protect ourselves against a possible attempt upon our lives.

An endless stream of callers, mostly inquisitive newsmongers, kept us on tenterhooks. We had constantly to be on the alert lest we should give ourselves away by a word or a look which would have been enough to confirm the suspicions of those who harried us with questions. They were often filled with the best intentions, which made things no easier, and we hailed the end of each day with relief.

The rumor of our impending execution caused great agitation among the factory workers, and they decided to form a bodyguard for our protection.

The Czar returned to Tsarskoïe-Selo on the morning of January first. Members of his suite said that he received the news of Rasputin's death without comment, and his cheerfulness had struck those around him. Never since the beginning of the war had he seemed so lighthearted. No doubt he thought that the death of the starets had put an end to the bondage from which he had been too weak to free himself. But no sooner had he reached Tsarskoïe-Selo than he fell once again under the influence of certain of his intimates, and once again his outlook changed.

Although only members of the Imperial family were allowed to enter the Grand Duke's palace, we contrived to receive our friends in secret. Several officers called to assure us that their regiments were ready to protect us. They even went so far as to propose that Dimitri should take the lead in a coup d'état. Many of the Grand Dukes thought that an attempt should still be made to save the régime by a change of rulers. Their plan was to march on Tsarskoïe-Selo by night, along with some of the Guards regiments. The Emperor was to be persuaded to abdicate, the Empress shut up in a convent, and the Czarevitch proclaimed Emperor with the Grand Duke Nicolas Nicolaïevitch as Regent. It was considered that Dimitri's participation in Rasputin's assassination made him the ideal person to head this movement, and they implored him to complete the good work he had begun for the salvation of the nation. The Grand Duke's loyalty did not permit him to accept these proposals.

The very evening of the Emperor's return, the Grand Duke Nicolas Mikhaïlovitch told us that Rasputin's body had been found near the Petrovski Bridge, in a hole in the ice. We heard later that it had been taken to the Veterans' Home at Tchesma, a short distance from St. Petersburg, on the road to Tsarskoïe-Selo. When the post mortem was over, Sister Akoulina, the young nun who had been exorcized by Rasputin, arrived bearing an order from the Czarina and laid out the corpse with the help of a male nurse. She placed a crucifix on the starets' breast and the following message from the Empress in his hands:

> *My dear martyr, give me your blessing, that it may always be with me for the rest of my sorrowful journey on earth. And from Heaven, remember us in your holy prayers!*
>
> Alexandra

On the evening of January first, a few hours after the discovery of Rasputin's body, General Maximovitch came to notify the Grand Duke Dimitri—this time in the Emperor's name—that he was to consider himself under arrest in his palace.

We spent an agitated night. At about three in the morning, several suspicious-looking men, who pretended they had been sent to protect us, tried to make their way into the palace through the back entrance. As they could not produce a written authority, they were turned out, and trustworthy retainers were placed on guard at all the palace entrances.

The next day, as usual, nearly all the members of the Imperial family forgathered in Dimitri's palace; his arrest was on everyone's mind and was the sole topic of conversation. To take such a step against a member of the Imperial family was apparently an event of such importance that everything else faded into the background. It never occurred to anyone that interests far greater than our own were at stake, and that the future of the country and of the dynasty depended on the decisions taken by the Emperor in the days to come; not to speak of the war, which could only be brought to a victorious end if the people and the Sovereign were united. Rasputin's death made a new policy possible, which would have rid Russia once and for all of the network of criminal intrigues in which she was involved.

On the evening of the 3rd, several men of the secret police turned up at the palace. They had been sent by Protopopoff to guard the Grand Duke Dimitri. The latter sent word that he needed no help from the Minister of the Interior, and that he refused to allow the police to enter his palace. Soon after, another guard arrived—a military one, this time—sent by General Kabaloff, Governor of St. Petersburg, at the request of Trepoff, the Prime Minister, who had discovered that Rasputin's followers were plotting to murder us. And so, what with Kabaloff's soldiers watching Protopopoff's spies, we could not complain that we lacked protection.

At the outbreak of war, the Grand Duke had given the first floor of his palace to be used as an Anglo-Russian hospital. This communicated with Dimitri's apartments by a private staircase. Some of

Rasputin's partisans entered the hospital on the pretext of visiting the wounded, but really with the intention of trying to gain access to the Grand Duke's apartments. The attempt failed, for they were stopped at the bottom of the stairs by a sentry, placed there by the head nurse, Lady Sybil Grey.

We lived in a state of siege. We could follow events only in the newspapers or from what our visitors told us. They gave us their views and expressed their personal opinions, but they all seemed chary of taking any initiative, and no one had any concrete plans for the future. Those who could have acted stayed in the background and left Russia to her fate. They were so fainthearted that they could not combine to take joint action.

Toward the end of his reign, Nicolas II was crushed by anxiety and disheartened by his political misadventures. He was a confirmed fatalist, and convinced that it was useless to struggle against destiny. If, however, he had seen the Grand Dukes joining with some of the leading and more loyal politicians in an effort to save Russia, this would have given him the courage and the energy to try to retrieve the situation.

But where were the right men to be found? For many years, Rasputin had by his intrigues demoralized the better elements in the Government, and had sown skepticism and distrust in the hearts of the people. Nobody wanted to take a decision, for nobody believed that any decision would be of any use.

After all our visitors had gone, we summed up what we had heard during the day, and the result was disheartening. All our fine hopes, all the ideals for which we had fought during the dreadful night of December 29, had come to naught. And we realized then how difficult it is to change the course of events even when one is actuated by the loftiest motives, and prepared to make great sacrifices.

Yet we did not give up all hope. The country was with us, full of confidence in the future. A wave of patriotism swept over Russia, particularly in St. Petersburg and in Moscow. The papers published enthusiastic articles, in which they claimed that Rasputin's death meant the defeat of the powers of evil and held out golden hopes for the future. This corresponded with public opinion. Unfortunately the press was not able to express itself so freely for long. On the third day after the starets' disappearance, an order was issued forbidding the papers even to mention the name of Rasputin. This did not prevent the crowds in the streets from giving vent to their feelings. Complete strangers stopped to congratulate each other on the death of the evil genius. People knelt to pray before the Grand Duke's palace, and before our house on the Moïka. The Te Deum was sung in the churches, and at the theaters, audiences insisted on the national anthem being played again and again. We were toasted in regimental messes; factory workers gave cheers in our honor. Letters from all parts of Russia brought us thanks and blessings. True, Rasputin's partisans did not forget us either; they covered us with abuse and uttered dire threats.

Dimitri's sister, the Grand Duchess Marie Pavlovna, arrived from Pskoff where the headquarters of the armies of the North were established; she described the wave of enthusiasm which swept over the troops when they heard that Rasputin was dead. They were convinced that, delivered at last from the starets' evil influence, the Emperor would now be able to choose wise and experienced advisers among his loyal subjects to help him govern the country.

A few days later, my hopes were raised by a summons I received from Trepoff the Prime Minister, but I was once again to be disappointed. He had been ordered by the Emperor to find out at all costs the name of the man who had murdered Rasputin.

I was taken under escort to the Ministry of the Interior. The Minister greeted me in the most friendly way and asked me not to consider him as an official, but as an old friend of the family.

"I presume that you sent for me by order of the Emperor?" I asked.

"That is so."

"Then everything I tell you will be reported to His Majesty?"

"Naturally. I can conceal nothing from my Sovereign."

"In that case, do you really expect me to admit anything, even supposing it was I who killed Rasputin? And do you imagine for one moment that I would give away my accomplices? Be good enough to let His Majesty know that those who killed Rasputin had only one object: to save the Czar and Russia. Excellency," I continued, "allow me to ask you a question, to ask you personally: is it possible that precious time is going to be wasted in tracking Rasputin's assassins at this critical moment when the future of our country is at stake? This is her last chance of salvation. Look at the enthusiasm Rasputin's death has roused all over Russia; look at the panic of his partisans. As to the Czar, I am convinced that at the bottom of his heart he is overjoyed, and expects all of you to help him in his task. Unite and act before it is too late. Is it possible that no one realizes that we are on the eve of a terrible disaster and that, unless there is a radical change in our home policy, the Imperial régime, the Emperor himself, and all his family, will be swept away on the wave of a revolution which threatens to break over Russia and in which we shall all be lost?"

Trepoff listened to me in silence: "Prince," he asked, "where did you gain such self-possession and surprising clearness of vision?"

I left this question unanswered. This was the last attempt we made to win over any of the high government officials.

Meanwhile, Dimitri's fate and mine remained undecided. It was the subject of endless discussions at Tsarskoïe-Selo. On January 3, the Grand Duke Alexander Mikhaïlovitch arrived from Kiev, which was his headquarters as Chief of Military Aviation. On hearing of the danger we were in, he telegraphed the Emperor, asking for an audience. He came to see us for a few minutes before going to Tsarskoïe-Selo.

As a result of his intervention, the Grand Duke Dimitri received the order transmitted by General Maximovitch to leave immediately for Persia, where he was to remain under the supervision of General Baratoff, who commanded a detachment of our troops in that country. General Leiming and Count Koutaïsoff, aide-de-camp to the Emperor, were appointed to go with him; his train left at two in the morning.

I also was exiled from St. Petersburg. I was to go that night to our estate of Rakitnoïe and remain there until further orders. Captain Zentchikoff, instructor at the Corps des Pages, and Ignatieff, an agent of the secret police, were to go with me and see that I spoke to no one until I reached my destination.

Both Dimitri and I hated being separated. We had grown to know each other better in the few days we had spent together as prisoners in his palace than in all the long years of our friendship. What high hopes we had had! . . . And all our golden dreams had come to naught! When should we meet again, and under what circumstances? The future was black, and we were filled with dark forebodings.

At half past twelve, the Grand Duke Alexander Mikhaïlovitch came to take me to the station. The platform was closed to the public, and detachments of police were stationed everywhere.

I entered my coach with a heavy heart. The bell rang, the engine whistled shrilly, the platform seemed to glide away and disappear. St. Petersburg vanished into the night as the train started on its lonely journey across the shadowy plains which lay asleep under the snow. My thoughts were dark indeed as the wheels thudded monotonously over the tracks.

chapter XXV

The journey was long and unpleasant, but I had the delightful surprise of finding Irina and my parents at Rakitnoïe. They had been warned of my arrival by my father-in-law, and had immediately left the Crimea to join me, leaving our daughter and her nurse at Aï-Todor.

I knew that my letters would be opened by the police, so I had been unable to write more than a few brief words to my wife. My family, therefore, knew nothing of the events in St. Petersburg, beyond what people were saying, and had naturally been seriously alarmed. Two telegrams received almost simultaneously put the finishing touch to their anxiety. One from the Grand Duchess Elisabeth in Moscow ran thus: "My prayers and thoughts are with you all. God bless your dear son for his patriotic act." The other, from St. Petersburg, was from the Grand Duke Nicolas Mikhaïlovitch: "Body found—Felix quite calm." My part in Rasputin's assassination had all at once become official.

Irina told me that she had wakened during the night of December 29 and, on opening her eyes, had suddenly seen Rasputin. He was dressed in an embroidered silk blouse and seemed immensely tall. The vision lasted only a second.

My arrival at Rakitnoïe did not pass unnoticed, but the inquisitive found that strict orders had been given that no one was to be admitted. I had a visit from the magistrate entrusted with the inquiry into Rasputin's death. Our meeting was a complete farce. I expected to see a cold and dignified official, severe and uncompromising, with whom I would have to wage a battle of wits. But instead, I found a man so deeply moved and so emotional that I thought he was going to fling himself into my arms. During lunch, he rose to make a patriotic speech and to drink my health. The conversation turned on life in the country, and my father asked him if he was fond of shooting. "No," replied the worthy official, who had a one-track mind, "I've never shot anybody." He looked very uncomfortable when he realized what he had said.

After lunch, he and I had a long talk. For some time he talked at random not knowing how to broach the subject. I came to his rescue by telling him that I had nothing to add to my previous statements. He at once seemed much relieved, and during the rest of our conversation Rasputin's name was not even mentioned.

Life at Rakitnoïe was monotonous. We often went for long sleigh drives. It was a beautiful winter, cold and dry. The sun shone brightly and there was not a breath of wind, so we could drive in open sleighs with the temperature well below zero, without feeling the cold. In the evening, we read aloud.

The news from St. Petersburg was most alarming. It was obvious that the people had all lost their heads and that the *debacle* was imminent.

The Revolution broke out on March 12. Buildings all over the capital were set on fire, and there was heavy shooting in the streets. A great part of the Army and of the police joined the Revolution—among them the Cossacks of the Household, the elite of the Imperial Guard.

After long discussions with the Soviet of Workmen's and Soldiers' Representatives, a Provisional Government was formed under the presidency of Prince Lvow, with Kerensky as Minister of Justice at the demand of the Socialist Party.

The Emperor abdicated on March 15. So as not to be separated from his delicate son, he handed over the crown to his brother, the Grand Duke Michael. The text of this historic document is well known, and I recall its noble words with the deepest emotion:

We, Nicolas II, by the grace of God Emperor of all the Russias, Czar of Poland, Grand Duke of Finland, etc., etc., hereby make known to all Our loyal subjects:

At this time of bitter strife against a foe who for nearly three years has been striving to invade Our country, it has pleased God to send down on Russia a fresh and grievous trial. The disturbances which have begun in our midst threaten to have a disastrous effect on the conduct of this fearful and relentless struggle. The destiny of Russia, the honor of Our heroic army, the welfare of the people, the whole future of Our beloved country, make it imperative that the war be brought at all costs to a victorious end.

The enemy is making his last efforts, and the hour is at hand when Our valiant army, with the help of Our gallant Allies, will defeat him conclusively.

In these decisive days so critical for the very existence of Russia, We deem it Our duty to do Our utmost to facilitate the close union of Our people so that in a common effort of the whole nation a rapid and decisive victory may be won.

That is why, in agreement with the Duma of the Empire, We have thought fit to abdicate the throne of Russia and relinquish Our sovereign power.

Not wishing to be parted from Our beloved son, we bequeath Our heritage to Our brother, the Grand Duke Michael Alexandrovitch, and we give him Our blessing on His accession to the throne. We urge Him to govern Russia in close communion with the Representatives of the legislative Assemblies, and to swear inviolable allegiance to them in Our beloved country's name.

We appeal to all the loyal sons of Russia, and ask them to fulfill their sacred and patriotic duty by obeying the Czar and, in this time of grave national crisis, helping Him, together with the Representatives of the Nation, to lead the Russian State into the path of glory, prosperity, and victory. God save Russia!

NICOLAS

On the following day, March 16, the Grand Duke Michael signed his provisional abdication. Kerensky, who had practically extorted this from him, was most eloquent in his thanks.

The government having given the Emperor "permission" to bid farewell to the Army, the Dowager Empress and my father-in-law immediately left for Kiev, and from there went to General Headquarters in Mohilev.

At the station, Nicolas II remained alone with his mother in her private train for two hours. Their conversation was not divulged.

When my father-in-law was invited to join them, the Empress was weeping bitterly. The Czar stood motionless and silent, smoking.

The Provisional Government yielded to the demands of the Soviet and ordered the Czar's immediate arrest. The infamous order of the day Number One was published; it empowered the soldiers to choose their own officers and to form regimental soviets, and it abolished saluting. This meant the end of all military discipline. In certain garrisons the men were already massacring their officers. It was the end of the Russian Imperial army.

Three days later, the Emperor left for Tsarskoïe-Selo where he was to be interned with his family. He wore a plain khaki tunic and the cross of St. George. His train was standing side by side with that of the Dowager Empress, who stood weeping at the window. She made the sign of the cross and a gesture of benediction. As the train moved out, the Czar waved good-by. This was the last time he was to see his mother.

On reaching Tsarskoïe-Selo, the Emperor was forsaken by all. The only one to accompany him to the Alexander Palace was Prince W. Dolgoroukoff.

I was allowed to leave Rakitnoïe at the end of March and we all returned to St. Petersburg. Before we left, a service was held at Rakitnoïe; the church was full of weeping peasants. "And how are we going to live?" they asked. "Our Czar has been taken from us!"

At Kharkov station we wanted to go to the buffet. We had to force our way through a crowd of jostling men and women hailing each other as "comrade." Someone recognized me and spoke my name. The crowd closed in on us, and in their enthusiasm started to shove and push, till we were almost suffocated. I had the unpleasant feeling that the very people who were cheering us today might just as easily lynch us tomorrow. Some soldiers came to our help, and cleared a way for us to the refreshment room. The crowd tried to rush in after us, and the doors had to be closed. They called on me to make a speech but I refused, saying that I was unable to speak in public. Just then, we were told that the train in which the Grand Duke Nicolas Nicolaïevitch was returning from the Caucasus had arrived in the station. To reach him, we had to make our way once more through the howling mob, which was now cheering the Grand Duke. He embraced me warmly, exclaiming: "At last we'll be able to triumph over Russia's enemies!" Our meeting was brief, as his train was leaving almost immediately. On getting back to ours, I met a singer called Altchevsky in the corridor. He told me that he had been in the country getting treatment for a serious nervous complaint; he came into our compartment and offered to sing for us. Suddenly in the middle of a song he stopped, and staring at me wildly asked: "Why are you looking at me like that? I can't sing any more." Taken aback, I begged him to continue, but he refused and launched into a long diatribe in a voice which grew louder and louder. His shouting attracted the attention of a friend of his in the next compartment who managed to find a doctor on the train to give him an injection. But in the dead of night, his howls echoed through the train, louder than ever. In the general atmosphere of strain and tension, this ghastly encounter with a madman was the highlight of our nightmare journey.

We found St. Petersburg very much changed. The confusion in the streets was indescribable. Most people were wearing red cockades. Our own chauffeur had thought it would be prudent to wear a red bow when meeting us at the station. "Take it off!" my mother cried indignantly.

One of the first things I did was to see the Grand Duchess Elisabeth in Moscow; I had not seen her since the tragic events in March. She came up to me with her eyes full of tears, and blessed and kissed me. "Poor Russia," she said, "what a terrible ordeal lies ahead of her! But we must bow before the will of Heaven. We are helpless. We can only pray and beseech God's mercy."

She listened with close attention to my account of the tragic night of December 29. "You could not act otherwise," she said when I had finished. "You made a supreme attempt to save your country and the dynasty. It is not your fault if the result is not what you hoped for. The fault lies with those who failed to do their duty. It was no crime to kill Rasputin; you destroyed a fiend who was the incarnation of evil. Nor is there any merit in what you did: you were destined to do it, just as anyone else might have been."

She told me that a few days after Rasputin's death the mothers superior of several convents had come to see her, to tell her of the disturbing events that had taken place in the communities on December 29. During the night offices, priests had suddenly gone mad, blaspheming and shrieking; nuns ran about the corridors howling like souls possessed and lifting their skirts with obscene gestures.

"The Russian people cannot be held responsible for events to come," continued the Grand Duchess. "Poor Nicky, poor Alix, what suffering awaits them! God's will be done. But even though all the powers of hell may be let loose, Holy Russia and the Orthodox Church will remain unconquered. Some day, in this ghastly struggle, Virtue will triumph over Evil. Those who keep their Faith will see the Powers of Light vanquish the Powers of Darkness. God punishes and pardons."

From the day of our arrival in St. Petersburg, our house on the Moïka was filled with a continuous stream of people; we found this very exhausting. Michael Rodzianko, President of the Duma and a distant relative, was among our most frequent visitors. One day my mother sent for me. Irina and I went up to see her and found her deep in conversation with Rodzianko. The latter rose as I came in, walked up to me, and said point-blank: "Moscow wishes to proclaim you Emperor. What do you say to that?"

This did not come as a surprise, as I had been approached several times since our return by people of different classes: officers, politicians, priests. Later on, Admiral Koltchak and the Grand Duke Nicolas Mikhaïlovitch also discussed the matter with me. The Grand Duke said: "The throne of Russia is neither hereditary nor elective: it is usurpatory. Take advantage of the circumstances; you hold all the trumps. Russia cannot go on without a monarch, and the Romanoffs are discredited; the people don't want them back."

I was deeply dismayed by the irony of the situation. The very man who had killed Rasputin in order to save the dynasty was himself requested to play the part of usurper!

Meanwhile, I was becoming very anxious about Dimitri, who had fallen ill at Teheran and was in despair at being so far from home.

The author in 1918

• • • • • • • • • chapter XXVI

Life in St. Petersburg grew daily more depressing. Revolutionary ideas had spread to all classes, even to the well-to-do and to the people who had always considered themselves conservatives. Rosanoff, a Russian author who had escaped the general contagion and remained unbiased, describes in a play entitled *The Revolution and the Intellectuals* the predicament in which the liberals found themselves when faced with the triumph of the Soviets: "After witnessing an admirable performance of the Revolution with the keenest enjoyment, the intellectuals wanted to fetch their warm fur-lined overcoats and return to their fine comfortable homes; but the coats had been stolen and the houses burned."

In the spring of 1917, many people left St. Petersburg and sought refuge in the Crimea. The Grand Duchess Xenia and her three eldest sons, my parents, and Irina and I, followed the general exodus. The wave of revolution had not yet reached southern Russia, and the Crimea was comparatively safe.

My young brothers-in-law, who had remained at Aï-Todor, told us that when news of the Revolution reached the Crimea the inhabitants of the two neighboring villages came to congratulate them on the change of regime—singing the Marseillaise and waving red flags. M. Niquille, their Swiss tutor, took the children and their governesses out onto a balcony from which he harangued the crowd. His country, he said, had been a republic for three hundred years, everyone there was perfectly happy, and he wished the same to the Russian people. Frenzied applause greeted this speech. Feeling extremely embarrassed, the poor boys did not know which way to look, but it all ended peaceably and the enthusiastic demonstrators went home singing the Marseillaise.

The Dowager Empress, accompanied by my father-in-law, her youngest daughter, the Grand Duchess Olga Alexandrovna, and the latter's husband, Colonel Koulikovsky, also arrived at Aï-Todor.

After the Emperor was arrested, the Empress Marie, who wanted to be as near her son as possible, stubbornly refused to leave Kiev. Fortunately the Government ordered all members of the Imperial family then in Kiev to leave the town. The local Soviet having given their approval, preparations were made for leaving at once, but it was not an easy matter to persuade the Empress to go.

Life in the Crimea was peaceful enough until May. But, as our stay there threatened to be a long one, I thought I ought to see what was happening to our house on the Moïka and also to the hospital in our house in Liteinaïa Street. I left for St. Petersburg with my brother-in-law Theodore, who insisted on coming with me. I brought back with me two Rembrandts, which were among the finest portraits in our picture gallery: "The Man in the Large Hat" and "The Woman with the Fan." Unframed and rolled up, the paintings were easy to carry.

Our journey back to the Crimea took place under most unpleasant conditions. A crowd of soldiers who had demobilized themselves, but kept their arms, filled the train. There were as many piled on the roofs of the coaches as inside them. In fact one coach collapsed under their weight. As they were all more or less intoxicated, several fell off during the journey. The farther south we went, the more crowded the train became, chiefly owing to the civilians who were seeking shelter in the Crimea. Eight of us, including an old woman and two children, were huddled together in what was once a compartment of a sleeping car.

We reached the Crimea at the same time as the all-too-famous Brechko-Brechkovskaïa, nicknamed "the grandmother of the Russian Revolution," who came to the Crimea for a rest after her long imprisonment in Siberia. She traveled in the Imperial train, and Kerensky had placed the Palace of Livadia at her disposal. The city of Yalta, gay with red bunting, turned out to give this old termagant a rousing welcome. The most ridiculous stories went round about the Brechkovskaïa. Popular report had it that she was the daughter of Napoleon I and a Muscovite shop assistant. On arriving at the station in Yalta, the crowds hailed her with cries of "Long live Napoleon!"

While we were in St. Petersburg, an alarming incident had disturbed the peaceful life of Aï-Todor.

One morning at dawn, my father-in-law was wakened by the barrel of a revolver being pressed against his forehead. A band of sailors, sent by the Sebastopol Soviet with a search warrant, had invaded the house. The Grand Duke was requested to hand over his keys and any arms he might possess. The Dowager Empress was forced to get up and allow her bed to be searched. Standing behind a screen and powerless to protest, she saw the leader of the gang make off with her papers and private correspondence; he had already taken all my father-in-law's papers. He even seized an old Bible which the Empress had had with her since the day she left Denmark to marry the Emperor Alexander III. The search lasted the whole morning. Nothing was found in the way of weapons excepting some twenty old Winchester rifles which came from a yacht my father-in-law used to own. In the afternoon the officer commanding the search party, an extremely disagreeable and arrogant man, informed the Grand Duke that he was obliged to arrest the Empress—"Marie Feodorovna," as he called her—as she had, according to him, insulted the Provisional Government. My father-in-law managed with great difficulty to calm him down. He reminded him that it was not customary to allow sailors to enter an old lady's room at five in the morning, and that it was natural for her to resent it.

This individual was to rise to an important post in the Bolshevik government, but eventually came to a bad end and was shot.

That the Provisional Government had allowed Aï-Todor to be searched was a further proof of their weakness. Acting on trumped-up information about the anti-revolutionary activities of my father-in-law's family, the St. Petersburg Soviet had insisted on a search warrant being issued by the Crimean authorities.

On hearing of what had happened, Irina hastened to Aï-Todor, but was not allowed to enter. There were guards at every entrance and even on the little footpaths known only to those familiar with the estate. It was only when the search party had left that she was able to join her family.

From then on, the inmates of Aï-Todor were subjected to every kind of annoyance. A guard of some twenty soldiers and sailors, all of them rough and insolent, settled down on the estate. The commissar who accompanied them produced a set of regulations by which the prisoners had to abide. After a list of things they were not allowed to do came the names of the people they were permitted to receive: Irina, myself, the boys' tutors, the doctor, and certain tradesmen. From time to time, and without the shadow of a reason, they were forbidden to see anyone, even Irina; then, without further explanation, the ban was lifted.

On my return to the Crimea, when Irina told me what was happening, we agreed that she ought to see Kerensky and ask him to intervene. So we left for St. Petersburg once more, but it was a whole month before Irina could get an audience with the head of the Provisional Government.

On reaching the Winter Palace she met a few old servants whose joy on seeing her again was very touching. She was shown into the Emperor Alexander II's study. Kerensky came in almost immediately; he was most polite and even a little embarrassed. He asked his visitor to sit down, and she immediately chose her great-grandfather's armchair, thereby obliging the head of the Government to take the seat reserved for visitors. As soon as he understood what had brought her, Kerensky tried to explain that it was no responsibility of his. But Irina paid no attention and continued her narrative without sparing him a single detail. In the end she had to be satisfied with his promise to do what he could, and left her ancestor's palace forever, after saying good-by to the staff for the last time.

In spite of what was happening and the general uneasiness, social gatherings were numerous in St. Petersburg. Even during the darkest days, young people must find an outlet for their high spirits.

Small parties were given almost every night, either at the Moïka or at the houses of friends who were still in town. We even spent an evening at Tsarskoïe-Selo with the Grand Duke Paul Alexandrovitch. After dinner his two daughters Irene and Natalie gave a charming performance of a French play written for them by their brother Wladimir. The Grand Duke Nicolas Mikhaïlovitch paid us long visits, always thundering against everything and everybody.

Toward the end of our stay in St. Petersburg the Bolsheviks made their first attempt to seize power. Trucks filled with troops drove through the city, shooting off machine guns; soldiers crouching on the running boards shot at any unfortunate pedestrians who had failed to take cover. The streets were strewn with the dead and wounded; the capital was in a state of panic. This time, however, the insurrection petered out and comparative calm was restored for a time.

Shortly after this, we returned to the Crimea. During our absence an inquiry had been held at Aï-Todor, following a complaint lodged by my father-in-law about thefts committed by the search party in May. All the inmates of the house were questioned separately. When the Dowager Empress' turn came she was requested to sign her statement: "the *ex*-Empress Marie." She picked up a pen and signed: "the widow of Emperor Alexander III."

It was not till a month later that Kerensky's emissary arrived on the scene. He was scared of everybody and everything, and did nothing whatever to improve conditions.

In August we heard that the Czar and his family had been taken to Tobolsk, in Siberia. Whether this measure had been forced upon the Government by the Bolsheviks or whether, as Kerensky stated, it was a first step toward action against them, it was impossible not to be extremely anxious about their fate. King George V had invited them to come to England, but this had met with the opposition of the British government in the person of Lloyd George. The King of Spain had also offered them hospitality, but the Emperor had refused, saying that no matter what happened neither he nor his family would ever leave Russia.

* * *

When autumn came, I decided to go to St. Petersburg again; I wanted to find a hiding place for our jewels and more valuable objets d'art. When I arrived I set to work at once with the help of the most trustworthy of our servants. I then went to the Anichkoff Palace and took out of its frame, and rolled up, a large portrait of the Emperor Alexander III which the Empress Marie was particularly fond of and had asked me to bring back with me. Unfortunately I came too late to save her jewels; they had been taken to Moscow by order of the Provisional Government. When I had completed my task at the Moïka, I went to Moscow with our faithful major-domo, Gregory Boujinsky. I took all our diamonds with me as I wanted to conceal them separately. The hiding place I chose was a recess under one of the staircases. I have already told how, thanks to Gregory Boujinsky's heroic devotion, this hiding place escaped the Bolshevists' investigations for a long time. Our jewels fell into their hands eight years later, when some workmen discovered them while repairing a step.

Before leaving Moscow I had a long talk with the Grand Duchess Elisabeth, whom I found full of courage. She had few illusions about the seriousness of the situation and was greatly alarmed over the fate of the Emperor and his family. After a short prayer in the chapel I took leave of the Grand Duchess, with a heavy foreboding that I should never see her again.

I left that same evening for St. Petersburg. The day after I arrived, the Provisional Government collapsed and the Bolshevik party, with Lenin and Trotsky at its head, assumed power. Indescribable confusion reigned in the capital; bands of soldiers and sailors broke into people's houses, pillaging and murdering. The town was in the hands of a frenzied, bloodthirsty populace, eager for destruction.

Those were days and nights of terror and anguish. One evening I witnessed a horrible scene from my window: a group of sailors had fallen on an old general; they were kicking him, and had half-stunned him with the butts of their rifles. The wretched man dragged himself along the ground, whimpering piteously. To my horror, I saw the blood streaming from two gaping holes in his swollen face, where his eyes had once been.

Many friends, and even strangers, took refuge at the Moïka, thinking they would be safer there. It was quite a problem to house and feed them all. One day a detachment of soldiers came to occupy the house. I showed them over it, and tried to make them understand that it was more fitted to be a museum than a barracks. They went away without pressing their point, but obviously meaning to come back.

A few days later, on leaving my room I stumbled over the bodies of some soldiers sleeping, fully armed, on the marble floor. An officer came up to me and said that he had been ordered to guard my house. I did not like this at all; it meant that the Bolsheviks considered me a sympathizer, which was a compliment I did not appreciate in the least. I decided to leave immediately for the Crimea. That same evening a young officer whom I knew, and who commanded our district, came to see me with a stranger in civilian clothes. They told me I was to leave St. Petersburg at once, and suggested that I should accompany them to Kiev. They handed me some faked identity papers which they had brought for me, saying they would call for me and take me to the station.

As this fell in with my own plans, I thought it best to obey what seemed more like an order than a piece of advice. As a matter of fact, I felt quite excited by the adventure. What could their intentions be? I wondered what awaited me. As I got into the car with them, I noticed that a great red cross had been painted on the front of our house.

The train was crammed; people, as usual, sat on the tops of the coaches, the windows of which were all broken and the blinds torn down. To my great surprise I was led to a private compartment, apparently reserved for us, which was then locked, and we spent a peaceful and comfortable night.

At Kiev, the hotels were full. The officer invited me to stay with him but I was not anxious to accept his hospitality. However, the only alternative was sleeping in the streets, so we got into a cab and drove off. I suddenly saw a friend of mine, Princess Gagarine, coming out of one of the houses. She recognized me and waved to me. I stopped the cab and asked my companion to wait while I went to speak to her. She seemed surprised to see me. "What are you doing here?" she asked. "And how have you managed to find a room?"

"I wish I knew myself what I was doing here," I answered, "and I have got a room, but I am not very happy about it."

She then offered to put me up, and I eagerly accepted. The next day I heard that the telegraph was still working, so I set out for the post-office to send my family a wire; they had been without news of me for some time and must have been anxious. But this proved no easy matter. Conditions were as bad as in St. Petersburg. There was a lot of firing going on in the streets, and one ran the risk of being hit by a stray bullet. Occasionally sporadic outbursts of machine-gun fire swept the pavements. I got to the post-office as best I could, dodging around corners, hiding in doorways, and lying flat on my stomach each time the firing came nearer. My hostess was appalled to see me return with my clothes all torn, my face and hands covered with mud.

My friend the officer came to see me a few days later, and told me that his house had been destroyed by a bomb the night before. He owed his life to the fact that, quite by chance, he had not slept there.

One morning, glancing through the newspaper, I saw that the police were on the track of a well-known criminal. I suddenly realized that my fake papers were made out in his name. I immediately got in touch with the officer, who produced a second set of papers with the greatest of ease.

At the end of a week I told him that I had no intention of staying in Kiev indefinitely. I had nothing to do there, and meant to join my family in the Crimea; but, before that, I wanted to go back to St. Petersburg and pick up the valuables I had left there when I came away in a hurry. This did not seem to suit the officer at all. However, he promised to let me know when it would be possible for us to go; he seemed determined not to part company with me. Two days later, he came back: "Be ready to leave tomorrow." He called for me the next day, accompanied by his mysterious acolyte.

At the station in St. Petersburg, I bought a newspaper and read: "Prince Youssoupoff has been arrested and imprisoned in the Fortress of St. Peter and St. Paul."

I handed the paper to my companions.

"Are you sure of your servants?" asked the officer.

"Absolutely sure."

"In that case, go home and don't move until you hear from me. Don't see a soul and don't answer the telephone. I hope to be able to get you off to the Crimea very soon."

I turned up my collar and set out for the Moïka. When I arrived I found my servants in tears. They had read of my arrest in the papers and were overjoyed to see me. In spite of the advice I had been given, I did see a few trusted friends. A few days later, still accompanied by my guardian angels, I left for the Crimea. Again a compartment had been booked for us and everything went smoothly. My efforts to get an explanation from my mysterious companions were all in vain: they met all my questions with blank silence. They both got out at Baktchisaraï and I have never seen them since. I found out later on that they were both Freemasons and were apparently acting on instructions issued by their Order. In any case, whatever their motives were, I feel I owe them a deep debt of gratitude.

Judging by the big Delaunay-Belleville car which met me at the station, flying a pennant with an enormous crown on it and our coat of arms on the doors, life in the Crimea was still comparatively normal. A few months previously, after a long struggle to maintain discipline, Admiral Koltchak, who was then commander-in-chief in the Black Sea, broke the Golden Sword he had been awarded for outstanding valor, threw the pieces into the sea, and resigned his command. Then one day soon after my arrival, the Black Sea Fleet went over to the Bolsheviks. There followed a terrible massacre of naval officers in Sebastopol. Bands of sailors broke into houses, looting and murdering, raping women and children in front of their husbands and parents; torturing men to discover their valuables. I happened to see some of these sailors, pearl and diamond necklaces hanging on their hairy chests, their arms and fingers loaded with bracelets and rings. Among them were youngsters of fifteen. Many were grotesquely powdered and made up. It was like a masquerade in hell. In Yalta, mutineers tied stones to the feet of their officers before shooting them, and then tossed their bodies into the sea. Later, a diver sent down to explore the bottom of the bay went out of his mind at the sight of these corpses standing upright in ghostly array and swaying in the current. We were never sure, on going to bed at night, of waking up alive in the morning. One afternoon a band of sailors came to Yalta to arrest my father. I told them that he was ill, and asked to be shown their warrant. Of course they did not have one, and I played for time by telling them to go and fetch one. After endless discussions, two of them reluctantly consented. As they had not returned several hours later, their companions grew tired of waiting, and left.

A few days later, another band of sailors came down from the hills behind Koreïz. They called themselves "naval cavalry." They were well-known for their cruelty and were dreaded even by the Soviets. Armed to the teeth and mounted on stolen horses, they rode into our courtyard brandishing flags with the most promising slogans such as "Death to the bourgeois! Death to the anti-revolutionaries! Death to the landlords!" A terrified servant came to tell me that they were demanding food and wine. I went into the courtyard. Two of the sailors dismounted and came to meet me. They had degenerate and brutal faces; one wore a diamond bracelet, the other a brooch. Their uniforms were stained with blood. They said they wanted to speak to me in private, so I took them to my room after sending the rest of the band to the kitchen for refreshments. Irina's face was a study when she saw me come in with my two ruffians! I sent for some wine and we all four settled down to a cosy talk. Our visitors did not seem at all embarrassed, but stared at us with curiosity. Suddenly one of them asked me if I was really the man who had murdered Rasputin, and on receiving my reply they both drank to my health, declaring that that being the case neither my family nor I had anything to fear from them. They began recounting their heroic feats against the White Army. Then, catching sight of my guitar, they asked me to sing. I did so, feeling rather relieved to put a stop to their unsavory reminiscences. I sang several songs and they joined in the choruses; one bottle after another was emptied and our guests got more and more boisterous. My parents, whose room was above mine, wondered what all the noise was about. But all things come to an end, and the sailors finally went off after shaking hands with us again and again, and thanking us effusively for our hospitality. The whole band jumped into their saddles, waved farewell in the most friendly fashion, and brandishing their flags disappeared into the hills.

Kerensky's commissar at Aï-Todor had been dismissed and a new man appointed by the Soviets. My father-in-law, in his book, describes this arrival as follows:

> *We are feeling the effects of the new Revolution. Djordjuliani, our head jailer, has been replaced by a sailor called Zadorojny. I was introduced to him on his arrival, in the room occupied by our guards. He is an enormous, savage-looking brute, yet there is a certain kindliness about him withal. Most fortunately our first conversation was in private, and from the beginning he was extremely polite. I asked him where he had served. In the Air Force, he replied, adding that he had seen me several times at Sebastopol. We then talked about the general situation, and from what he said I gathered that he was on our side, although he frankly admitted that he had at first allowed himself to be drawn into the revolutionary movement. . . . We parted the best of friends. It is a great comfort to know that we can depend on him. He treats us roughly before his comrades to disguise his real feelings.*

Meanwhile a man by the name of Spiro appeared at Aï-Todor and assembled all its inmates for a roll call. The Dowager Empress refused to come down, merely showing herself for an instant at the top of the stairs.

Zadorojny first came to Aï-Todor in December; in February he told my father-in-law that all the Romanoffs residing in the Crimea were to be interned along with their suites at Dulber, an estate belonging to the Grand Duke Peter Nicolaïevitch. He explained that this was being done to ensure their safety. It appeared that the Yalta Soviet was insisting on their immediate execution, whereas the Sebastopol Soviet—from which Zadorojny took his orders—wanted to await Comrade Lenin's instructions, and feared that the Yalta Soviet might attempt to seize the prisoners by force. The reason why Dulber had been chosen was that it would eventually prove easier to defend than Aï-Todor, as it had high thick walls and was more like a fortress than a palace. Among those who were interned were: the Dowager Empress, my parents-in-law and their six sons; the Grand Duke Nicolas Nicolaïevitch, his wife, and her two children from a first marriage; the Grand Duke Peter and the Grand Duchess Militza and their children, Princess Marina and Prince Roman. As for their youngest daughter, Princess Nadejda who was married to Prince Orloff, the Grand Duchess Olga Alexandrovna, and my wife, who were all married morganatically, they were allowed to go free.

At Dulber, the prisoners were completely cut off from the rest of the world. The only person allowed to visit them was our daughter Irina, then two years old. Through her, we managed to communicate with them. Her nurse took her to the gates of the park and the child entered it alone, with our letters pinned inside her coat. The answers reached us in the same way. Our little messenger never let us down. The conditions in Dulber were none too good; things were very uncomfortable and food was very scarce. Korniloff, the chef, who later kept a famous restaurant in Paris, did the best he could with the little he had: mostly buckwheat and pea soup. Once, for a treat, the prisoners of Dulber had donkey for lunch and billy goat for dinner.

Knowing that her brothers were allowed out in the park, my wife invented a system by which we could communicate with them. We used to go for a walk with our dogs under the walls of the estate. Irina would call the dogs and instantly one of her brothers would appear on top of the wall. If he caught sight of a jailer, he would slip to the ground and we walked on looking as innocent as we could. Unfortunately our stratagem was found out before long.

I met Zadorojny one afternoon and we walked a little way together. After asking for news of his prisoners, I told him that there was something I wanted to speak to him about; he seemed surprised and a little embarrassed. Presumably he did not want his men to see him with me. So I asked him to come one evening to my house, where he could be sure of not meeting anyone he knew. To get into the house unobserved, all he had to do was to climb over the balcony of my room, which was on the ground floor. He came that evening and several times afterward. My wife was often present at our meetings. We spent hours trying to find some way of saving the Empress Marie and her family.

It became more and more evident that this fearsome-looking giant was sincerely devoted to us. He explained that he was fighting for time by exploiting the rivalry that existed between the two soviets: that of Yalta which wanted to shoot the royal prisoners on the spot, and that of Sebastopol which, in agreement with Moscow, wanted them to be tried. I suggested his telling the Yalta Soviet that the Romanoffs were shortly going to be transferred to Moscow for trial, and that if they were shot out of hand important state secrets, known only to them, would be lost. Zadorojny took my advice. He had managed to protect his prisoners until then, but the situation grew daily more difficult, as the Yalta Soviet suspected that he was trying to save them, and his own life was in danger. A few days later he came to our house in the middle of the night to tell me that he had received information from a reliable source that a large party of sailors was coming the next day to take the prisoners to Yalta and shoot them. He had decided to be away when they arrived, as he was sure of his men and knew that in his absence they would not allow anyone to enter the estate. He added that the young princes had already, for several nights, taken turns at mounting guard, and that arms were held in readiness for them in case of alarm. He also announced that there was going to be a general massacre in which no one would escape. . . . The news was all the more unpleasant as we were incapable of defending ourselves, for all our arms had been confiscated.

Sure enough, the troop of sailors arrived next day from Yalta and tried to enter Dulber. As Zadorojny had foreseen, his men said that in the absence of the commissar, their orders were to admit no one. The walls were bristling with machine guns, and when they saw that the guards were prepared to use them the aggressors left, shouting insults and threats as they went.

We knew that after this unsuccessful venture, Yalta would take steps to end the matter once and for all. Foreseeing that a massive attack was imminent, Zadorojny went to Sebastopol himself to fetch reinforcements. He was expected back the same evening. But Yalta lay closer to Dulber than Sebastopol. . . .

We spent the night on the roof of our house, from which we could see the towers of Dulber and keep an eye on the road by which both the reinforcements from Sebastopol and the bandits from Yalta would arrive. It was dawn when we saw the armored trucks from Sebastopol drive past. As nothing appeared from Yalta, we went to bed. We awoke to be told that the Germans had arrived. This was a solution of our difficulties that no one had foreseen.

It was then April and a few days before Easter. On March 8, the Soviet government had signed the peace of Brest-Litovsk, and the Germans had begun occupying certain parts of Russia. They liked to pose as liberators to an over-credulous population who were exhausted by trials and privations and only too happy to welcome them as such. It was, in fact, their arrival that saved the lives of the prisoners of Dulber. The general rejoicings over their sudden and unexpected release can well be imagined. The German officer wanted to hang Zadorojny and his men. He was thunderstruck when the Grand Dukes begged him not to dream of such a thing. On the contrary, they asked him to leave Aï-Todor under the protection of their late jailers. The German finally consented, on condition that he was relieved of all responsibility should anything go wrong. It was quite clear that he was convinced that their prolonged detention had driven the poor Grand Dukes mad.

A few days later, after touching farewells, the jailers and their prisoners parted. The younger ones cried and kissed the hands of their former captives!

In May, one of the Kaiser's aides-de-camp arrived in Yalta. He brought with him an offer from his Imperial master to proclaim Czar of all the Russias any member of the Imperial family who would consent to countersign the Treaty of Brest-Litovsk. All the Romanoffs present rejected the proposal with indignation. The Kaiser's envoy then asked my father-in-law to arrange a meeting with me. The Grand Duke refused, saying that no member of his family would ever turn traitor.

After their release, the prisoners remained for some time at Dulber; then the Empress went to live at Harax, an estate belonging to the Grand Duke George, one of my father-in-law's brothers, and the rest returned to their homes.

As time went by, things became more or less normal. The relief felt by the older generation was tinged with a certain uneasiness, but the young people gave themselves up to the joy and excitement of being alive and free. Life became a round of pleasures: picnics, tennis parties, outings of all kinds.

We found a new distraction in the founding of a weekly magazine. A friend of ours, Olga Wassilieff, a charming and intelligent girl, was editor. We used to meet at Koreïz every Sunday evening. After the latest news, Olga would read aloud the articles that each of her sixteen correspondents had written during the week on a subject left to their own choice. This was usually either some fabulous adventure, or an imaginary journey to some distant land, which was rather touching when one thinks how uncertain was the future of the youthful authors. The meetings began and ended with a hymn to the glory of the newspaper, which we sang in chorus. As the electric current was cut off at midnight, these evenings generally ended in candlelight.

The interest which our parents took in our magazine and the amusement they derived from it did not prevent their feeling a trifle uneasy, for they knew that, in such troubled times, the most innocent pastimes were dangerous.

Our periodical had a short life. It appeared only thirteen times; then all the members of the staff, one after the other, were laid low with Spanish flu. When, later on, we were obliged to fly for our lives and had to reduce our luggage to a minimum, the first thing that my wife packed was the gazette.

The Grand Duke Alexander had given his daughter a grove of pine trees, perched on a cliff above the sea, an enchanting spot. In 1915, we had built a little country house there; it was whitewashed inside and out, and had a green-tiled roof. As it was on a slope it was all lopsided, and its greatest charm lay in its complete lack of symmetry. A carpet of flowers stretched before the front door. A few steps led down from the entrance to a gallery overlooking the hall, which gave onto a terrace with a fountain in the center. Through another door one reached the swimming pool, which was surrounded by a pergola smothered in roses and wisteria, as was the house. As the cottage was all on different levels, it lent itself to a profusion of funny little staircases, unexpected corners, landings, and balconies. The furniture was of oak with chintz cushions, and was somewhat like old English country furniture; there were rush mats on the floor instead of carpets. We were, alas, never able to live in the place, but during the comparatively happy days of the summer of 1918 we sometimes had picnics there. Food was scarce and the guests had to bring their own, but there was plenty of wine as everyone in the Crimea owned vineyards. There was also no lack of gaiety, for the young are ever ready to forget the trials of the day and look forward with eagerness to the future, however threatening it may be.

It was the day before one of these picnics that we heard that the Czar and his family had been assassinated. But there were so many wild rumors afloat at the time that nobody believed them any longer, and the party was not even canceled. The news was denied a few days later, and a letter was published purporting to have been written by the officer who had saved their lives. Soon, alas, it was no longer possible to doubt the terrible truth. But even then the Empress Marie refused to believe it, and to her dying day treasured the hope of seeing her son again.

The terrible events of the last few months sometimes made me wonder whether, as some people claimed, the death of Rasputin had not been the cause of the calamities which had overtaken our unfortunate country. When I think of those tragic days, I cannot imagine how I could have planned and committed a deed so contrary to my nature and principles. I was like a man in a dream, a dream that was a horrible nightmare. And to think I went home that night and slept like a child! I never had the slightest qualms of conscience; the thought of Rasputin never troubled my sleep. I had the feeling that it was someone else and not I who had done the deed, and I always spoke about it as if I had had no part in it.

The Grand Duchess Elisabeth had said that I was guided by a Force beyond my control. But was it a Force for Good or a Force for Evil?

There was an old nun of great saintliness who lived in Yalta and who was reputed to have the power of prophecy. She had been stricken by some mysterious complaint which had baffled all the doctors and left her half paralyzed, and had not stirred from her bed for nine years. She had a deep-rooted horror of fresh air, and never allowed the window of her cell to be opened. And yet, the story went, it smelled deliciously of flowers.

I decided to go and see this woman who was the object of so much veneration, but without revealing my identity. As I entered her cell, she stretched out her arms: "You have come!" she cried. "I've been expecting you. I dreamed of you as the savior of our country." I went up to her bed and she gave me her blessing, and, seizing my hand kissed it. I felt both moved and embarrassed as she looked at me with glowing eyes. I stayed with her for a long time, and I told her of my fears.

"Don't be unhappy," she said. "You are under the protection of God. Rasputin was a fiend whom you destroyed as St. George slew the dragon. Rasputin himself is grateful to you and protects you, for in killing him you prevented him from committing even greater sins.

"Russia must go through terrible trials to atone for her sins. Many years will pass before her resurrection. Few of the Romanoffs will escape death, but you will survive. You will take an active part in the restoration of Russia. Remember that he who opened the door must be the one to close it."

When I left her I was in a very confused state of mind. The idea of being protected at the same time by God and by Rasputin was hard to grasp. And yet I must admit that several times in the course of my life the name of Rasputin has saved both myself and my family from great dangers.

chapter XXVII

The series of odious crimes committed by the Bolsheviks against the Imperial family began with the murder of the Grand Duke Michael, the Czar's younger brother. He was arrested in February 1918 at his residence of Gatchina, and shot at Perm, in Siberia, in June of the same year. The second crime was the assassination of the Czar, the Czarina, and their children.

Since the first days of the Revolution, the Emperor and his family had been interned in Tsarskoïe-Selo. Then one day in August 1917 they learned that the Provisional Government had decided to change their place of detention, and their hopes rose high as they thought they might be sent to the Crimea. They were deeply disappointed when they were told that they were going to Tobolsk, in Siberia.

A small group of staunch friends was granted permission to share their lot. They were: Countess Hendrikoff, lady-in-waiting; Mlle Schneider, *lectrice* to the Empress; Prince Dolgoroukoff, Marshal of the Court; General Tatistcheff; Dr. Botkine and Dr. Derevenko; M. Gilliard and Mr. Gibbs, the Swiss and English tutors; Nagorny, the sailor attached to the Czarevitch, who carried the little invalid when he was unable to walk; and several other loyal servants.

The river boat which conveyed the prisoners from Tyumen to Tobolsk passed through Pokrovskoïe, Rasputin's native village. From the deck, the Imperial family could distinctly see the house of the starets. The events which had taken place since his death had strengthened the Empress' faith in her Siberian prophet, and she saw in this a fresh sign of his protection.

The prisoners were lodged in the governor's house at Tobolsk. Their jailers were continually obliged to disperse the faithful people who would come and stand under their Sovereigns' windows and raise their caps and cross themselves when passing the house.

At first the Imperial family lived under fairly tolerable conditions. The soldiers who guarded them behaved decently, and their colonel, Kobylinsky, was sincerely attached to his prisoners and did all in his power for their comfort. But, after the Bolshevik coup d'état, the Soldiers' Committee usurped the authority vested in Kobylinsky, and the prisoners were subjected to every sort of unpleasantness. In February 1918, after the Army was demobilized, the old soldiers who made up the guard were replaced by arrogant youngsters, and the plight of the prisoners grew worse each day. All attempts to liberate them had failed. In the first place, the Emperor had repeatedly declared that he would not attempt to escape if it meant his having to leave Russia. Another reason for the failure of these attempts was the presence of one Solovieff, Rasputin's son-in-law, sent to Tobolsk by Anna Wirouboff with the object of forming a clandestine center with a view to preparations for the Imperial family's escape. It turned out that this sinister personage—in whom Anna Wirouboff had complete faith—was a secret agent of both the Bolsheviks and the Germans. The latter, who then occupied part of Russia, wanted to bring the Emperor back to Moscow so that he might ratify the Treaty of Brest-Litovsk. It was therefore imperative that no one who was loyal to the Czar should have any contact with the prisoners. Solovieff took good care of that. He established relations with the prisoners through Father Alexis, their father-confessor, and managed to convince the Empress that he alone, guided by Rasputin's spirit, could ensure the safety of the Emperor and that of his family. He made her believe that a group of three hundred loyal officers stood ready to deliver them when he gave the word. Anyone belonging to the royalist organizations formed for the purpose of rescuing the Emperor and his family inevitably fell into his hands, and, no less inevitably, disappeared. When Solovieff and his wife were arrested at Vladivostock by the White Army in 1919, an examination of their papers gave ample proof of their guilt, but the couple managed to escape and take refuge in Germany.

In April 1918, Commissar Yakovleff, vested with unlimited powers, was sent from Moscow with a detachment of a hundred and fifty men. Three days after his arrival, he informed the Emperor that he had come to take him away, but gave him no hint as to his destination. He merely assured him that he would not be harmed, and that if anyone wished to accompany him he would raise no objection.

This placed the Czarina in a cruel dilemma, for the Czarevitch had been taken seriously ill a few days before and was not in a condition to be moved. The unhappy mother was torn both ways: she could not bring herself to leave her son, nor could she let her husband set off without her for an unknown destination. Finally she decided to follow her husband, leaving her son in the care of three of her daughters, his tutor M. Gilliard, and Dr. Derevenko. The Grand Duchess Marie, Prince Dolgoroukoff, Dr. Botkine, and three servants went with the Emperor.

The journey was extremely tiring and arduous. It was made in a tarantass (a wicker cart without seats, used by peasants in the Ural district), over terrible roads with deep ruts. They changed horses in Pokrovskoïe, under the windows of Rasputin's house. The next stop, an unexpected one, was in Ekaterinburg. The prisoners were confined in the house of a certain Ipatieff, a wealthy local merchant.

It has since been proved that Yakovleff was supposed to take his prisoners to Moscow, and that the reason he stopped in Ekaterinburg was to avoid a trap to seize the Emperor which had been set by the Ural Government, probably in conjunction with Moscow. Yakovleff's real intentions have never been fully cleared up. Some people believe that he was trying to save the prisoners. One fact is certain, however: that later on, having joined the White Army, he was captured by the Bolsheviks and shot.

Three weeks after the departure of their parents the Czarevitch, whose health had improved, and the three Grand Duchesses, were also removed from Tobolsk to Ekaterinburg. The joy of being together again somewhat mitigated the Imperial family's misery and suffering.

A wooden barricade reaching to the second story had been rapidly built around Ipatieff's home, to turn it into a prison. Sentries and machine guns were placed everywhere, inside the house and out.

Escape was now impossible. Germany, having lost all hope of obtaining the Emperor's signature to the Treaty of Brest-Litovsk, abandoned the Imperial family to its fate.

The prisoners could no longer have any doubt as to what this would be. The conditions under which they lived during this last stage of their martyrdom defy description. No humiliation was spared them, but they suffered most from being forced to live in such close contact with their jailers, who were unspeakably boorish and offensive, and almost always drunk. The doors of the room occupied by the Grand Duchesses had been removed, and the soldiers entered it as and when they pleased.

Yet, upheld by an unshakable faith in God, the prisoners seemed to be no longer affected by their surroundings. They were already living in another world, on another plane. Their calmness and gentleness made a deep impression upon their jailers, who gradually treated them with less brutality. Since their arrival at Ekaterinburg, the prisoners had been separated from most of their companions.[1] Fortunately, Dr. Botkine was allowed to stay with them, and a few servants as well. These faithful and devoted friends were a great consolation to the Imperial family during the last days of their lives.

The assassination of the prisoners had been decided on. The White Army, created in Siberia by Koltchak, was drawing nearer and nearer. This settled their fate.

I will not give an account of this abominable crime; the facts are now too well known. In spite of the care taken by the murderers to

[1]With the exception of the two foreign tutors, all those who followed the Imperial family into captivity paid for their devotion with their lives. The sailor Nagorny, a humble Ukrainian peasant, could have saved his life by disowning his Emperor; he preferred death.

remove all traces of their crime, all the facts have been collated with untiring patience and devotion by Sokoloff, the examining magistrate who directed the inquiry into the massacre of the Imperial family. These records have been published[2] and M. Gilliard, the Czarevitch's tutor, has told the whole story in his book *The Tragic Fate of Nicolas II*. In 1920, after the collapse of Admiral Koltchak's government, M. Gilliard met Sokoloff and his chief, General Dietrichs, in Harbin. They were very anxious to place the records of the inquiry in safekeeping, as the Bolsheviks were trying to lay hands on them. General Janin, Head of the French Mission which had been evacuated to Manchuria, consented to bring them back to Europe, along with the few remaining relics of the Imperial family. This explains how all the details of the crime and the names of the actual murderers came to light. One thing is not explained, and that is a strange discovery made by Sokoloff, the examining magistrate, which he described to me himself. On the wall of the cellar in Ipatieff's house, he found two inscriptions. The first was a copy of the twenty-first verse of Heine's poem "Balthazar": "*Balthazar war in selbiger Nacht von seinem Knechten umgebracht.*" (That same night, Balthazar was murdered by his servants.) The second was in Hebrew and was later translated: "Here was slain the Head of the Church and of the State. The order has been obeyed."

Twenty-four hours after the assassination of the Imperial family, another tragedy was enacted in the little town of Alapaïevsk, about a hundred and fifty versts away (roughly, ninety miles).

The Grand Duchess Elisabeth, the Grand Duke Serge Mikhaïlovitch, Princes John, Constantine and Igor (the sons of the Grand Duke Constantine), Prince Wladimir Paley, Sister Varvara, and the Grand Duke Serge's secretary—all were arrested in the spring of 1918, taken to Alapaïevsk, and imprisoned in the schoolhouse.

Their life at first was bearable. They were even allowed to go to church; but soon things changed and the odious ill-treatment inflicted on them was aggravated by the brutality and insolence of their jailers.

[2]*An Inquiry into the Assassination of the Russian Imperial Family*, by Nicolas Sokoloff, examining magistrate at the Omsk law court. Payot, Paris.

I have already referred to the death of the Grand Duchess and her companions. In October 1918 their bodies were found in the shaft of a deserted mine into which they had been thrown alive, after being stunned with blows from rifle butts.

After these assassinations in Siberia and the Ural came the murder of the Grand Dukes who had remained in St. Petersburg. My father-in-law's two brothers, the Grand Duke Nicolas and the Grand Duke George Mikhaïlovitch, the Grand Duke Paul Alexandrovitch, the Grand Duke Dimitri Constantinovitch, and his nephew Prince Gabriel had all been arrested and imprisoned. Thanks to the energy and devotion of his wife, Prince Gabriel was freed and escaped the fate of his relatives. The others were all transferred to the Fortress of St. Peter and St. Paul and soon afterward were shot. The Grand Duke George and the Grand Duke Dimitri died praying; the Grand Duke Paul, who was very ill, was shot on a stretcher; the Grand Duke Nicolas joked with his executioners, and held a favorite kitten in his arms.

They were the last Romanoff victims of the Bolshevik Revolution. Thus ended in blood and ashes the reign of one of the world's most powerful dynasties which, after ruling over Russia for more than three centuries and serving as the instrument of her greatness, was the involuntary cause of her downfall.

According to the terms of the Armistice signed on November 11, 1918, the Germans were to evacuate the Crimea and all the other parts of Russia they had occupied during the previous spring. Several hundred Russian officers who had succeeded in making their way to the Crimea with the object of protecting the remaining members of the Imperial family now announced their intention of joining the White Army. My brothers-in-law Andrew, Theodore, and Nikita, and I decided to do likewise, and we wrote to General Denikin, the commander-in-chief, asking him to enroll us. He replied that, for political reasons, members or connections of the Romanoff family were undesirable in the ranks of the White Army. This was a great disappointment, for it was our earnest wish to take part in the unequal struggle against the destructive forces which had taken possession of our country. A great wave of patriotism swept over those parts of Russia in which the new army was being raised under the leadership of some of Russia's best soldiers. The names of Generals Alexeeff, Korniloff, Denikin, Kaledin, Youdenitch, and of Admiral Koltchak will go down in Russian history as those of great national heroes.

Toward the end of 1918, the Allied Fleet arrived in the Crimea. My father-in-law left Russia on a British ship, accompanied by his son Andrew and Andrew's wife. His object was to see the heads of the Allied governments and explain to them the situation in Russia, as they were apparently far from realizing its gravity. Clemenceau could not receive him, but his secretary was most charming and very polite. The Grand Duke met with no better response elsewhere, and was even refused a visa for England. We are now facing the consequences of the tragic lack of foresight of the politicians who then governed Europe.

When the Red Army approached the Crimea, we realized that as far as we were concerned the end had come. On the morning of April 7, the commander of the British Naval forces at Sebastopol called at Harax, where the Dowager Empress lived. King George V had placed the dreadnought *Marlborough* at her disposal, as he considered that events called for her immediate departure from Russia. The British commander insisted that she should go aboard that very evening. At first she flatly refused, and it was only with the greatest difficulty that he finally persuaded her to go. As it happened, we were all at Harax at the time of his visit, for it was the Grand Duchess Xenia's birthday. The Empress gave me a letter for the Grand Duke Nicolas Nicolaïevitch, in which she told him of her decision to leave, and asked him and his family to come with her.

The news that the Dowager Empress and the Grand Duke Nicolas were on the verge of departure spread through the town like wildfire and caused a panic. Requests poured in from thousands of refugees, begging to be evacuated. But one warship could not take off all those whose lives would be endangered by the arrival of the Bolsheviks. Irina and I went on board the *Marlborough* after the Empress, the Grand Duchess Xenia, and my brothers-in-law had embarked.

When Irina told the Empress that nothing had been organized or provided for the evacuation of all these poor people, Her Majesty told the Allied authorities that she refused to leave unless immediate steps were taken to rescue them.

As a result of her firmness, a number of Allied warships steamed into Yalta to fetch away the refugees. Next day, together with my parents, we joined the Empress on the *Marlborough*.

Another ship left Yalta just before we did; on board her were the Crimean officers, en route to join the White Army. The *Marlborough* had not yet weighed anchor; standing in the bow, the Empress watched the ship pass by. Tears streamed down her cheeks as these young men, going to certain death, saluted her. Behind their Empress, they could discern the tall figure of their former commander-in-chief, the Grand Duke Nicolas.

On leaving our country with heavy hearts, that 13th day of April 1919, we knew that we were going into exile; but how long it would last, none of us could tell. Who could have dreamed that thirty-three years later it would still be impossible to foresee the end?

index